Witness

Exploring and Sharing Your Christian Faith

Dr. Ronald K. Crandall

Welcome to *Witness*!

Inside you will find twenty-five group sessions that will help
you and your congregation become more proficient at and more excited
about Christian witnessing. The first session is an orientation to the format and
expectations of the experience. Your group leader will guide and assist you through
this session as you begin with others in your group the journey of a lifetime.

---

*May God grant you a sense of joyful awe as you uncover
the wonder of amazing grace and learn how to pass it on!*

THE GENERAL BOARD OF
DISCIPLESHIP
THE UNITED METHODIST CHURCH

Sponsored by the Foundation for Evangelism and the General Board of Discipleship of The United Methodist Church

THE GENERAL BOARD OF
DISCIPLESHIP
THE UNITED METHODIST CHURCH

The Foundation for Evangelism and the evangelism staff of the General Board of Discipleship have been in conversation, prayer, and development of this study for more than three years. We hope that you will share in our excitement and commitment to exploring and sharing the Christian faith.

For information about *Witness:* www.gbod.org/witness

For information about the Foundation for Evangelism: www.evangelize.org

Cover and book design by Nanci H. Lamar
Edited by Linda R. Whited and Heidi L. Hewitt

ISBN 0-88177-322-0
Library of Congress Catalog Card No. 00-105381

The journal entries in this workbook © by Ken Evans. Used by permission.

DR322

Contents

SETTING OUT

Every year more than four million hikers of all ages and degrees of fitness take time to explore some part of the Appalachian Trail. This escape to fresh air, magnificent vistas, and nature's hidden wonders beckons to people bogged down in the hectic pace and high-tech pressures of modern living. The entire trail is 2,160 miles of snaking switchbacks and mountainous undulations. It runs from Springer Mountain near Atlanta, Georgia, to Mt. Katahdin, Maine, and lies within a day's drive of two-thirds of America's population.

Only a small percentage of the people who tackle the trail do so as thru-hikers. These brave souls, numbered in thousands not millions, undertake the ultimate test of mind and body and set out to hike the entire trail. With everything you have on your back, fifteen miles a day is a good day. There are also bad days and days for healing. Overall, a six-month commitment is required. Most hikers set out from Georgia early in the spring and hope to arrive in Maine before the first frost. Only fifteen to twenty percent make it; the rest succumb to injury, sickness, family emergencies, or just plain old mental and physical exhaustion. But for those who make it, and even for those who simply give it their best, thru-hiking the Appalachian Trail is life changing.

Recently, a friend of mine, Ken, wanting to get his life in focus and desiring to be a better Christian witness in today's world, set aside six months to become a thru-hiker. He began the journey on Easter Sunday, and wrote in his journal:

> *For me it was the perfect symbol to start on—through death comes life. Today we celebrate the new life of Jesus, rising from the tomb.*

Two days later came the reality check:

> *I pray I can cut the weight and that my foot heals.... We are not yet at the shelter, and exhaustion is taking over. We walked miles without the energy to do so, but had to press on. I can understand why people end their hike; it is not always fun. In those moments they drop out and miss all that God has for them.*

Camp Notes

Use this column to jot down ideas and responses, either while the group is meeting or during the week.

We will keep up with Ken's adventures on the trail through some of his journal entries.

To ensure a record of your own journey, take good Camp Notes and use your *My Witness Journal* to record your thoughts and feelings as you go.

Camp Notes

Q1

Can you recall an occasion when you set out on an adventure or tackled a task that seemed far beyond your abilities? When? What was the challenge? How did it turn out? What did you learn about yourself? about others? about life? about God?

_____

_____

_____

_____

_____

_____

Now when they saw the boldness of Peter and John and realized that they were uneducated and ordinary men, they were amazed and recognized them as companions of Jesus.

(Acts 4:13)

Why would anyone want to set out on a six-month trek full of challenges around every bend? Haven't you at times wanted to do something out of the ordinary? Haven't you at one time or another wanted to begin a journey full of possibilities, where you would be stretched and challenged to discover more of who you really are and what in your life is really valuable? On the Appalachian Trail the challenges are blisters, blood, aching muscles, sprained ankles, sickness, and days alone. But there are also serendipitous encounters with both the beauty and beasts of nature, friends and antagonists met along the way, sacred personal reflections, and intimate conversations with others looking for life's answers.

Witness is an invitation to just such a journey. Though not nearly as physically challenging as the Appalachian Trail, *Witness* is a life-changing adventure—a trek for you and for your congregation. The goal is much more than just completing the trail. It is making discoveries: self-discoveries, discoveries about God and God's purpose for all of creation, and discoveries about being God's children and disciples of Jesus Christ. The ultimate goal is to create a culture of vital Christian witness in individuals and congregations all across the church.

As we enter a new millennium, more and more people are looking for spiritual answers to life's questions, but an expanding array of competing truth-claims leave many confused and skeptical about religion. Nevertheless, millions of people all around the world are coming to new faith in Jesus Christ. At the same time, many of us have taken our faith for granted and are now finding ourselves unprepared to boldly bear witness to what we believe in order that others may discover a vital relationship with God.

"Companions of Jesus" (Acts 4:13) will quite naturally find themselves nudged by the Holy Spirit to witness to all of God's purposes in the world. But most of us are all too aware of our shortcomings. How can we be more faithful and fruitful as individual witnesses and as witnessing congregations? How can we become more sensitive to the Holy Spirit's guidance? How can we have more confidence in what we know and Whom we know?

Answers to these and other questions are found on the journey as we encounter the risen Jesus, the Lord, who longs to instruct us and inspire us. For most of us it's not so much a matter of getting new information as it is discovering a new perspective. But like those two disciples on the road to Emmaus described in Luke 24:13-35, we are changed by walking with Jesus. We are transformed from those who seem dejected and confused to those who are anxious to tell others of the amazing reality of the kingdom of God and the risen Savior.

Preparing for the Journey

On this *Witness* adventure we will explore five trails. As we follow each trail for several weeks, we will be challenged to learn more about what it means to be a Christian witness.

Trail 1: What is God's purpose in the world, and how can I be part of it?

Trail 2: Who is Jesus Christ, and how can I know him?

Trail 3: Who is the Holy Spirit, and how can I experience the Spirit's presence in my life?

Trail 4: What is the nature and purpose of Christ's church, and how can I contribute to its work?

Trail 5: Who am I as a Christian witness, and how is God calling me to respond?

Since you have already arrived at this point in your reading, more than likely you are at least curious or perhaps even committed to undertaking the pilgrimage we call *Witness*. The five trails are listed above; but to get ready for the trek and to equip you to be a thru-hiker, it is time to clarify expectations, check the list of equipment, review the disciplines involved, and establish a proposed schedule.

Expectations: What are your expectations, and what are the expectations of your *Witness* leader?

Equipment: What equipment will each person need for the trail? Remember that we're packing light!

1. An easy-to-read (and/or old favorite) translation of the **Bible** (Old and New Testaments) with a concordance.
   You may find an annotated study Bible helpful, too.
   There will be daily readings from the Bible and opportunities each week to discuss insights and learnings from these readings.
2. A copy of this **workbook.**
3. A copy of *My Witness Journal* for your personal reflections.
4. An **open attitude** and a **cooperative spirit**.

Disciplines: Each day we will be on the trail walking individually with Jesus, and once a week we will gather at a campfire to have some trail talk—insights, experiences, stories, and encouragement—as we seek to grow together as Christ's witnesses. What disciplines will be required for succeeding at this undertaking that stretches us and asks for our best?

1. **Attending weekly team meetings,** usually lasting one to one and a half hours. There are twenty-four sessions after this introductory session. Clearing your calendar for full participation is important.
2. **Completing weekly assignments,** including reading and written reflection, along with stretching exercises related to the *Witness* terrain explored during the week.
3. **Talking openly** with your team to enhance one another's vision and encourage one another for the challenges encountered.

Q2
What are your expectations, hopes, and fears as you begin this journey? Tell the group the reasons you are interested in this faith adventure and what you hope to gain over the next several months of walking with others on the *Witness* trail.

Camp Notes

Record the names of your group members on the lines below. Remember each one in prayer each day you are on the trail.

_____

_____

_____

_____

_____

_____

_____

4. **Praying daily** for yourself and for each team member. Pray for faithfulness, courage, an open heart and mind, and for the Holy Spirit of God to use your time on the trail for both personal and congregational renewal as a witnessing community.

Schedule: We need to clarify the schedule. Perhaps the dates and times for the group meetings have already been established. If not, clarify them now and record them below.

> **Meeting day:** _____
>
> weekly except for _____, _____, _____
>
> **Meeting time:** _____ to _____
>
> **Meeting place:** _____

Getting Started

We're ready to begin! Discovering God's purpose for the world and our role as witnesses to it constitutes our first major undertaking: Trail One. Readings this week will focus on biblical images to help us discover the big picture.

READING ASSIGNMENTS

1. Record your reflections, questions, and insights from these daily Bible readings in your *My Witness Journal.*
   Day 1: Genesis 1:26-31 (Creation)
   Day 2: Exodus 3:1-12 (Moses before God)
   Day 3: Isaiah 58:1-12 (God's word to Israel)
   Day 4: Matthew 5:1-20 (Jesus' teachings)
   Day 5: Luke 4 (Jesus in Galilee)
   Day 6: Ephesians 3 (Paul's prayer)
2. As you read the chapter for next week (pages 10–14), underline or highlight special thoughts and answer the questions in the Q boxes.

ACTION ASSIGNMENT

Sometime this week ask at least one friend, coworker, or family member what he or she thinks is God's ultimate purpose for the world. In the space provided in your *My Witness Journal,* write down some thoughts you hear and the insights you gain.

Come next week ready to tell about your observations from your Bible reading and the perspectives about God's purpose for our lives discussed in your conversation.

Pray together for the journey.

Trail One
Exploring God's Purpose

As we set out on the trail, it is important to get a clear overview of the terrain ahead, a sort of conceptual map laying out the overarching purpose of God. The first two vistas on this trail will establish a grounding in some of the basics. What is God's purpose for creation? for humanity? for you and me?

As those who are setting out to become better witnesses to God's purpose, we must begin with as much clarity as possible. So let's get started on the trail!

Camp Notes

Today was not a hard hike, which was a good introduction so I can ease myself into the challenge…. I hope this feeling continues all the way up.

Ken (trail name: Wadi)

Biblical Images of God's Purpose

VISTA ONE

Prayer

Protect me, O God, for in you I take refuge.
I say to the LORD, "You are my Lord;
  I have no good apart from you."…
I bless the LORD who gives me counsel;
  in the night also my heart instructs me.
I keep the LORD always before me;
  because he is at my right hand,
    I shall not be moved.
Therefore my heart is glad, and my soul rejoices…
You show me the path of life.

  (Psalm 16:1, 7-9, 11)

Trail Talk

Picture yourselves as hikers who have just finished a week on the trail and are together to tell your stories around the campfire. What adventures have you had? What dangers and delights have you encountered on the trail?

Use the notes in your *My Witness Journal* to guide the discussion of your reading assignment. What do the Scriptures you examined this week reveal as God's design and purpose for creation and for humanity? Don't get bogged down in details yet, but do notice differences and similarities as various group members speak.

Next, think about your action assignment interviews. Were there any surprises? How clearly do people seem to understand the purpose of God? Were your own perspectives challenged or enlarged by what you heard?

Finish your Trail Talk time by letting one or two people tell a brief campfire story of their own about how they came to discover more of what the psalmist calls "the path of life."

Q1

On the trail, most hikers don't use their given names, but rather they choose a handle that has meaning for them. A wadi in Palestine is a steep-sided riverbed. The contrast between its seasons of rushing water and complete dryness make it a good symbol of both life and death.

What trail name would you choose to describe yourself?

_____

Why?

_____

_____

_____

What are the trail names of others in your group?

_____

_____

_____

_____

_____

_____

Q2

If you were asked to name some key words that describe God's purpose for the world, what would they be?

_____

_____

_____

Trail Markers

This week and next our goal is to explore some of the vistas of God's purpose as revealed in the Bible. We will be looking at major themes that run through both the Old and New Testaments. We will look at key words and images such as *shalom, salvation,* and *eternal life.* We won't examine all of the themes you might name, so feel free to use a concordance and/or a commentary to explore some on your own. If you are not sure how to use these resources, ask for help from your leader or pastor.

Together we will look at six themes. Let's begin by examining two of those already mentioned: shalom and salvation.

Shalom

Shalom is both an ancient and a contemporary Hebrew greeting meaning peace. The term can refer to either personal or political peace, but it always has a religious overtone. In fact, the deeper meaning of the word is more like completeness or total well-being. In the context of Israel's political survival, peace was then, even as it is today, often short lived and subject to fragile treaties and human deceit. Ultimately, peace could be secured only by divine intervention. Shalom is always a gift—a blessing, not an achievement.

The prophets often challenged God's people to recognize that true peace is not merely the absence of temporal conflict, but that true peace is wholeness and harmony with God's design for all creation. In fact, as a facet of God's own nature, shalom is intimately connected to righteousness, faithfulness, justice, mercy, and truth. The problem was that God's people usually fell short of this kind of living. What was needed was "a spirit from on high" (Isaiah 32:15).

It became clear that only a special messenger, a messiah, could bring this ultimate gift. The Messiah would be the "Prince of Peace," bringing "endless peace" (Isaiah 9:6-7), and would establish God's "covenant of peace" (Ezekiel 34:25).

The prophet Micah announced that Bethlehem would be the birthplace of the Messiah. In God's time Jesus was born. Jesus began to teach, saying, "Blessed are the peacemakers, for they will be called children of God" (Matthew 5:9). To the wind and the waves, he said, "Peace! Be still!" (Mark 4:39), and his disciples were stunned at the cosmic power of his shalom. In the upper room, as these same disciples struggled to understand that Jesus was leaving them and returning to the Father, he said, "My peace I give to you.... Do not let your hearts be troubled" (John 14:27).

Camp Notes

The ichthus, or sign of the fish, was an early Christian acronym that stood for Jesus Christ, Son of God, Savior.

I have observed the misery of my people who are in Egypt; I have heard their cry... So come, I will send you to Pharaoh to bring my people, the Israelites, out of Egypt.

(Exodus 3:7, 10)

Thus the LORD saved Israel that day from the Egyptians. (Exodus 14:30)

Following the Crucifixion, the risen Lord appeared to his disciples, who were hiding behind locked doors, and said, "Shalom" (John 20:19). As the "spirit from on high [was] poured out" at Pentecost, this gospel of shalom as God's completeness and wholeness spread to men and women of all races and tongues. The disciples, full of this heavenly Spirit, went forth "preaching peace by Jesus Christ" (Acts 10:36).

The apostle Paul had his own encounter with the risen Lord and boldly witnessed everywhere: "We have peace with God through our Lord Jesus Christ" (Romans 5:1). This peace is not a personal possession to be enjoyed in isolation from the rest of humanity. We are now peacemakers as the children of God.

Writing to the Christians in Ephesus, Paul told them to put on "the whole armor of God" as they confronted a world that knew little of this peace that makes us whole and holy and one body in Christ. He said, "Fasten the belt of truth around your waist, and put on the breastplate of righteousness. As shoes for your feet put on whatever will make you ready to proclaim the gospel of peace" (Ephesians 6:14-15). In the words of the old Negro spiritual, "All God's children got shoes." So, children, have you got your shoes?

Salvation

Probably the most common term used by Christians to describe God's purpose for the world is *salvation.*

In Hebrew the word for salvation is *Yeshua,* which in English is Jesus. The word describes an action of deliverance, such as an assisted escape from captivity, disease, danger, or even death. But salvation's rescue is not only *from* enslavement; it is also *to* wholeness, health, freedom, life, and spaciousness.

The Old Testament contains several images of deliverance, but the Exodus story provides the best drama of salvation. The Hebrew male children, including Moses, were saved from Pharaoh's death sentence by the midwives (Exodus 1:15–2:10). But all the Israelites were in need of rescue, so God called Moses to be an instrument of divine deliverance and salvation.

The Hebrews were saved from the deadly pestilence that struck down all of Egypt's firstborn. Because faithful Hebrews obediently smeared lambs' blood on their doorposts, death passed over their homes. Pharaoh relented, and Moses led the Hebrews out of slavery and toward the Promised Land. The journey itself, however, was treacherous. Again and again, God intervened with saving acts: parting the sea, providing manna from heaven, supplying water from a rock, and protecting them from marauding tribes. But were they grateful and ready to serve the Lord with gladness? No, they complained at every turn; and, in their rebellion, even talked frequently of returning to Egypt (Numbers 14:1-4).

This pattern of forgetfulness dominates much of the Old Testament. Five centuries after Moses, God declared through the prophet Isaiah: "I reared up children and brought them up, but they have rebelled against me" (Isaiah 1:2). God's salvation, always offered as amazing grace, did not produce a grateful and witnessing people whose purpose was to be "a light to the nations, that [God's] salvation may reach to the end of the earth" (Isaiah 49:6).

The problem was clearly identified by King David when he faced his own sin against God and prayed:

> *Create in me a clean heart, O God,*
> *and put a new and right spirit within me....*
> *Restore to me the joy of your salvation...*
> *Then I will teach transgressors your ways.*
> *(Psalm 51:10-13)*

God's ultimate salvation coming in the Messiah would need to address this soul sickness. Yeshua is born, and the angel declares "good news of great joy for all the people: to you is born this day in the city of David a Savior, who is the Messiah, the Lord" (Luke 2:10-11). And when he was grown, Jesus announced that he came "to seek out and to save the lost" (Luke 19:10).

The New Testament Gospels use the words *saved* and *salvation* sparingly. Other expressions such as *finding life* and *entering the Kingdom* take center stage. Several verses in Acts come to mind: 2:21, 2:47; 4:12; and 15:6-11. But Paul is the one who carefully reminds us that salvation comes not by anything we can do for ourselves or for God. It is only by grace, through faith, that we have been saved (Ephesians 2:1-10).

This salvation is an already accomplished reality (Ephesians 2:8), a continuing reality (1 Corinthians 1:1-8), and a future reality (Romans 5:8-10) for all those who have faith. It is the great salvation (Hebrews 2:3) by the blood of the Lamb that brings an eternal passing over from death into life everlasting and makes us joint heirs with Christ, even to sharing as "participants of the divine nature" (2 Peter 1:4).

> *They have no knowledge—*
> *those who carry about their*
> *wooden idols,*
> *and keep on praying to a god*
> *that cannot save....*
> *There is no other god besides me,*
> *a righteous God and a Savior.*
> *(Isaiah 45:20-21)*

> *God did not send the Son into the world to condemn the world, but in order that the world might be saved through him.*
>
> *(John 3:17)*

Camp Notes

We sat around laughing all night and looking for satellites. I found four, forcing me to fight off a new name, Satellite Guru.... Crazy but nice people out here.

Wadi

Moving On

Well, there's more to see as we begin our second week of exploring the vistas of God's purpose. Like last week, there will be daily prayer and reading assignments, and an action assignment.

Take a few minutes in breaking camp to tie up any loose ends and to clarify next week's assignments.

READING ASSIGNMENTS

1. Record your reflections, questions, and insights from these daily Bible readings in your *My Witness Journal.*
   - **Day 1:** John 17 (eternal life)
   - **Day 2:** Jeremiah 31:31-34 (the new covenant)
   - **Day 3:** Ezekiel 36:22-32 (the new covenant)
   - **Day 4:** 2 Corinthians 3 (the glory of God)
   - **Day 5:** Matthew 6:19-33 (the Kingdom)
   - **Day 6:** Matthew 13:44-58 (the Kingdom)
2. As you read the chapter for next week (pages 15–20), underline or highlight special thoughts and answer the questions in the Q boxes.

ACTION ASSIGNMENT

Sometime this week continue your research about what people think God's purpose is. Ask two or three more people what they think is the ultimate purpose of God. In the space provided in your *My Witness Journal,* write down some thoughts you hear and insights you gain.

End your time together in prayer.

See you on the path!

Biblical Images of God's Purpose

VISTA TWO

Prayer

> *Make me to know your ways, O LORD;*
> *teach me your paths.*
> *Lead me in your truth, and teach me,*
> *for you are the God of my salvation;*
> *for you I wait all day long.*
> (Psalm 25:4-5)

Trail Talk

Congratulations! You've made it through two weeks on the trail. Have you enjoyed the vistas? Have you witnessed some of the glories of God's creation and heard God's voice as you've walked along some biblical paths?

Tell the group about some of the insights and reflections from your reading assignment recorded in your *My Witness Journal* for this week. Did you take a side trail and hunt for themes of God's purpose other than those we looked at last week? What extra discoveries did you make?

Report the results of your action assignment for the week. How many people did you ask to help with your research? Were they surprised at your request? Were they cooperative? Did they seem to be interested in the subject matter? Did you have any surprises? Was it fun? Was it frightening? Was it helpful? How?

It's time to explore a few more of the vistas of God's purpose for the world revealed in Scripture. Last week we discussed the images of shalom and salvation. This week your reading opened up the vistas of eternal life, the new covenant, the glory of God, and the kingdom of God. Here we will focus on the first two, with just a glance at the Kingdom and the glory.

I've met Mac and Cheese, Mark Canadian Goose, Dawn Treader, and Shiver.... One guy made it up here to the shelter but left the backs of both heels on the trail. He's going to try to use duct tape to solve it, hoping to build a new foot.

Wadi

Camp Notes

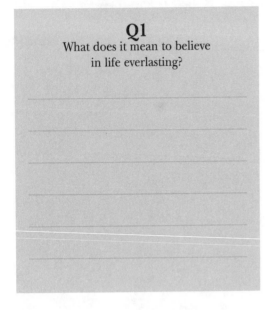

Q1
What does it mean to believe in life everlasting?

_____

_____

_____

_____

_____

Lord, you have been our dwelling place
in all generations.
Before the mountains were brought forth,
or ever you had formed the earth
and the world,
from everlasting to everlasting
you are God.   *(Psalm 90:1-2)*

He was in the beginning with God. All
things came into being through him, and
without him not one thing came into being.
What has come into being in him was life.
(John 1:2-4)

Eternal Life

The Apostles' Creed ends with the words "I believe in…the life everlasting." What is eternal life, or the life everlasting?

To some, the answer is obvious. It means life without end. It means going to heaven and living there forever. To be sure, these are part of the gift of eternal life, but there is more, much more.

The words *forever* and *everlasting* both refer to the ages or eons. Everlasting life is life to the ages, or life outside of and beyond time. It is life that is lasting or indestructible. In the Old Testament, any number of things are referred to as everlasting: the everlasting arms of God, the everlasting covenant, the everlasting kingdom, the everlasting righteousness, along with joy, priesthood, salvation, mercy, and love. But all references are connected in some way to the everlasting God. What is everlasting is not a *what* but a *Who*!

Perhaps the biggest mistake we make when we talk about everlasting or eternal life is to think of it as a quantity instead of a quality. We think of it as living somewhere (heaven? hell?) forever. But everlasting life is God's life. The focus is on the nature of this life, not simply on the duration. The nature of this life is glimpsed in the Old Testament in Psalm 133.

> *How very good and pleasant it is*
> *when kindred live together in unity!…*
> *For there the* LORD *ordained his blessing,*
> *life forevermore.*
> *(Psalm 133:1, 3)*

Eternal life is perfect unity and harmony. We can catch a glimmer of it here on earth when love is most alive, but it is perfected only in the eternal life and love that is divine.

In the New Testament, John prefers the image of eternal life to all others when he describes in his Gospel the gift Jesus has brought to us. He begins by announcing that Jesus is eternal life. He had always existed, and when he appeared we saw life full of glory and truth. He came from the love of God "so that everyone who believes in him may not perish but may have eternal life" (John 3:16).

When Jesus prayed to his Father about his mission, he said:

> *Father, the hour has come; glorify your Son so that the Son*
> *may glorify you, since you have given him authority over all*
> *people, to give eternal life to all whom you have given him.*
> *And this is eternal life, that they may know you, the only true*
> *God, and Jesus Christ whom you have sent.*
> *(John 17:1-3)*

Eternal life as defined by Jesus is knowing God in full intimacy as a child knows a completely trustworthy and loving father. Later, Jesus prayed:

> *I ask not only on behalf of these, but also on behalf of those who will believe in me through their word, that they may all be one,...so that the world may know that you have sent me and have loved them even as you have loved me.*
>
> *(John 17:20-23)*

The gospel of eternal life is about knowing God the way Jesus knows God. It is about being one with God and with one another through believing in and living in Jesus Christ as the complete revelation of true life and true love. This is the experience that awaits those who come to Christ in faith This is the gospel to which we are called to bear witness.

New Covenant

It is clear from the earliest biblical record that God values relationships. The first aspect of creation reported to be "not good" is "that the man should be alone" (Genesis 2:18). When Adam and Eve were in loving harmony with each other and with God's design, they "were both naked, and were not ashamed" (2:25). Their disobedience, however, brings more than an expulsion from the garden; it also produces guilt, anxiety, and a desire to hide from each other and from God (3:8). The good of being together has turned sour, and the rest is history, as they say.

Actually, there is a bit more to history as the Bible reports it. God's design for humanity will not be thwarted. Again and again God seeks faithful people who will help form a community that lives for God's glory and reveals the beauty of love and righteousness. This pursuit of a faithful covenant community is one of the most important concepts in the Bible. The word *covenant* appears more than three hundred times in the Bible, woven around faithful servants such as Noah, Abraham, Moses, David, the prophets, and finally Jesus. In fact, the word we use to describe the two major parts of the Bible—*testament*—is a word meaning covenant.

While there were several versions or variations of the old covenant (recorded in the Old Testament), none of them produced the desired results for long. God's covenant law, summarized in the Ten Commandments, clarified what was expected and promised; but the destructive infection of human sin always turned the beauty of covenant love for God and neighbor into lies, lust, greed, divisiveness, and destruction. God's name was neither honored by the covenant community nor carried as "a light to the nations" (Isaiah 49:6), but God remained faithful and focused.

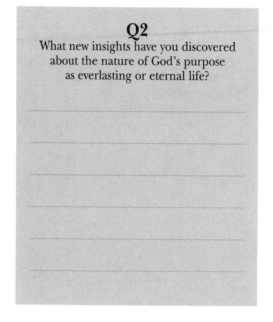

Q2
What new insights have you discovered about the nature of God's purpose as everlasting or eternal life?

_____

_____

_____

_____

_____

When Abram was ninety-nine years old, the LORD appeared to Abram, and said to him, "I am God Almighty; walk before me, and be blameless. And I will make my covenant between me and you, and will make you exceedingly numerous."

(Genesis 17:1-2)

I am God, and there is no other like me, declaring the end from the beginning and from ancient times things not yet done, saying, "My purpose shall stand, and I will fulfill my intention."

(Isaiah 46:9-10)

Camp Notes

Q3

Compare Jeremiah's new covenant with Ezekiel's (this week's reading for Days 2 and 3). What are the similarities? What stands out in your mind as the real difference?

_____

_____

_____

_____

_____

For the law of the Spirit of life in Christ Jesus has set you free from the law of sin and of death. For God has done what the law, weakened by the flesh [human nature on its own], could not do.

(Romans 8:2-3)

You are a chosen race, a royal priesthood, a holy nation, God's own people, in order that you may proclaim the mighty acts of him who called you out of darkness into his marvelous light. *(1 Peter 2:9)*

The glory of the LORD shall be revealed, and all people shall see it together.

(Isaiah 40:5)

I am coming to gather all nations and tongues; and they shall come and see my glory... From them I will send survivors...to the coastlands far away that have not heard of my fame or seen my glory; and they shall declare my glory among the nations.

(Isaiah 66:18-19)

God used both Jeremiah and Ezekiel to announce that the coming *new* covenant would be different. There would be radical (to the root) forgiveness and cleansing, new hearts, a new spirit; and the law would be written inside on their wills instead of outside on tablets of stone. God promised: "I will be their God, and they shall be my people" (Jeremiah 31:33).

Jesus reminded those who wished to accuse him of breaking God's covenant law that the true essence of the covenant was relational. It was total love for God, self, neighbor, and even one's enemies (Luke 10:25-37). But how is this possible?

It's not a patch job on the old covenant, any more than one can patch an old wineskin when putting new wine into it (Mark 2:21-22). Although the purpose of God is the same, to create a community of righteousness and holy people ruled by love, the covenant is different. Actually, it is a covenant designed to make us "a new creation" (2 Corinthians 5:17), not a patched-up old creation. Paul clarifies it as "a new covenant, not of letter but of spirit; for the letter kills, but the Spirit gives life" (2 Corinthians 3:6). Indeed, the prophets promised it (Ezekiel 36:26-27); Jesus manifested it (Luke 4:16-21); and as the crucified and risen Messiah of God, Jesus established it as the new covenant for all (Jew and Gentile) who would repent of their sins, believe in him, receive him, and be filled with his Spirit. Simply put, the new covenant is "Christ in you, the hope of glory" (Colossians 1:27) and "You are the body of Christ" (1 Corinthians 12:27).

Glory

Perhaps this is a good time for a quick look at another vista of God's purpose. By now you are probably recognizing recurring patterns in these images. Indeed, these vistas are like the multifaceted radiance of a lovely diamond—they are cuts in the same Stone. Each image reveals the glory of the Stone itself.

The glory of God is a theme running through the Bible. The creation reveals God's glory (Psalm 8; Romans 1:18-23), and humanity is also designed to reveal the glory of God. (Of course, there is a problem with humanity. We'll see more about that next week.) God's purpose is that "the earth will be filled with the knowledge of the glory of the LORD, as the waters cover the sea" (Habakkuk 2:14).

God's children "fall short of the glory of God" because of their sin (Romans 3:23); but the true Child, Jesus, reveals "the glory...of a father's only son, full of grace and truth" (John 1:14). And this is not the end of the story.

In John 17 (which you read this week), Jesus prays to his Father, asking on behalf of his disciples "that they may be one." He then announces that the glory, which he had with the Father from the beginning, he has given away—*to them!* Yes, Jesus gives the glory of God as a gift to his disciples.

God's glory is a shining radiance, a beautiful manifestation of the presence of God. Jesus lived constantly in that presence and gave (and continues to give) that gift to his disciples. How? "Christ in you, the hope of glory" (Colossians 1:27). "The Spirit of him who raised Jesus from the dead dwells in you" (Romans 8:11). As God's new creations and the body of Christ, we are meant to reveal the beauty of oneness with God and with one another.

> *Beloved, let us love one another, because love is from God; everyone who loves is born of God and knows God. Whoever does not love does not know God, for God is love.*
>
> *(1 John 4:7-8)*

"God is love" (1 John 4:16). This is our witness. How are we doing?

The Kingdom

One last vista of God's purpose to examine is the kingdom of God. The Gospel writers remind us that Jesus came "proclaiming the good news of God and saying, 'The time is fulfilled, and the kingdom of God has come near; repent, and believe in the good news'" (Mark 1:14-15). This was the message Jesus sent his disciples out to announce and to demonstrate, and it was John Wesley's favorite text to preach on.

Much like the new covenant, the kingdom of God is a fulfillment of an old promise. The kingdom of God is the realm and rule of God on earth. It is not where people say, "Lord, Lord," but where people do the Father's will (Matthew 7:21) on earth as it is in heaven. We probably pray for this regularly, as Jesus taught us, but do we realize it is already here? Jesus brought it with him. There is more to come; but until he returns, the doors to the Kingdom are still open to all, including those whom many would not expect to be welcome: the poor, the oppressed, the outcasts, the sinners, and any willing to be "born from above" by the Spirit (John 3:1-10).

Q4

Look again at the passage from John 17. What, do you think, is the glory?

Q5

As you have prayed the Lord's Prayer over the years, what was your image of the Kingdom? What is it now?

Camp Notes

Q6

E. Stanley Jones, a famous writer, missionary to India, and evangelist, described the kingdom of God as "Christlikeness universalized."[1]

Does Jones' phrase describe the heart of all of the vistas we have examined? How does this description help clarify our task as witnesses?

Moving On

Before breaking camp and heading out to the trail, take a moment to review next week's assignments.

READING ASSIGNMENTS

1. Record your reflections, questions, and insights from these daily Bible readings in your *My Witness Journal.*

Day 1: Genesis 3:1-4 (original sin)
Day 2: Proverbs 3 (wisdom versus foolishness)
Day 3: Ezekiel 18 (turning from righteousness)
Day 4: Matthew 9 (forgiveness as a healing)
Day 5: Romans 5–6 (sin, death, and life)
Day 6: 1 John 1 and 3 (sin in contrast to love)

2. As you read the chapter for next week (pages 21–26), underline or highlight special thoughts and answer the questions in the Q boxes.

ACTION ASSIGNMENT

During the week think about how you would define sin. Think about the consequences of sin. Then ask at least two friends or coworkers for their thoughts about what sin is and about what its consequences are. In the space provided in your *My Witness Journal,* write down some thoughts you hear and the insights you gain.

Close your time together with the Lord's Prayer.

See you on the path!

Camp Notes

The Human Problem: Sin

Prayer

Have mercy on me, O God,
*   according to your steadfast love;*
according to your abundant mercy
*   blot out my transgressions.*
Wash me thoroughly from my iniquity,
*   and cleanse me from my sin.*

For I know my transgressions,
*   and my sin is ever before me.*
Against you, you alone, have I sinned,
*   and done what is evil in your sight,*
so that you are justified in your sentence
*   and blameless when you pass judgment....*

Hide your face from my sins,
*   and blot out all my iniquities.*
Create in me a clean heart, O God,
*   and put a new and right spirit within me.*
*   (Psalm 51:1-4, 9-10)*

Trail Talk

We don't have to go far or look deep to see the evidence of human sinfulness. We all share, in one way or another, in its destructive and life-twisting impact.

David was "a man after [God's] own heart" (1 Samuel 13:13-14), but sin in the guise of lust caught him in its grip. He surrendered to the temptation of adultery, and then to murder. He ran from the truth, hiding from its piercing light, until God sent the prophet Nathan to confront him face to face (2 Samuel 11–12). Psalm 51 captures David's repentant spirit.

We're not all murderers or adulterers; but if we are honest, we have discovered ourselves to be sinners in need of forgiveness and heart cleansing.

We made it to the top of Blood Mountain (4,458 feet).... Many thru-hikers believe it is named that because their blisters are breaking and some are getting infected. Actually, there were mighty battles on this mountain between the Creek and Cherokee Indians.

Wadi

Camp Notes

Exercise

Take a few minutes to discuss together what you learned this week about sin. Then try to answer these questions openly.

1. When was the first time you can remember being aware of your own sin and the need for forgiveness?
2. Were you aware of God being part of this experience?
3. Was there a time you can remember when you actually asked, like David, for a deep cleansing of your heart? What was the outcome?

Sin Is Serious

It's not fun to talk about sin. There's something about the word itself and all the images it brings up that puts our teeth on edge. But how can we deny the power of sin in our world? Read any newspaper or magazine; listen to news on the radio or to the heartache in much of today's music; or watch on television or in movies the stories of bigotry, degradation, and hate that bombard us constantly. It's an old story, but it hasn't gotten better with time. It gets better only with a divine touch of healing for the human heart.

The word *heart* is often used in a metaphorical way to describe the center or core of something, as in the expression "the heart of the problem." It is this metaphor the Bible often uses when describing the human heart as the source of the sin problem. Obviously, sin involves our whole being, our thoughts and feelings as well as our wills and our choices. The heart could best be described as the center of our desires. One's heart would then be the wellspring of one's desires. Does it run pure, or is it contaminated?

Dwight Moody said, "Character is what you are in the dark." There is a dark side to everyone, whether large or small, deep or shallow. As I walked in the woods, I was praying for someone back home, and I broke down when I thought how I had hidden issues in my life.... I was so ashamed of ignoring my conscience to maintain my own control. I fell before God all around me and begged for forgiveness.

Wadi

According to Jeremiah, "the heart is devious above all else; it is perverse—who can understand it?" (Jeremiah 17:9). If a spring is defiled, can it be restored? Or is the source of the problem so deep and so hidden that there is no hope? This is the level of debate we get into when discussing sin. Some would say there are good souls and bad souls, no saints and no sinners. That's all there is to it. Others, especially those who have experienced the touch of heaven to sweeten their own lives from a poisoned past, know there is more to the story; there is hope for healing and living water available to all.

The Bible recognizes sin as a serious problem that affects the whole stream of human history. "Sin is lurking at the door; its desire is for you, but you must master it" (Genesis 4:7). All of us find part of our own story in the recounting of Adam and Eve's disobedience and their resulting enmity with each other, with God, and with creation itself. "All have sinned and fall short of the glory of God" (Romans 3:23). Sin poisons life, and the final result is death (Genesis 2:17; Romans 6:23).

Today, however, such language seems too drastic for the moral relativism that is so dominant in our secular postmodern society. "After all," we say, "we all make mistakes." But if we speak only of mistakes, our vocabulary leads us to assume either that

1. there is no ultimate standard given by God, and therefore both sin and forgiveness are unnecessary concepts; or
2. sin is just another word for mistake, and surely God is big enough to forgive us readily, no matter what errors we may have made.

Tragically, both of these efforts to take the sting out of sin also take the healing balm out of salvation. In telling us that our inner springs are not so much poisoned as they are muddied, these optimists not only eliminate the biblical record of the human predicament but also make unnecessary God's wondrous intervention in the Messiah. There is no longer any need for a truly Christian gospel.

Sin Distorts and Destroys

From the biblical perspective, it is not surprising that the truth of sin's seriousness is frequently downplayed. This is precisely what is depicted in the temptation scene with the serpent in Genesis 3:1-7. Sin willfully walks in where temptation distorts truth.

In previous weeks, we have explored God's purpose for humanity. Sin is any exercise of will contrary to God's purpose. It is making a choice that seems to offer *more* but turns out to be *less*. It is opting for no restrictions as the meaning of freedom, but discovering that such liberty leads to bondage. Jesus was perfectly free, and yet he said, "I seek to do not my own will but the will of him who sent me" (John 5:30). Sin is failure to recognize and respond, in faith and love, to the true identity of God, God's word, God's creation, and God's children (including my own true self).

All of us have been disoriented and confused by countless years of sin's impact on our cultures and communities. Racism, bigotry, haughtiness, and selfish pursuits of every kind emerge as the offspring of pride in societies and families as well as in individuals. Many suffer extensive disorientation resulting from the sin of others. Consider the enormous obstacles facing children scarred by abuse in all of its horrible forms. And even in families and Christian fellowships where the gospel has been taught and lived, the capacity to sin always remains alive. We are given opportunities every day to choose to walk in the light or in darkness, the way that leads to life or the way that leads to destruction. In the shadows it is always easier to lose our bearings and wander off the path and get lost.

In fact, the Bible announces that we all have wandered from the path and are lost. Yet when we hear the sound of the Savior's voice and cry out, "Here I am. Save me!" he does.

Q2
What do you think? Are the following sins or the results of sin? Is there any difference?

People will be lovers of themselves, lovers of money, boasters, arrogant, abusive, disobedient to their parents, ungrateful, unholy, inhuman, implacable, slanderers, profligates, brutes, haters of good, treacherous, reckless, swollen with conceit, lovers of pleasure rather than lovers of God, holding to the outward form of godliness but denying its power.
(2 Timothy 3:2-5)

Q3
How would you define sin?

If we say that we have no sin, we deceive ourselves, and the truth is not in us.
(1 John 1:8)

Camp Notes

Enter through the narrow gate; for the gate is wide and the road is easy that leads to destruction, and there are many who take it. For the gate is narrow and the road is hard that leads to life. (Matthew 7:13-14)

Q4

How does our society try to address the sin problem? What is our church's approach? Is there any real hope for humanity's ills?

If we confess our sins, he who is faithful and just will forgive us our sins and cleanse us from all unrighteousness.

(1 John 1:9)

Sin's Solution

Sin poisons life. Sin breaks relationships. Sin separates us from God and God's design for our lives. Sin leads us to doubt rather than to entrust ourselves in "faith, hope, and love" (1 Corinthians 13). It's an old story and, apart from God's intervention, there is little good news for humanity's future.

Earlier we posed the question, "If a spring is defiled, can it be restored? Or is the source of the problem so deep and so hidden that there is no hope?" Can the wellspring of sinfulness found in the human heart be saved, cleansed, and sweetened? When Jesus' disciples were confounded by the overwhelming impossibility of anyone being saved, Jesus said, "For mortals it is impossible, but for God all things are possible" (Matthew 19:26).

When Moses and the Israelites entered the wilderness after their escape from Pharaoh's armies, they walked three days into the desert without water. When they came to a well at Marah, it was bitter. God intervened and "the water became sweet" (Exodus 15:22-25). When the prophet Elisha arrived in Jericho, the city complained that the water was bad. God intervened and "the water has been wholesome to this day" (2 Kings 2:19-22).

God instructs Jeremiah to declare:

> *My people have changed their glory*
> *for something that does not profit.*
> *Be appalled, O heavens, at this,*
> *be shocked, be utterly desolate,*
>   *says the LORD,*
> *for my people have committed two evils:*
> *they have forsaken me,*
> *the fountain of living water,*
>   *and dug out cisterns for themselves,*
> *cracked cisterns*
> *that can hold no water.*
>   *(Jeremiah 2:11-13)*

There is a solution, but it is not a simple admonition to try harder. It is a miraculous healing of our poisoned waters through divine intervention by "the fountain of living water" (Jeremiah 2:13). The hope of our salvation lies with God, not with us.

Waters of Life

Living water, the water we need for living, flows only from one Source. Living water heals the bitterness and death in waters soured and poisoned by sin. When God imparts to Ezekiel a vision of the restoration of heavenly glory upon the earth, the prophet is shown a sacred river flowing from the throne of God toward the Dead Sea:

> *And when it enters the sea, the sea of stagnant waters, the water will become fresh...and everything will live where the river goes.*　*(Ezekiel 47:8-9)*

In a similar scene, John's Revelation finishes the story of the New Testament. Jesus, the Lamb of God, is at the center of the throne and "will guide them to springs of the water of life, and God will wipe away every tear" (Revelation 7:17).

Perhaps Jesus himself best describes this living water image of God's solution to our sin problem. While in the city of Jerusalem during the festival commemorating the wilderness wanderings, Jesus cries out:

> *Let anyone who is thirsty come to me, and let the one who believes in me drink. As the scripture has said, "Out of the believer's heart shall flow rivers of living water."*
> *(John 7:37-38)*

John goes on to explain: "Now he said this about the Spirit, which believers in him were to receive" (John 7:39).

Is there a solution to the human problem? Can the poisoned life that flows from our sin-sick souls be sweetened and the glory of God flood the earth? Yes. The Savior announces, "Come to me," and the angel proclaims that the Savior will save his people from their sins. Yes, the final notes of the New Testament ring out:

> *Then the angel showed me the river of the water of life, bright as crystal, flowing from the throne of God and of the Lamb through the middle of the street of the city. On the other side of the river is the tree of life...; and the leaves of the tree are for the healing of the nations....*
> 　*And let everyone who hears say, "Come."*
> 　*And let everyone who is thirsty come.*
> 　*Let anyone who wishes take the water of life as a gift.*
> *(Revelation 22:1-2, 17)*

Later we will examine how Jesus enables this healing of our heart problem to become a reality. For now, though, let's join in the victory celebration. There is forgiveness and cleansing for all who will drink of the living water.

Q5

Has this image of living water been helpful? Is there another way you prefer to describe sin's problem and God's solution?

Camp Notes

Moving On

The trail we've been on this week is pretty steep. Before breaking camp and heading out again, take a few minutes to tell one another your thoughts and feelings about being on the trail so far. What has been the best part for you? What are you still looking forward to?

Make sure you take a moment to review next week's assignments.

READING ASSIGNMENTS

1. Record your reflections, questions, and insights from these daily Bible readings in your *My Witness Journal.*
   Day 1: Genesis 12:1-9 (God evangelizes.)
   Day 2: Exodus 3:7–4:20 (God accompanies.)
   Day 3: Isaiah 55 (God sends the word.)
   Day 4: Hosea 2:13–3:5 (God courts the beloved.)
   Day 5: Mark 1:1-39 (Jesus declares his mission.)
   Day 6: John 4:1-42 (Jesus evangelizes.)
2. As you read the chapter for next week (pages 27–32), underline or highlight special thoughts and answer the questions in the Q boxes.

ACTION ASSIGNMENT

During the week think about the images and feelings the word *evangelism* evokes in you. Then ask two or three others for their responses to the word. Write in your *My Witness Journal* the ideas you hear and the insights you gain.

End your time together in prayer.

See you on the path!

God as the Evangelist

Prayer

*God of heaven and of earth,
Thank you for leaving the glory
 of heaven to search the earth
 for lost children;
Thank you for seeking and finding me
 as I wandered in a dry and barren wilderness
 longing for living water;
Thank you for inviting me to join you
 on this trail of exploring how to offer
 your life-giving gift to others.
Make us all more beautiful revelations of your love
 and witnesses to your Son, our Savior,
In whose name we live and pray.*

Amen.

Trail Talk

Let's sing "O For a Thousand Tongues to Sing" together as we meet to discuss the week and wind up four weeks on the trail.

Charles Wesley wrote this hymn in 1739, just one year after both he and his brother John had experienced having their hearts "strangely warmed." In response to their own new assurance of God's forgiving and cleansing love through trusting in Christ alone for salvation, they began:

> *So far as we were able (and we knew God could work by whomsoever it pleased him) to* convince *those who would hear what true Christianity was, and to* persuade *them to embrace it.*[2]

The Wesleys and early Methodists never called this activity evangelism. That word was just not part of their vocabulary. Instead, they often referred to their efforts as "spreading scriptural holiness" or preaching "salvation," "true religion," or "true Christianity."

So, where did the words *evangelism, evangelist,* and *evangelize* come from? Actually, they have a strong biblical heritage. But before we get to that, take a few minutes to talk about notes from this week's *My Witness Journal* and the responses of others to the word *evangelism.*

O For a Thousand Tongues to Sing

*O for a thousand tongues to sing
my great Redeemer's praise,
the glories of my God and King,
the triumphs of his grace!*

*My gracious Master and my God,
assist me to proclaim,
to spread through all the earth abroad
the honors of thy name....*

*He speaks, and listening to his voice,
new life the dead receive;
the mournful, broken hearts rejoice,
the humble poor believe.*[3]

Q1
How would you define evangelism?

Camp Notes

There is a hiker on the trail named Hard Rock, who is out to use a sword and cut the darkness, to save the lost and free their souls at every shelter. He is loud and forward and has stepped on numerous toes. People are searching for something, some peace,...and Hard Rock headlocks them and gives them a Bible pile driver to set them straight. That hurts my heart.

Wadi

The Evangel Words

Over the last several years, many groups like yours have created a list of images and feelings in response to the word *evangelism*. Often, the list is divided between positive images and feelings and negative ones. It's not unusual for words like *pushy, manipulative,* and *emotional* to show up along with *gospel, salvation,* and *friend*. Frequently, people describe a number of evangelistic methods they either like or dislike, such as two by two, big tent, tracts, or loud. Did your group experience some of this diversity and tension in their interviews this week?

The original word *evangel* is a Greek word meaning good news. In old English it was known as *godspell* and later simplified to *gospel*. To deliver the evangel, or the gospel, is to evangelize or to do evangelism. In the Old Testament, the word most commonly used is to *herald* good news. The earliest heralds were runners who carried the good news of victory in battle (2 Samuel 18:19-33). In time, the idea of the victory message was enlarged to include God's total salvation, and the herald became all God's people and, ultimately, the Messiah (Isaiah 40:6-11; 52:7).

Exercise

Turn to Chapter 8 in the Book of Acts. Notice that in this time of persecution, the apostles (the evangelists) remained in Jerusalem (8:1-3). All the others were scattered and went evangelizing (8:14). Look at verses 4, 12, 25, and 35. In each of these verses the same verb, *evangelize*, is used. Read the verses, if you can, from several different Bible translations. Then record how this gospeling action is most commonly translated.

Acts 8:4 _____

or _____

Acts 8:12 _____

or _____

Acts 8:25 _____

or _____

Acts 8:35 _____

or _____

Q2

How beautiful upon the mountains
are the feet of the messenger
who announces peace,
who brings good news,
who announces salvation.
(Isaiah 52:7)

Why, do you suppose, does it say the messenger's feet are beautiful?

_____

_____

_____

_____

Sadly, in English we have almost always translated the verb *evangelize* as *preached* or *proclaimed* the gospel. Isn't it interesting that we have translated the verb, even as Philip sits next to a man in his taxi, as "he proclaimed [or preached] to him the good news" (Acts 8:35)? Isn't our image of preaching the gospel different from that of two people talking about the things of God? The sad thing is, this translation through the years has essentially removed the task of evangelizing from those who thought of themselves as others instead of as preachers. We are not all evangelists. We are not all preachers. We *are* all witnesses to God's good news, who need to be attentive to God the Evangelist.

Before we move on to explore the meaning of that last phrase, "God the Evangelist," take a few minutes to tell your ideas from the passages you read this week.

God the Evangelist

God is personally involved in both the desire and the activity needed to bring new life to all people. A summary of this week's reading assignments might look something like this:

God speaks to all creation, to chosen servants, and to all peoples.

God seeks Adam and Eve in the garden, Abraham and Sarah in far-off Mesopotamia, and all the nations of the earth through witnesses scattered everywhere.

God saves Moses from Pharaoh's wrath, the Hebrew children from slavery, and all humanity from the ravages of sin.

God sends the word of liberating power through an old hardheaded shepherd, a love-scorned prophet, and finally through the perfect messenger: God's own Son.

To Abraham God announced the word of covenant hope for all nations to be blessed through an old couple's faithful willingness to be instruments of God. To Moses God declared a longing for Abraham's offspring, the Israelites, to be set free and reminded the chosen but hesitant messenger, "I will be with you" (Exodus 3:12).

God speaks and God acts, and the two are one. God speaks the whole of creation into existence (Genesis 1). It is God's word that goes forth, accomplishes that which God intends, and does not return empty (Isaiah 55:11). Everything in the Bible reminds us that the spoken word is powerful. Each name in the Bible has meaning; it is not just a pleasant sound. We could say that the Bible believes in the power of words, and especially in the power of God's words. And God is absolutely committed to delivering the word of salvation to all people.

In order to demonstrate the steadfast and patient love God has for his unfaithful "wife," Israel, Hosea delivers God's gospel both as words to hear and as drama to behold—the spurned prophet buys back out of prostitution (redeems) his unfaithful wife, Gomer (Hosea 3).

Q3

What did you find in the Bible this week to help clarify God's design for evangelism?

Q4

Do you know the meaning of your name? Is it a biblical name?

Name: _____

Meaning: _____

_____

Camp Notes

Q5
Can you recite Isaiah 52:7?

_____

_____

_____

_____

The gifts he gave were that some would be apostles, some prophets, some evangelists, some pastors and teachers.

(Ephesians 4:11)

Name someone you think
of as an evangelist.

_____

Name someone (or several people)
you think of as a witness.

_____

Witness: one who tells out of personal experience what he or she has seen or heard or knows.

You are my witnesses, says the LORD.
(Isaiah 43:10)

When the Holy Spirit has come upon you,…you will be my witnesses.
(Acts 1:8)

Jesus asserts that it is inherent in his purpose for being here to "proclaim the message" (Mark 1:38). And in John's Gospel we read how Jesus practiced this message-bearing with a woman not normally seen as worthy, except in the eyes of God (John 4:7-27).

All of these snapshots are glimpses into the true meaning behind the evangel words. Evangelism is God's message, God's presence, God's power, God's salvation, God's Messiah, God's Spirit, and our feet. Maybe hiking and getting our feet in shape is a good metaphor after all!

We Are All Witnesses

God's greatest desire is to get our feet moving. Above all things, it is our feet that are "beautiful upon the mountains" as we seek to be God's runners, heralds, and witnesses. We often think witnessing and evangelism are mostly about being wonderfully gifted speakers; and since few of us are, we figure that lets us off the hook. Moses reminded God that he could hardly carry on a normal conversation because he was "slow of tongue" (Exodus 4:10-12). But God was less interested in his mouth than in his feet. I believe that is true for us as well. If we move our feet for God—that is, if we go where God leads us—we are reminded both by Scripture and by the Spirit, "I will be with you."

In evangelism, God uses us all. Was Mother Teresa an evangelist? Probably not. Was she a witness? Absolutely! Did she have a part to play in evangelism? Without question. It has already been said that we are not all evangelists, but that we are all witnesses. It is probably time to distinguish between these two complementary roles and responsibilities.

There are different gifts. Some are evangelists, and some evangelists are preachers; but some are also plumbers or homemakers or pediatricians. Many gifted evangelists are soft spoken, and that may include the person next to you in your Trail Talk circle. Or *you* may have this gift. Evangelists sense that telling others of God's gift in Christ is their passion and is naturally (or, we might better say, supernaturally) what they do with love for God and love for those needing to hear the gospel. We may all have this desire and opportunity from time to time, but an evangelist feels this is his or her number-one task and feels called and gifted to be about this ministry above all others.

Finding and encouraging those who have the gift to be evangelists is an important undertaking. It may even be a byproduct of what we are about on this journey. Our primary focus, however, is more on helping everyday Christians who aren't gifted as evangelists discover how to fulfill their responsibility as Christian witnesses. To be such Christian witnesses means learning how to move their feet (and tongues) in their churches and in their everyday environments to the tune of the gospel following the rhythm of God's Holy Spirit.

Something for the Trail

In the New Testament there are hundreds of pages describing how we should live in response to the grace of God. There are dozens of pages describing how a few of Christ's disciples, the apostles, carried out their assigned mission of taking the gospel to the ends of the earth. There are a few pages describing the impact ordinary Christians have on others as they live out God's salvation and become a divine fragrance for refreshing the world. And there is one exceptionally helpful text informing us all how to bear our witness with both feet and lips when the opportunity presents itself.

> *In your hearts set apart Christ as Lord. Always be prepared to give an answer to everyone who asks you to give the reason for the hope that you have. But do this with gentleness and respect.*
> (1 Peter 3:15, New International Version)

Can you see a threefold responsibility here? First, establish in the center of your own hearts the priority of Christ as Lord. Second, as you live your lives, exuding the gospel fragrance brought by the presence of Christ in you, be ready to answer people's questions about the hope that you have. Third, when the opportunity comes, speak in love to people, with gentleness and respect. Learning how to make this simple yet profound formula our daily reality is the goal for the rest of the journey. I hope you're happy to be part of the hike and ready to press on to Trail Two.

Moving On

Well, we've come to the end of Trail One. There is much more ahead, but this first trail has helped us get used to the gear, the group, and the pace. Our focus has been on expanding our view of (1) God's purpose, (2) our problem (sin), (3) God's provision for us in Christ and the Holy Spirit, and (4) our response as Christian witnesses. How are you doing?

Here are a few questions to consider: What has been most helpful? What is your greatest new discovery? What still needs more clarity for you? How are you feeling about having conversations with others in your group and with those outside your group?

Trail Two takes us up the mountain with Jesus. Who is Jesus? What is it that Jesus has really done, and what is he doing now? What does it mean to say, "I am Jesus' disciple" or "I am Jesus' witness"?

Take a moment to hear any announcements and to get any needed clarification of next week's assignments.

Camp Notes

Thanks be to God, who in Christ always leads us in triumphal procession, and through us spreads in every place the fragrance that comes from knowing him.
(2 Corinthians 2:14)

I had a great talk with Stray about God and faith. He used to go to church as a kid, until he saw it as a social event of prestige by appearance.... He is willing to go back if he does not have to appear a certain way to please others.... We have really clicked.

Wadi

Trail One, Session 5

READING ASSIGNMENTS

1. Record your reflections, questions, and insights from these daily Bible readings in your *My Witness Journal.*
   - **Day 1:** Ecclesiastes 12 (the Teacher and Truth)
   - **Day 2:** Luke 2:21-40 (a prophet's prophecy)
   - **Day 3:** Mark 6:1-16 (a prophet's hometown)
   - **Day 4:** Matthew 22 (challenging the Teacher)
   - **Day 5:** John 3:1-10 (two teachers)
   - **Day 6:** John 13:1-17 (the Teacher's example)
2. As you read the chapter for next week (pages 34–38), underline or highlight special thoughts and answer the questions in the Q boxes.

ACTION ASSIGNMENT

During the week find at least one time to mention the name Jesus in a conversation with someone outside your church circles. Note any response and write down your observations in your *My Witness Journal.*

Close camp with prayer or another round of songs. Perhaps you will want to sing "O For a Thousand Tongues to Sing" again. Or perhaps someone in the group will want to suggest another song.

See you on the path!

Trail Two
Up the Mountain With Jesus

When Jesus saw the crowds, he went up the mountain.

(Matthew 5:1)

Jesus as Prophet-Teacher

Prayer

Gracious God of all truth and wisdom,
thank you for granting to us through Jesus
a clear revelation of your will,
and for instructing us
in the way that leads to life eternal.
He who is the light of the world
has illumined our path
and saved us from stumbling in the dark.
Grant, as we gather once more at Jesus' feet,
that we would hear your word,
that we would sense your presence,
and that we would be better witnesses.
In Jesus' name we pray.

Amen.

Trail Talk

Jesus was sometimes referred to as a prophet. The Samaritan woman he met at the well said to him, "Sir, I see that you are a prophet" (John 4:19). Likewise, the man born blind, when describing Jesus as the one who had healed him, said, "He is a prophet" (John 9:17). But more often he was simply called Teacher, a designation he readily accepted for himself.

> *Go into the city to a certain man, and say to him, "The Teacher says, My time is near; I will keep the Passover at your house with my disciples."* (Matthew 26:18)

Jesus was both a prophet and a teacher. As we head up the mountain with him, our goal, like those early disciples, is to learn from one whose words and deeds reveal the things of God and offer unusual wisdom for living.

> *When Jesus saw the crowds, he went up the mountain; and after he sat down, his disciples came to him. Then he began to speak, and taught them.* (Matthew 5:1)

What is the heart of his message? How do his signs and wonders contribute to this message? How was he similar and how was he different from the other teachers and prophets? These are some of the questions we will explore together. But first, report your own observations from this week's readings, and then talk about any responses you received when you mentioned Jesus' name in conversations.

Jesus as Prophet

Jesus was a prophet. Sometimes it seems strange for those of us who acknowledge that he is more than a prophet to say that Jesus was a prophet. We do not want others to think of Jesus as only one among many messengers of God. But Jesus carried all the marks of a prophet; he was nothing less even if something more.

And what might these marks be? Actually, it could be a rather long list. However, prophets, both men and women, were more often recognized intuitively than by a checklist of characteristics. Nevertheless, let's start with a short checklist.

Prophets had a special call from God to speak and act for God. Moses is perhaps the archetype of this call. On the backside of nowhere while tending sheep, Moses was found by God and called to be God's spokesman (Exodus 3–4).

Jeremiah recorded his own story this way:

> Now the word of the LORD came to me saying,
> "Before I formed you in the womb I knew you,
> and before you were born I consecrated you;
> I appointed you a prophet to the nations."
> Then I said, "Ah, Lord GOD! Truly I do not know how to
> speak, for I am only a boy." But the LORD said to me,
> "Do not say, 'I am only a boy';
> for you shall go to all to whom I send you,
> and you shall speak whatever I command you.
> Do not be afraid of them,
> for I am with you to deliver you,
>   says the LORD."
> Then the LORD put out his hand and touched my mouth; and
> the LORD said to me,
> "Now I have put my words in your mouth."
>
> *(Jeremiah 1:4-9)*

Prophets knew they had little choice but to say, "Thus says the LORD!" Sometimes they received the words of the Lord, as with Jeremiah, and sometimes they had a vision. Like John the Baptist, they delivered their message with unusual boldness, often challenging the established social-political-religious order and calling for repentance and actions befitting God's concern for justice, mercy, and truth. Both Jesus and John came declaring, "Repent, for the kingdom of heaven has come near" (Matthew 3:2; 4:17). And Jesus said, "I do nothing on my own, but I speak these things as the Father instructed me" (John 8:28).

Prophets sometimes knew intuitively what others did not. In this sense they were gifted with what some call psychic powers. The prophet Elisha knew the things that were spoken only in the king's bedchamber (2 Kings 6:12).

Q1
What descriptive words come to mind when you think of a prophet?

Q2
Do you know any modern-day prophets?

When the chief priests and the Pharisees heard his parables, they realized that he was speaking about them. They wanted to arrest him, but they feared the crowds, because they regarded him as a prophet.

(Matthew 21:45-46)

Camp Notes

Q3
Which fulfilled prophecies about Jesus as the Messiah come to your mind?

_____

_____

_____

_____

One day, while he was teaching, Pharisees and teachers of the law were sitting near by (they had come from every village of Galilee and Judea and from Jerusalem); and the power of the Lord was with him to heal.
(Luke 5:17)

They were astounded at his teaching, for he taught them as one having authority, and not as the scribes. *(Mark 1:22)*

Q4
Who was one of your favorite teachers? Why?

_____

_____

_____

_____

The Lord GOD has given me
the tongue of a teacher,
that I may know how to sustain
the weary with a word.
Morning by morning he wakens—
wakens my ear
to listen as those who are taught.
(Isaiah 50:4)

Nathan was sent by God to confront David with his secret sin of adultery and murder (2 Samuel 12:1-14). Jesus was recognized as a prophet by the woman at the well (John 4:19) because he knew her story without anyone to inform him. On occasion, prophets also announced what was to come in the future, and people waited for their prophecies to be fulfilled. Many of these foretellings concerned the Messiah, and Matthew is especially careful to remind his Jewish audience that Jesus fulfilled these prophecies. Jesus also prophesied the future, including his death and resurrection (Mark 9:31–32) and his return in glory (Mark 13:24-27).

Great prophets were sometimes recognized by their part in God's miraculous interventions. Moses, Elijah, Elisha, and Jesus all manifested this miracle-working power. Some saw the miracles of Jesus as signs that he was Satan's tool, but Jesus and those he healed declared such thinking foolish (Matthew 12:22-32; John 9:16-17) and reminded everyone to see instead the activity of the Spirit of God. When Jesus took Peter, James, and John up the high mountain with him (Matthew 17:1-8), they witnessed his transfiguration; but they also noticed the company he kept: Moses and Elijah. Jesus was indeed a prophet among prophets, even prophets from beyond the grave.

Jesus as Teacher

As might be expected, although both prophets and teachers were acknowledged as devout and gifted servants of God, there were more teachers than prophets. In Jesus' day a teacher, or rabbi, was usually a scholar well trained in Jewish law who frequently had an entourage of disciples (males only!) and often a school of his own. Jesus had disciples (both men and women) who accompanied him (Luke 8:1-3). But Jesus had no formal training, and his school was wherever he was as he wandered from place to place. Another troublesome characteristic of this rabbi, Jesus, was his age. A true and respected teacher had to be at least forty, but Jesus was barely thirty when he began his ministry (Luke 3:23). The whole scene around Jesus was nonconformist, and many who knew and followed the normal social rules were confused. In spite of all that seemed against it, Jesus almost immediately established himself as a rabbi, a teacher who "taught them as one having authority" (Matthew 7:29).

A teacher was expected to possess wisdom, not just information or knowledge. A teacher was to write "words of truth plainly" (Ecclesiastes 12:10) and "sustain the weary with a word" (Isaiah 50:4). Jesus clearly seemed to be one who in the spirit of Isaiah listened to the Lord God so that he might be taught. He often said things such as the following:

> *My teaching is not mine but his who sent me. Anyone who resolves to do the will of God will know whether the teaching is from God or whether I am speaking on my own.*
> *(John 7:16-17)*

And what was it that this teacher taught? It's not an easy question to answer quickly, but in reality this is all we sometimes have the chance to tell others. Remembering the passages you read this week and anything else that comes to mind, what would you say are the four or five most important things Jesus wanted people to learn from his teaching? Use the space available in the side column to create your list; then listen at the campfire as the others in your trail group tell their ideas.

It would be a good idea to keep working on this list as you read from the Bible in the weeks ahead. Some would say the heart of Jesus' teaching is contained in the Sermon on the Mount (Matthew 5–7). Indeed, these words are close to the essence of his instructions on how to live in the kingdom of God, but there are other even more difficult sayings.

Exercise

Read the passages listed below and take notes as you try to get to the heart of Jesus' message. Note especially the teachings that created the most debate and discussion about Jesus. Would these be controversial today?

Matthew 22:34-46

_____

_____

Luke 15:1-10

_____

_____

Luke 24:13-27

_____

_____

John 6:25-42

_____

_____

Jesus teaches us about God, ourselves, our neighbors, his own true identity, and about finding eternal life. He is Prophet and Teacher. Who else is he?

Q5
What did Jesus teach?

Your List

What Others Thought

Camp Notes

Masada is a mountaintop near the Dead Sea that is difficult to access and was used as a fortress by the Jewish people. David wrote in Psalm 18:2: "The LORD is my rock, my fortress (Masada), and my deliverer." My body is being broken upon the rocks of the Appalachians, but my soul and spirit are being built on Jesus, the Rock.

Wadi

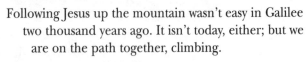

Moving On

Following Jesus up the mountain wasn't easy in Galilee two thousand years ago. It isn't today, either; but we are on the path together, climbing.

Take a few minutes for any announcements and to review the assignments for next week. You will be looking at the Jesus who is more than a teacher and a prophet—much more.

READING ASSIGNMENTS

1. Record your reflections, questions, and insights from these daily Bible readings in your *My Witness Journal*.
   - **Day 1:** Matthew 8 (many titles, take your pick)
   - **Day 2:** Luke 19:1-10 (why the Son of Man came)
   - **Day 3:** Mark 10:32-45 (what the Son of Man must do)
   - **Day 4:** John 1:1-18 (the word of God made flesh)
   - **Day 5:** Philippians 2:1-11 (Christ Jesus in the form of God)
   - **Day 6:** Colossians 1:1-20 ("the image of the invisible God")
2. As you read the chapter for next week (pages 39–44), underline or highlight special thoughts and answer the questions in the Q boxes.

ACTION ASSIGNMENT

During the week ask at least one person, "Have you ever really wondered who Jesus is?" Encourage some conversation that includes more than a yes or no answer. Write down in your *My Witness Journal* the ideas you hear and the insights you gain.

See you on the path!

Jesus as Son of Man and Son of God

Prayer: A Statement of Faith

The Nicene Creed

We believe in one God,
the Father, the Almighty,
maker of heaven and earth,
of all that is, seen and unseen.

We believe in one Lord, Jesus Christ,
the only Son of God,
eternally begotten of the Father,
God from God, Light from Light,
true God from true God,
begotten, not made,
of one Being with the Father;
through him all things were made.
For us and for our salvation
he came down from heaven,
was incarnate of the Holy Spirit and the Virgin Mary
and became truly human.

(The Nicene Creed was composed over a period of 126 years, A.D. 325 to A.D. 451. English translation of the Nicene Creed prepared by the English Language Liturgical Consultation [ELLC], 1988. Used by permission.)

Trail Talk

Over the centuries the Christian church has tried to clarify for itself and for the world the unique nature of Jesus. Both the Bible and Christian experience, from the earliest disciples until today, testify that Jesus is a truly unusual person. Who is he?

> *Now when Jesus came into the district of Caesarea Philippi, he asked his disciples, "Who do people say that the Son of Man is?" And they said, "Some say John the Baptist, but others Elijah, and still others Jeremiah or one of the prophets." He said to them, "But who do you say that I am?" Simon Peter answered, "You are the Messiah, the Son of the living God."*
> *(Matthew 16:13-16)*

Is he a prophet? the Son of Man? the Son of God? the Messiah? Jesus answered Peter:

> *Blessed are you, Simon son of Jonah! For flesh and blood has not revealed this to you, but my Father in heaven.*
> *(Matthew 16:17)*

Our Trail Talk in this session explores the meaning of Jesus' identity as Son of Man and Son of God.

Son of Man

How do you picture Jesus? What does he look like? Do you have a favorite artist's painting of him? Does the image of an actor who played the role of Jesus in a movie come to mind? Do you enjoy the great Renaissance depictions of Jesus or the Orthodox icons of Jesus, or do you find them strange? What would Jesus look like today? How would you recognize him? Have you ever had a dream or vision of Jesus? When you say or hear the name Jesus, what do you see?

Have you noticed that down through the ages, and even today in varying cultures and lands, we portray Jesus like us—and yet different. Is this right? Well, the answer is both yes and no. The Jesus of history, who was baptized in the Jordan River, who stripped grain in his hands as he walked through fields, who wept over the city of Jerusalem, and who died a common criminal's death on a Roman cross, was a young Jewish male from Nazareth in Galilee. He spoke a language none of us would understand, Aramaic, with a northern accent that was looked down on by sophisticated big-city people. He walked around days at a time homeless (Luke 9:58), and he did not bother to wash when invited into a home for a meal (Luke 11:37-38). Is this the Jesus you picture? Actually, we know almost nothing about his appearance, except that he probably looked quite different from the way we usually picture him.

Jesus was the Son of Man. What was he saying by choosing this title for himself? To begin with, the designation simply means human or mortal. He knew hunger and thirst (John 19:28) and digested food the same as we do. He grew tired after a long day's walk (John 4:6), and he sometimes fell asleep when others thought he should be awake (Matthew 8:23-25). And Jesus could suffer and die, just as we do. As we acknowledge in the Nicene Creed, Jesus was fully human.

The writer of Hebrews saw this as a critically important piece of the gospel:

> *It was fitting that God, for whom and through whom all things exist, in bringing many children to glory, should make the pioneer of their salvation perfect through sufferings. For the one who sanctifies and those who are sanctified all have one Father. For this reason Jesus is not ashamed to call them brothers and sisters… For it is clear that he did not come to help angels, but the descendants of Abraham. Therefore he had to become like his brothers and sisters in every respect, so that he might be a merciful and faithful high priest in the service of God, to make a sacrifice of atonement for the sins of the people. Because he himself was tested by what he suffered, he is able to help those who are being tested.*
> *(Hebrews 2:10-11, 16-18)*

Camp Notes

Q1
What characteristics would you want to make sure were included in your favorite picture of Jesus?

_____

_____

_____

_____

_____

Today was one of the hardest for me in many ways. If it were possible to quit, I would have. The 83-degree sun beat down upon me, adding to the struggle of the several thousand feet gain I had to face…. I was tired of taking breaks, tired of praying for strength, tired of walking forward when I had no energy, tired of sweating, and tired of the challenge.

Wadi

For we do not have a high priest who is unable to sympathize with our weaknesses, but we have one who in every respect has been tested as we are, yet without sin. Let us therefore approach the throne of grace with boldness, so that we may receive mercy and find grace to help in time of need.

(Hebrews 4:15-16)

Jesus can be the perfect pioneer or trail guide who opens the way for all humanity to come to God. He can do this because he knows by experience every rebuff, every pain, every trial, every temptation that we face—yet without sin. He understands. He has been there. We can come to him because he is one of us, yet different in the best way.

Have we at times made Jesus too distant, too clean, too divine? Have we seen him as other than human to the degree that he could not possibly understand what we think or feel? To think of Jesus this way is a grave mistake. Jesus is fully human. That's why he can be "the pioneer and perfecter of our faith" (Hebrews 12:2).

But there is more to the expression *Son of Man* than "fully human." *Son of Man* is a special term selected by Jesus from the Old Testament prophets, especially Ezekiel and Daniel. The expression in Hebrew is *ben 'adam*, or son of adam. The Adam of Genesis 1 is the first man created by God. In the Old Testament Book of Ezekiel, the expression *Son of Man* occurs ninety-three times. "Son of man" is the way God addresses the prophet. The New Revised Standard Version of the Bible simply translates it "O mortal," but most versions keep the translation "Son of Man." Notice the assignment given to Ezekiel as Son of Man:

> *He said to me, "Son of man, stand up on your feet and I will speak to you." As he spoke, the Spirit came into me and raised me to my feet, and I heard him speaking to me. He said: "Son of man, I am sending you to the Israelites, to a rebellious nation... Say to them, 'This is what the Sovereign LORD says,' whether they listen or fail to listen."*
>
> *(Ezekiel 2:1-3; 3:11, New International Version)*

"In the thirtieth year,...the heavens were opened," and Ezekiel received his calling as a prophet (Ezekiel 1:1). He was both a priest and a prophet. He announced both hope and judgment. He clarified that each individual is personally responsible for his or her own righteousness or sin. If "the wicked turn away from all their sins..., they shall surely live," and if the "righteous turn away..., they shall die" (Ezekiel 18:1-4, 19-32). Full of divine love and compassion for errant children, God proclaims the warning:

> *Get yourselves a new heart and a new spirit! Why will you die, O house of Israel? For I have no pleasure in the death of anyone, says the Lord GOD. Turn, then, and live.*
>
> *(Ezekiel 18:31-32)*

Q2

How does the fact that Jesus is "fully human" affect your faith in him and your commitment to him as one of his disciples?

_____

_____

_____

_____

_____

Living in mainstream America, one concentrates on the extras of life and not simplicity or just needs. How little we truly need. By living a material life, we forget how to be open to a more vulnerable way of living.... The first lesson in hiking and in following the lead of God is pain and suffering. It hurts. But in knowing hurt we are refined.

Wadi

Can you see the ministry of Jesus, the Son of Man, in Ezekiel's message?

But even more important than Ezekiel's frequent use of the term *Son of Man* is Daniel's single reference to the Son of Man. In his strange vision of the judgment of the world's kingdoms and the arrival of the kingdom of God, Daniel sees one like a Son of Man, "coming with the clouds of heaven":

> *And he came to the Ancient One*
> > *[God upon his throne]*
> > *and was presented before him.*
> *To him was given dominion*
> > *and glory and kingship,*
> *that all peoples, nations, and languages*
> > *should serve him.*
> *His dominion is an everlasting dominion*
> > *that shall not pass away,*
> *and his kingship is one*
> > *that shall never be destroyed.*
> > > *(Daniel 7:13-14)*

Jesus boldly selects the title Son of Man perhaps because of its dual meaning. Thus he protected his true identity from those who would not believe that in him God's kingdom had arrived. And truly this Son of Man was both human and heavenly.

Son of God

Jesus preferred to call himself the Son of Man, but others recognized him as the Son of God. The angel Gabriel announced to Mary that her child would be "holy" and "called Son of God" (Luke 1:35). The devil tempted Jesus in the wilderness, saying, "If you are the Son of God," do this or that (Matthew 4:1-11). The demons inhabiting tormented souls came forth at his touch, shouting, "You are the Son of God!" But Jesus "rebuked them and would not allow them to speak, because they knew that he was the Messiah" (Luke 4:41; see also Matthew 8:28-29).

Perhaps the turning point for accepting the title came at Caesarea Philippi when Peter put it all together and answered Jesus, "You are the Messiah, the Son of the living God" (Matthew 16:16). Although Matthew, Mark, and Luke all acknowledge this special identity of Jesus, no one makes more of it than John does. As the last of the Gospel writers, he reveals the clearest record of Jesus' special relationship with God as "his only Son" (John 3:16).

The crowd answered him, "We have heard from the law that the Messiah remains forever. How can you say that the Son of Man must be lifted up? Who is this Son of Man?" (John 12:34)

Then the sign of the Son of Man will appear in heaven, and then all the tribes of the earth will mourn, and they will see "the Son of Man coming on the clouds of heaven" with power and great glory. (Matthew 24:30)

Remember in your reading this week how John names Jesus as the active and creative word of God moving into this world, bringing light and life and giving to "all who received him, who believed in his name…power to become children of God" (John 1:12). John's Gospel, as well as the three letters of John, is full of insight into the meaning of Jesus' identity as God's Son. Jesus testifies:

> *God so loved the world that he gave his only Son.*
> *(John 3:16)*
>
> *The Father loves the Son and has placed all things in his hands. Whoever believes in the Son has eternal life.*
> *(John 3:35-36)*
>
> *Whatever the Father does, the Son does likewise.*
> *(John 5:19)*
>
> *For just as the Father has life in himself, so he has granted the Son also to have life in himself.* *(John 5:26)*

The claims of being a Son with a divine identity continued until Jesus uttered the words that led to his eventual crucifixion:

> *"The Father and I are one." The Jews took up stones again to stone him. Jesus replied, "I have shown you many good works from the Father. For which of these are you going to stone me?" The Jews answered, "It is not for a good work that we are going to stone you, but for blasphemy, because you, though only a human being, are making yourself God."*
> *(John 10:30-33)*

Even today many believe in Jesus the teacher or the prophet or the Son of Man, but they doubt that Jesus ever claimed or wanted to be thought of as the Son of God and "of one Being with the Father" (from the Nicene Creed). We will explore more of this later, but it is clear that Jesus is not someone who can easily be dismissed. His works and teachings and self-identity claims are such that his question to Peter still demands a decision: "Who do *you* say that I am?"

Camp Notes

Q3

What other characteristics of Jesus as the eternal Son of God emerged from the two passages read this week from Paul's letters?

Philippians 2:1-11

Colossians 1:1-20

Camp Notes

Q4
Looking back over your own life of faith, what are the stages you have gone through in terms of answering the question, "Who do you say that I am?"

Moving On

Next week we will look more closely at how these images fit together to reveal Jesus as Messiah, King, and God. But before we break camp, take a few minutes to tell your answers to the question in **Q4,** or to tell any new insights discovered in the last week or two that have made you more excited about being a witness for Jesus.

Review next week's assignments.

READING ASSIGNMENTS

1. Record your reflections, questions, and insights from these daily Bible readings in your *My Witness Journal.*
   - **Day 1:** Matthew 1:1–2:15 (the Messiah's arrival)
   - **Day 2:** John 1:19-51 (recognizing the Messiah)
   - **Day 3:** Luke 24:1-35 (the risen Christ Jesus clarifies)
   - **Day 4:** Deuteronomy 17:14-20 (qualities of God's true King)
   - **Day 5:** John 18:33–19:22 (King of the Jews)
   - **Day 6:** Revelation 19:1-16 ("King of kings and Lord of lords")
2. As you read the chapter for next week (pages 45–50), underline or highlight special thoughts and answer the questions in the Q boxes.

ACTION ASSIGNMENT

During the week listen to hear people's needs. Tell at least three people that you will be praying for them. List the names of those people and their needs in your *My Witness Journal.* Add any comments you wish about your experience of intercessory prayer.

Keep climbing. Pray for one another during the week.

See you on the path!

Jesus as Messiah, King, and God

Prayer

When Jesus saw people, he had compassion for them (Matthew 9:35-38). People with all kinds of needs flocked to him. One paralyzed man had friends who brought him to a house where Jesus was teaching and let him down through the roof. Jesus forgave the man's sins and sent him home walking and glorifying God (Luke 5:17-26).

Jesus equipped his disciples to minister to people in the same way he had. And as he prepared them for his departure, he told them:

> *Very truly, I tell you, if you ask anything of the Father in my name, he will give it to you. Until now you have not asked for anything in my name. Ask and you will receive, so that your joy may be complete.* (John 16:23-24)

Prayer in Jesus' name is a ministry and a source of joy. It is part of every Christian's heritage. Paul wrote:

> *I thank my God every time I remember you, constantly praying with joy in every one of my prayers for all of you… For God is my witness, how I long for all of you with the compassion of Christ Jesus. And this is my prayer, that your love may over-flow more and more.* (Philippians 1:3-4, 8-9)

Paul finished this Philippian letter by admonishing them:

> *Do not worry about anything, but in everything by prayer and supplication with thanksgiving let your requests be made known to God. And the peace of God, which surpasses all understanding, will guard your hearts and your minds in Christ Jesus.* (Philippians 4:6-7)

In one sense, Christian prayer is a mystery. It is not magic. It is not manipulation. It is a faithful and obedient effort to align our hearts with the will of God in the name and Spirit of Jesus. It is communion, a two-way conversation with the One who invites us to ask, search, and knock (Matthew 7:7) so that we might know God's presence and power. It is bringing our selves, our friends, and indeed the whole world to Jesus.

Camp Notes

In the morning, while it was still very dark, he got up and went out to a deserted place, and there he prayed. (Mark 1:35)

The Lord's Prayer

Our Father, who art in heaven,
hallowed by thy name.
Thy kingdom come,
thy will be done on earth
as it is in heaven.
Give us this day our daily bread.
And forgive us our trespasses,
as we forgive those who
trespass against us.
And lead us not into temptation,
but deliver us from evil.
For thine is the kingdom, and
the power, and the glory, forever.[4]
Amen.

Camp Notes

_____

_____

_____

_____

_____

_____

> ## Q1
> Does saying Jesus Christ when it means Jesus Messiah (anointed) feel any different? If yes, how?
>
> _____
>
> _____
>
> _____
>
> _____
>
> _____

The well-known star of David is today a symbol for the nation of Israel. In Jesus' day, it likewise was a common symbol of God's promise, and it decorated the synagogue in Capernaum where Jesus frequently worshiped.

Begin this time together with a few minutes of quiet reflection. In your mind's eye see Jesus in your midst. "Where two or three are gathered in my name, I am there among them" (Matthew 18:20). Praise God for what you have been learning. Offer yourself again to Christ as his instrument of love and grace. Pray again for each person you were led to this week as part of your witness.

Trail Talk

This week you focused on noticing others' needs and praying for them. Did you find it easy or difficult? What effect did this exercise in prayer have on you? What responses did it elicit from those you spoke with and prayed for? What answers to prayer do you have that you can celebrate?

For the last few weeks we have been trying to draw closer to Jesus and discover his true identity. We have walked with him as prophet, teacher, Son of Man, Son of God, and most recently as Messiah, King, and God Incarnate. Before heading up this last steep trail together, tell any observations or insights you have noted in your *My Witness Journal* from this week's readings.

Jesus Messiah

Hope for the arrival of an anointed one (*messiah* in Hebrew, *christos* in Greek) emerges slowly in the Old Testament. Anointing, or pouring oil from a horn held over someone's head, was a means of recognizing a servant chosen by God for a special purpose. The verb *anoint* occurs in various forms sixty-nine times in the Old Testament and most commonly describes the ritual of ordaining a high priest or enthroning a king.

> *Samuel said to Jesse, "Are all your sons here?" And he said, "There remains yet the youngest, but he is keeping the sheep." And Samuel said to Jesse, "Send and bring him; for we will not sit down until he comes here." He sent and brought him in. Now he was ruddy, and had beautiful eyes, and was handsome. The LORD said, "Rise and anoint him; for this is the one." Then Samuel took the horn of oil, and anointed him in the presence of his brothers; and the spirit of the LORD came mightily upon David from that day forward.*
>
> (1 Samuel 16:11-13)

David as God's anointed becomes a symbol of divine intervention through a human agent that is carried through the psalms and the prophets. God's chosen servants—intended to be Israel as a nation and the royal line of kings from David—turn out to be less than up to the challenge. The promises of an anointed (a messiah) who will fulfill all the designs of God's rule and reign move toward a heavenly figure who will come and establish justice and peace on earth (Isaiah 11:1-9).

As we have seen, the New Testament is full of quotations from the psalms and the prophets demonstrating that Jesus fulfills the role of Messiah. One key example is Jesus' own challenge to the Pharisees who were anxious to test him on all fronts: "Jesus asked them this question, 'What do you think of the Messiah? Whose son is he?'" (Matthew 22:41-42). This inquiry is prompted by the messianic promise of Psalm 110:1, a text that is referred to several times in the New Testament (Acts 2:34-35; Hebrews 1:13; 10:12-13).

Likewise, Jesus frequently referred to Isaiah and to passages from the psalms and other prophets to establish his own authenticity (Matthew 11:1-6; Luke 4:14-21; 24:13-53). And Philip explained to the court official from Ethiopia that Isaiah's suffering servant (Isaiah 53), who "like a lamb silent before his shearer...does not open his mouth," is none other than Jesus, the Messiah (Acts 8:26-39).

This final image of God's Messiah suffering and dying for the sins of the world is one of the most difficult for Jews and Muslims and some Buddhists to accept. Their thinking is that if divine favor were truly upon this man Jesus, God would not allow him to be humiliated and put to death as a common criminal. For them, whatever else Jesus was, surely he was not God's anointed Messiah or God's Son and Savior of the world. "Just look around," the argument goes, "the world is still a mess and unsaved."

King Jesus

In your reading this week, one early description of a true king of Israel was clarified in Deuteronomy 17:14-20. Was Jesus this king? Yes, but much more. The anointed King of the Jews, who would establish God's reign forever, seemed to be announced by the appearance of his star (Matthew 2). But King Herod's rule was threatened by such an untimely arrival.

Thirty years later, on what we call Palm Sunday, a multitude in Jerusalem shouted, "Blessed is the king" (Luke 19:38), as Jesus rode into the city on the back of a young donkey. Yet Jesus wept, realizing that most were blind to the truth of that announcement (Luke 19:41-46). Although he was crucified as King of the Jews, even his disciples wondered why he had not yet overthrown the Roman rule and set up his much-talked-about kingdom of God.

Jesus had modeled his kingdom and declared, "My kingdom is not from this world" (John 18:33-37). His kingdom was an alternative kingdom for all peoples. After his resurrection he continued to instruct his disciples about this kingdom and told them to prepare to be his witnesses (Acts 1:1-8) and make disciples of all peoples, since "all authority in heaven and on earth" had been given to him (Matthew 28:18-20). As one risen from the dead, he is King Jesus, but also the messianic Lamb and suffering Servant who will on one final day separate the sheep from the goats and conquer all who make war on God's Anointed. A day is coming when all will know he is "Lord of lords and King of kings" (Revelation 17:14). In fact, he is *Emmanuel,* God with us (Matthew 1:23).

The LORD says to my lord,
"Sit at my right hand
until I make your enemies
your footstool."
(Psalm 110:1)

Q2
Have you ever felt confused about Jesus' death or known someone who wondered why God would let his own Son die?

_____

_____

_____

How would you answer this argument against Jesus as the Messiah?

_____

_____

_____

_____

_____

_____

Where is the child who has been born king of the Jews? For we observed his star at its rising, and have come to pay him homage.
(Matthew 2:2)

Jesus, God Incarnate

Q3
Is it easy or difficult for you to think of Jesus as your King? Why?

_____

_____

_____

_____

_____

As if believing in Jesus as the long-awaited Messiah and King of Israel were not enough, the title Son of God and Lord added to the challenge. Human imagination was stretched to the breaking point when Jesus said, "The Father and I are one" (John 10:30) and "Whoever has seen me has seen the Father" (John 14:9). Yet, Emmanuel, God with us, had been promised; and Jesus accepted the God-Man identity both before and after his crucifixion and resurrection.

Jews knew from the heart of their history, the Shema (Deuteronomy 6:4-5), that the "LORD alone" was God. God was one; there were no others. Therefore, how could any sane or faithful Jew make the claims that Jesus seemed to and accept praise, honor, and glory that belonged only to the Lord God alone? This was the ultimate "Jesus problem." Perhaps it still is.

The Lord God had said:

> Turn to me and be saved,
>   all the ends of the earth!
>   For I am God, and there is no other.
> By myself I have sworn,
>   from my mouth has gone forth
>   in righteousness
>   a word that shall not return:
> "To me every knee shall bow,
>   every tongue shall swear."
>   (Isaiah 45:22-23)

In order for me to be who God wants me to be, I need to cease to be what I want to be. I need to identify myself with other creations of God, to try to see through their eyes instead of seeing my own views. Becoming incarnational always leads to death, death of things in and about me. But doing this will help me relate.

Wadi

But the disciples of Jesus apply such language to their Master and Messiah and Lord and announce that he is God. Recall Paul's words from Session 7:

> Let the same mind be in you that was in Christ Jesus,
>   who, though he was in the form of God,
>   did not regard equality with God
>   as something to be exploited,
>   but emptied himself,
>   taking the form of a slave, being born in human likeness.
>   And being found in human form, he humbled himself
>   and became obedient to the point of death—
>   even death on a cross.
>
> Therefore God also highly exalted him
>   and gave him the name that is above every name,
>   so that at the name of Jesus
>   every knee should bend, in heaven and on earth and
>   under the earth,
>   and every tongue should confess
>   that Jesus Christ is Lord, to the glory of God the Father.
>   (Philippians 2:5-11)

Jesus assumes a long list of prerogatives restricted to God: He forgives sins (Luke 5:20-21); he raises the dead (Luke 8:49-56; John 5:21; 11:38-44); he judges the nations (Matthew 25:31-46; John 5:22-23); he saves (Matthew 1:21; Acts 4:11-12; 1 Timothy 1:15); he is the resurrection (John 11:25); he is worshiped with the Father (Philippians 2:10-11; 2 Peter 3:18; Revelation 5:11-14); he receives prayers (Acts 7:59-60; 2 Corinthians 12:8-9); he is Lord (John 20:26-28; Acts 2:34-36); and he is preexistent and the Creator (John 1:1-4; Colossians 1:15-20).

In time the full meaning of this incarnation of God as a human being had to be clarified. The early church simply announced Jesus' teachings and their experience:

> *We declare to you what was from the beginning, what we have heard, what we have seen with our eyes, what we have looked at and touched with our hands, concerning the word of life—this life was revealed, and we have seen it and testify to it, and declare to you the eternal life that was with the Father and was revealed to us—...so that you also may have fellowship with us; and truly our fellowship is with the Father and with his Son Jesus Christ.*   *(1 John 1:1-3)*

Gradually, we came to understand and explain this mystery as the Holy Trinity—one God in three persons. We will examine this concept later, but Christians have always believed that in Jesus Christ (Messiah) we are in the presence of God Almighty.

Read again the lines from the Nicene Creed (page 39) and then the passage above from John's letter. Is this your witness? Have you seen, heard, and touched this reality? Do you have fellowship with the Father and with his Son Jesus Christ? If so, with Paul you can say, "I believed, and so I spoke" (2 Corinthians 4:13).

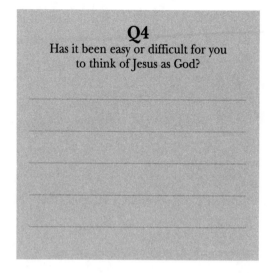

Q4
Has it been easy or difficult for you to think of Jesus as God?

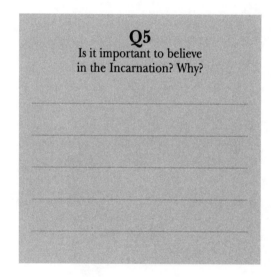

Q5
Is it important to believe in the Incarnation? Why?

Camp Notes

As I move through the world of mountains, sky, trees, and animals, I am seeing God through this creation. I am seeing Christ at the center of the cosmic community. I am seeing God reveal himself through who I am and seeing that he cares about the intimate issues of my life.

Wadi

Moving On

Take a few minutes to review next week's assignments.

READING ASSIGNMENTS

1. Record your reflections, questions, and insights from these daily Bible readings in your *My Witness Journal.*

Day 1: John 3:1-21 ("born from above")
Day 2: Luke 7:36-50 (Which one loves more?)
Day 3: Matthew 7:1-28 (saying, "Lord, Lord")
Day 4: John 15:1-17 (branches and friends)
Day 5: Romans 9:27–10:13 (your lips and your heart)
Day 6: Ephesians 2 (by grace through faith)

2. As you read the chapter for next week (pages 51–56), underline or highlight special thoughts and answer the questions in the Q boxes.

ACTION ASSIGNMENT

Last week we prayed for those whom we knew had an obvious need. This week we want to begin praying for people whose needs may not be so obvious. From all of the conversations you have had so far on the trail, prayerfully select three to six people you sense need a clearer understanding of and a more faith-filled relationship with Jesus Christ. Pray for those people daily. Be ready for any opportunity to tell them about what you believe and what you've been learning. Keep good journal notes.

Jesus said, "And remember, I am with you always" (Matthew 28:20).

See you on the path!

Jesus as Savior, Lord, and Friend

Prayer

Lord Jesus,
Thank you for leaving heaven's riches
  to come to earth,
  to be born in an animal's stable, and
  to join us as our brother.
Thank you for preaching good news to the poor,
  opening blind eyes,
  healing life's diseases, and
  setting captives free.
Thank you for dying on a cross for my sins,
  rising from the dead for my new life,
  reigning as Lord of my life forever,
  and sending your Spirit to fill me with divine love.
You are my Savior, my Lord, and my eternal Friend.
Enable me to be your faithful and fruitful witness,
  for God's glory, the salvation of others, and my joy.
                              Amen.

Trail Talk

The trail up the mountain with Jesus has reached the top. We are gathered here on the summit to be as face to face with him as we can this side of heaven. For weeks we have explored who he is as described by Scripture— quite a few layers—and today we explore who he is for each of our own lives.

For nearly two thousand years when people expressed their desire to become members of Christ's church, they answered questions something like those in the side column **(Q1).** Take a moment to read the questions.

In this lifetime we will probably never fully comprehend all that such questions may be implying. But having trudged up these trails with Jesus to the summit, we may have a better comprehension now than when we started.

In this session, we will explore three final images: Jesus as Savior, Jesus as Lord, and Jesus as Friend. Our focus will be on what these images and our confession of faith in Jesus Christ mean to us personally.

Q1

Do you renounce the spiritual
  forces of wickedness,
  reject the evil powers of this world,
  and repent of your sin?

Do you accept the freedom and
  power God gives you
  to resist evil, injustice, and oppression
  in whatever forms they present
  themselves?

Do you confess Jesus Christ as your Savior,
put your whole trust in his grace,
and promise to serve him as your Lord,
in union with the church which
  Christ has opened
to people of all ages, nations, and races?[5]

How well do these questions represent the meaning of being a Christian and a member of Christ's church?

Camp Notes

1. **John 3:1-21**

_____

_____

2. **Luke 7:36-50**

_____

_____

3. **Matthew 7:1-28**

_____

_____

4. **John 15:1-17**

_____

_____

5. **Romans 9:27–10:13**

_____

_____

6. **Ephesians 2**

_____

_____

_____

Let's begin by reflecting on this week's readings.

1. What have you come to understand as the meaning and importance of Jesus' words to Nicodemus about being "born from above" or "born of water and Spirit"? Is this image helpful to you? Has this experience happened to you?

2. What is the relationship Jesus describes between forgiveness and love? Do you identify more with Simon or with the woman? Have you recognized your own need for a savior who "forgives much," or have you struggled with a great need to feel forgiveness?

3. Jesus indicates it is much easier to say "Lord, Lord" than to live as though we mean it. What is your story about learning the difference? Can you identify an area of your life where Jesus seems to be pushing you to more faithfully acknowledge him as Lord?

4. Jesus describes an intimacy of love between himself and the Father, and between himself and his disciples. He calls his disciples friends. Is it easy or difficult for you to see Jesus as your friend? Why? Can we be fruitful branches if he is not our friend?

5. Paul explains that righteousness is by faith in what Christ has done. To be saved we must believe in our hearts and confess with our lips. Why, do you think, are both important? Is confessing with our lips needed only once (when we join the church), or more than once?

6. Salvation is a gift of grace, not something earned. We can receive it only by faith, not merit. When did you first understand this truth about salvation? Are you still tempted to earn God's grace? How does this shape your relationships with others? What is the place of good works in God's design for us?

Many of the ideas in these passages are at the heart of the transforming power of the gospel. Until we believe and have confessed some of this amazing grace, it is difficult to pray and live and speak so that others will discover it as good news for their lives. Speaking of praying, how did this week's action assignment go?

We have invested more time than normal in this opening Trail Talk. But don't let that bother you. We are on the summit with Jesus.

Q2
What did God do this week in answer to your prayers?

_____

_____

_____

Jesus as Savior

Back along the trail in Session 2, we noted that the biblical concept of salvation is deliverance from danger and healing from soul sickness. For someone to say "Jesus is my Savior" means he or she has recognized the need for a Rescuer-Healer, and that Jesus is his name.

As simple as this may seem to many, it is not by any means easy for all of us to get to this point. Sin and society often teach us to be measured by our own achievements, and we frequently label people as weak if they turn to someone else to bail them out. Frankly, most of us don't truly recognize how desperate our situation is until we reach some kind of bottom in life. Perhaps that is why it was the poor, the sinners, and the outcasts that most readily recognized Jesus and his kingdom, and why Jesus told the parable of the prodigal son (Luke 15:11-32).

The firstborn son was a good boy who did things right, stayed home, and followed the rules. It was that younger brother of his who messed up. He wanted more out of life than the humdrum existence of normalcy. So he took all that he had going for him and all that he had coming to him and set off on his own. Our culture values this kind of independence, and most of us can probably remember looking forward to leaving the nest.

Leaving home was not the problem Jesus wanted to highlight. But out in the world it didn't take long for the problem to show up. The lad decided to live against the grain of his best identity, and he made a wreck of his life. Only when he had no more options to buy friends or even to survive through the night did he come to his senses, acknowledge his condition, swallow his pride, and turn toward home.

It's hard to turn away from our own distorted views and self-willed investments and humbly acknowledge a desperate need for rescue and a savior. In a sense, it kills us to do so, or at least it kills our independence, which we mistake for freedom. But this awakening, as John Wesley called it, is something the Holy Spirit provides opportunity for again and again, until we are convinced that we are lost, are ready to repent, and see Jesus as the truth, the life, and the way home (John 14:6).

Interestingly enough, the good son who stayed home had a more difficult time accepting the gift of his father's love. He was unaware of any need for grace or salvation. And the one thing he knew was that he deserved more than his gutter-scum brother. He had kept the rules, so where was the payoff?

Paul understood the older brother's perspective perfectly. He saw himself as totally confident "in the flesh"—that is, in his own righteousness. He believed God would honor him because he had kept the rules. His eyes were so focused on proving himself before God and others that he missed the best gift, the Messiah.

Camp Notes

Q3
What kinds of people do you think face the greatest obstacles in coming to Jesus as Savior and Lord?

Q4
What hymns or songs best summarize for you the meaning of Christ's cross for your forgiveness and salvation?

The jailer…said, "Sirs, what must I do to be saved?" They answered, "Believe on the Lord Jesus, and you will be saved, you and your household." They spoke the word of the Lord to him and to all who were in his house. At the same hour of the night he took them and washed their wounds; then he and his entire family were baptized.
(Acts 16:29-33)

Camp Notes

Y P is a man who is aggressively seeking truth. He enjoys reading the Bible, especially the Book of Ecclesiastes because it outlines all that is not of worth. He believes God is to be sought after with all strength, but does not yet know what the religious form will be. He was raised in a Christian family, but is not sure that is the path he wishes to walk.... He gets frustrated with Christians because from what he has seen, they often seek wealth and status and then say it is the blessings of God.

Wadi

He died for all, so that those who live might live no longer for themselves, but for him who died and was raised for them.

(2 Corinthians 5:15)

All that Paul trusted in before coming to Christ as Savior, he came to

> *regard...as loss because of the surpassing value of knowing Christ Jesus my Lord. For his sake I have suffered the loss of all things, and I regard them as rubbish, in order that I may gain Christ and be found in him, not having a righteousness of my own that comes from the law, but one that comes through faith in Christ.* (Philippians 3:8-9)

This gift of salvation is free but also extremely costly. It cost the life of the perfect Lamb of God, sacrificed for the sins of the world. Jesus declared, "This is my blood,...poured out for many for the forgiveness of sins" (Matthew 26:28). Paul reminds us that "while we still were sinners Christ died for us" (Romans 5:8). This was to prove God's love for us and to demonstrate that forgiveness of sin against God is no small thing. It is a matter of life and death. In fact, through faith we can choose—his death to sin and his life toward God at work in us, or our life of sin and our death toward God. The Christian gospel asks, "Which death and which life do you want?"

Paul said the sacrament of baptism symbolizes the Christian's choice:

> *Do you not know that all of us who have been baptized into Christ Jesus were baptized into his death? Therefore we have been buried with him by baptism into death, so that, just as Christ was raised from the dead by the glory of the Father, so we too might walk in newness of life.... We know that our old self was crucified with him so...consider yourselves dead to sin and alive to God in Christ Jesus.*
>
> *(Romans 6:3-4, 6, 11)*

To say Jesus is my Savior is to accept a life transplant—old life for new life, decaying life for eternal life, my life by my rules for Christ's life and Christ's rule. And this is why we can't talk about Jesus as Savior without also talking about him as Lord.

Jesus as Lord

The man sitting next to me on the plane was going home after attending his brother's funeral. As we talked about life and death and the old family church he had grown up in, I asked if he had been "saved" in that church. "Oh, yes," he assured me, "and I sang in a traveling gospel quartet." It was a long flight, and eventually he told me of his seven marriages and fourteen children. Had he ever really understood or experienced being saved?

It's much too easy to separate *Savior* from *Lord*, but one does not exist without the other. Jesus is Savior *and* Lord. The passage we read from Ephesians 2 reminds us that salvation is a pure gift of grace through faith, but that we have been created in Christ Jesus for good works. Jesus was the perfect servant, who "humbled himself and became obedient to the point of death" (Philippians 2:8). His life in us is a life of obedience to the love and law of God. He is Lord of our lives, for our lives are his. He bought them and owns them. Surrender to this reality is joy. Continued rebellion is sin and sorrow.

Jesus as Friend

Anyone who knows Jesus as Savior and Lord knows him also as a true friend. He instructs us in obedience so that our joy will be full. Jesus told his disciples, "I have called you friends, because I have made known to you everything that I have heard from my Father" (John 15:15).

A true friend doesn't withhold vital information and speaks the truth in love. A true friend is interested in our happiness and fulfillment. A true friend listens and tries to explain anything that is unclear. A true friend knows us better than we know ourselves. A true friend is available when needed and loves to spend time with us. What would you add to the list if you were describing what a true friend is? How has Jesus been this kind of friend for you?

Perhaps the most important characteristic of Jesus as our true friend is that he wants to introduce us to his best friend—his *Abba*, Father. His whole goal in coming and dying and rising again from the dead was so that we might "be one," be reconciled, and thus live in true friendship with God. This was his prayer for us all (John 17:20-26). This is our calling as his friends, to enable others to find their best friend (2 Corinthians 5:17-20). This privileged ministry as witnesses, or friend-makers, is under the guidance of and in the power of the Holy Spirit. Thus we turn next to walking with and in the Spirit—Trail Three.

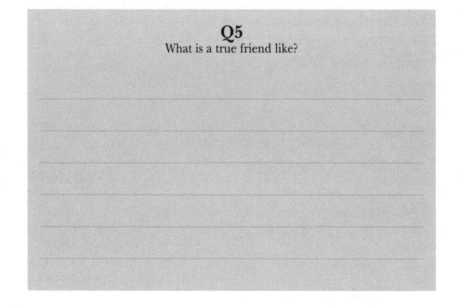

Q5
What is a true friend like?

Long Haul and Breathe Deep broke up their hiking partnership this morning…. Breathe Deep had insulted Long Haul and mocked her in front of others…. Long Haul said she could never believe in Christianity now…. I said, "I'm sorry that Breathe Deep insulted and hurt you, but I am even more sorry that it was a Christian who did it to you…. I ask for your forgiveness on behalf of all Christians, though many will hurt you again in the future; and that hurts me…. My wish for you is that this does not close doors for you in reaction to paths in life, but that you will see human nature for what it is." She accepted my apology and thanked me for speaking. She said it really helped her.

Wadi

Camp Notes

If you keep my commandments, you will abide in my love, just as I have kept my Father's commandments and abide in his love. I have said these things to you so that my joy may be in you, and that your joy may be complete. (John 15:10-11)

What a Friend We Have in Jesus

What a friend we have in Jesus,
*   all our sins and griefs to bear!*
What a privilege to carry
*   everything to God in prayer!*
O what peace we often forfeit,
O what needless pain we bear,
*   all because we do not carry*
*   everything to God in prayer.*[6]

Moving On

Take a few moments to review next week's assignments.

READING ASSIGNMENTS

1. Record your reflections, questions, and insights from these daily Bible readings in your *My Witness Journal.*

Day 1: Matthew 3 (three at a baptism—Spirit of God, Father, Beloved Son)

Day 2: John 14 (three in an upper room—Father, Son, Holy Sprit)

Day 3: Luke 24:36-53 (three at a resurrection—Messiah, Father, Power from on high)

Day 4: Acts 15:1-29 (three in the church's life—God, Holy Spirit, Lord)

Day 5: Romans 8:1-17 (three in one Spirit—Spirit, Spirit of God, Spirit of Christ)

Day 6: 1 John 4 (three in one God of love—Son, Father, Spirit)

2. As you read the chapter for next week (pages 58–62), underline or highlight special thoughts and answer the questions in the Q boxes.

ACTION ASSIGNMENT

Continue this week to pray for one another and for those you identified as your friends. Perhaps you've seen some individuals wearing the letters WWJD on items of clothing. I did this week, on a nurse in a surgical ward. I was encouraged by her presence and her witness. It's a good question: "What would Jesus do?" Try this week to pray that question through each day and to act accordingly as the Spirit leads you. Keep good journal notes about any insights you receive.

Take a few minutes for a closing prayer. Sing "What a Friend We Have in Jesus." Keep your eyes open for his friendly Spirit.

See you on the path!

Trail Three
Into Life in the Holy Spirit

The Holy Spirit, whom the Father will send in my name, will teach you everything.

(John 14:26)

Camp Notes

Q1
What would you write about the Holy Spirit if you were to create your own statement of faith?

I believe in the Holy Spirit, who...

_____

_____

_____

_____

_____

_____

_____

_____

Spirit of the Living God

Spirit of the living God,
*   fall afresh on me.*
Spirit of the living God,
*   fall afresh on me.*
Melt me, mold me, fill me, use me.
Spirit of the living God,
*   fall afresh on me.*[7]

Spirit of the Holy Trinity

Prayer: A Statement of Faith

The Nicene Creed
We believe in one God,
*   the Father, the Almighty,*
*   maker of heaven and earth,*
*   of all that is, seen and unseen.*

We believe in one Lord, Jesus Christ,
*   the only Son of God,*
*   eternally begotten of the Father,*
*   God from God, Light from Light,*
*   true God from true God,*
*   begotten, not made,*
*   of one Being with the Father;*
*   through him all things were made.*
For us and for our salvation
*   he came down from heaven,*
*   was incarnate of the Holy Spirit and the Virgin Mary*
*   and became truly human.*
*   For our sake he was crucified under Pontius Pilate;*
*   he suffered death and was buried.*
*   On the third day he rose again*
*   in accordance with the Scriptures;*
*   he ascended into heaven*
*   and is seated at the right hand of the Father.*
*   He will come again in glory*
*   to judge the living and the dead,*
*   and his kingdom will have no end.*

We believe in the Holy Spirit, the Lord, the giver of life,
*   who proceeds from the Father and the Son,*
*   who with the Father and the Son*
*   is worshiped and glorified,*
*   who has spoken through the prophets.*
*   We believe in the one holy catholic and apostolic church.*
*   We acknowledge one baptism*
*   for the forgiveness of sins.*
*   We look for the resurrection of the dead,*
*   and the life of the world to come. Amen.*

(English translation of the Nicene Creed prepared by the English Language Liturgical Consultation [ELLC], 1988. Used by permission.)

Yes, it's long, at least compared with many other common creeds. But its purpose (notice the structure) was to clarify that although our faith is centered in Jesus as the Christ, it is a faith that acknowledges one God in three persons—Father, Son, and Holy Spirit. No other creed gives as much attention to the Holy Spirit, limited though it is, as does this one.

Trail Talk

Who is the Holy Spirit of God? What is the Spirit's relationship to the Father and the Son? How should we picture and respond to this Spirit? This is the subject of our Trail Talk as we begin Trail Three.

Take a few minutes in camp to report lessons learned and new insights about the nature and work of the Holy Spirit from this week's assignments.

Who Is the Spirit?

We could begin by asking, "What is a spirit?" But in the Bible, *spirit* is a who, not a what, and that difference is significant.

In the Old Testament, the word used for spirit is *ruach* (pronounced "roo-akh"). It is used more than 350 times. It can be translated as wind, breath (especially breathing out), or spirit. Notice that in the verses from Ezekiel 37 (Ezekiel's vision of the valley of dry bones), the same word is translated all three ways (**Q3**). The power of the word is in the idea that God breathes life (spirit) into a human form, and it becomes a real, live, God-imaged being, person, or soul (Genesis 2:7).

In the New Testament, the idea is the same. The Greek word for wind and spirit is *pneuma* (a pneumatic tire is air- or breath-filled, and pneumonia is a breathing disease). Spirit is like the wind. Jesus said:

> *The wind blows where it chooses, and you hear the sound of it, but you do not know where it comes from or where it goes. So it is with everyone who is born of the Spirit.*
>
> *(John 3:8)*

But wind and spirit are not the same. A spirit is a personal life force, and as such has "person-ality."

"God is spirit," said Jesus (John 4:24); but because all spirits are not of God, we are to "test the spirits" (1 John 4:1). In other words, all spirits do not reveal the nature or personality of God. Some are contrary or evil spirits, and some are in harmony with the nature of God. Our concern here is to look at the one Spirit who is in perfect harmony with God, because this Holy Spirit is the Spirit of God.

Some would say, "Well, if God is Spirit, then isn't the Spirit of God simply the same as God?" Yes and no. Here the mystery grows more wondrous. Just as we discovered that Jesus was both God's Son (distinct from the Father) and God Incarnate (one with the Father), so also the Spirit is both distinct from and one with God the Father and God the Son. The best way we know to describe this is to say there are three persons but one Godhead. So let's look first at the person of the Spirit.

Camp Notes

Q2
What did you learn about yourself or the Spirit in your action assignment this week?

_____

_____

_____

_____

Q3
How does your version of the Bible translate these verses from Ezekiel?

Thus says the Lord GOD to these bones: I will cause _____ to enter you, and you shall live. (37:5)

Then he said to me, "Prophesy to the _____, prophesy, mortal, and say to the _____: Thus says the Lord GOD: Come from the four _____, O _____, and breathe upon these slain, that they may live." (37:9)

I will put my _____ within you, and you shall live. (37:14)

Camp Notes

> ### Q4
> When you try to picture the Holy Spirit, what images come to mind?

The Spirit as Person

The Spirit in the Old Testament frequently "comes upon" or "rests upon" those whom God chooses for a special task or ministry. This arrival of the Spirit of God enhances dramatically the strength, wisdom, life energy, and confidence of those on whom it rests. On occasion the Spirit speaks through some who are chosen to be God's voice to the people (Numbers 11:25-29). And in rare instances, the Spirit speaks to those whom he enters (Ezekiel 2:2-4). But much of the activity of the Spirit is influence and not necessarily indicative of the Spirit being a distinct person. Much like God's word that "goes out" (Isaiah 55:11), God sends the Spirit forth as an emissary to accomplish some creative or redemptive act (Psalm 104:30).

The personal nature of the Spirit is enhanced significantly by the New Testament. The Holy Spirit of God leads both Jesus and his disciples (Matthew 4:1; Romans 8:14). The Spirit speaks (John 16:13; Acts 8:29), teaches (John 14:26), testifies (John 15:26), comforts (Acts 9:31), convinces and convicts (John 16:7-11), intercedes for us in prayer (Romans 8:26), distributes gifts and maintains unity in the church (1 Corinthians 12:7-13), and is the Lord who transforms us (2 Corinthians 3:17-18). The list goes on and on, but whenever the work of the Spirit is mentioned in the Bible, the Spirit is person, never merely a force or influence.

Without doubt the Holy Spirit is more difficult to visualize as person than is God the Father or Jesus Christ the Son, but the Spirit is always a personal presence. Into the name of this one but tri-personal God—Father, Son, and Holy Spirit—we are baptized (Matthew 28:19).

The Spirit of the Holy Trinity

Did you ever try to explain the Trinity to anyone? Take a moment and note an illustration you might use. Over the course of history, many have tried to make sense of this holy mystery by analogy. Saint Patrick (c. A.D. 389–461) saw the Trinity in a cloverleaf. Saint Augustine of North Africa (A.D. 354–430) saw trinitarian footprints everywhere in creation, such as a single object having three dimensions and the human self having memory, understanding, and will. Many have used examples such as an orange or apple or egg, which have three distinct layers but only one identity. Others have seen the Trinity in three states of matter (water as solid, liquid, and gas), or in the various roles one person can have (child, parent, sibling), or in a human being consisting of body, mind, and will.

> ### Q5
> What are two or three of your favorite ways to explain the Trinity (one in three, three in one)?

These may in some ways be helpful analogies, but all of them have flaws. God does not have three parts; nor is each of the persons in the Godhead merely a role. They speak to one another and interact with one another, yet each has unique contributions to make. All are involved in every divine action, and all are Lord; only the Son takes on flesh and dies on a cross; the Spirit empowers us for witnessing (Acts 1:8); and only the Father sets the times and seasons (Acts 1:7). They are distinct persons (or we might say centers of consciousness), yet they are one personality. The Father's will is the will of the Son and the Spirit. The Father is not cold and distant and the Son warm and friendly. The Spirit is not wild and crazy and the Father orderly and judgmental. There is one God, one nature, one essence, but three persons who are totally interconnected and yet distinct.

Does it still sound hard to imagine or explain? Try imagining the following: Saint Augustine, reflecting on God's nature as love, realized that love requires at least two people, since people are agents for sending and receiving love. The Father loves the Son, and the Son loves the Father. The love bond, or Spirit of this divine love, is actually a third person generated from this eternal relationship. The Spirit is the love connection and spreads this love of God.

Every relationship has its own unique spirit. You can tell the spirit of a marriage, friendship, or athletic team. It is the interactive presence of that community that can be sensed as something special that emerges from the relationship. The divine community or relationship between the Father (source) and the Son (reflection) has a Spirit. This Spirit of God is a third person bound into the Godhead, yet dancing through all space and time and offering the possibility of our coming home to divine love through the Son to the Father.

In a nutshell, the love of God moves from the Father and the Son out through the Spirit to touch our lives. In turn we are invited by the Spirit to come to the Son, who opens the door for us into the Father's presence where there is joy forever. And in God's presence, like our Maker-Redeemer-Sanctifier, we become one (John 17), and thus the world knows love.

Much is being written on the Trinity these days. If your interest has grown through this discussion, ask your pastor for additional reading suggestions.

Camp Notes

I in them and you in me, that they may become completely one, so that the world may know that you have sent me and have loved them even as you have loved me.

(John 17:23)

Q6
What adjectives come to mind when you think of the Father?

_____

_____

_____

_____

What adjectives come to mind when you think of Jesus the Son?

_____

_____

_____

What adjectives come to mind when you think of the Holy Spirit?

_____

_____

_____

_____

Camp Notes

Five years ago, I went to a new church with my best friend.... This Spirit-filled church was empowered by God, though far out of my comfort zone.... At the end of the sermon, the speaker pointed straight at me and began to say things that were direct answers and confirmations to many of my silent prayers.... "I see you walking through forests, splitting them open.... You will be a bright light in the darkness that will attract others to you."... As I hiked in last night, it jumped in front of my eyes with clarity and blew me away. I have seen much of this come about especially in the last week as people have been seeking me out to talk about life and God.

Wadi

Moving On

Whatever else the Holy Spirit does, the Spirit breaks into our lives in times and places we don't always anticipate. The Spirit is Lord, and the Spirit is freedom (2 Corinthians 3:17-18). This week we explore the creative and liberating energy of the Spirit, and pray that the Spirit will re-create us too.

READING ASSIGNMENTS

Begin each day's assignment by singing or reading "Spirit of the Living God" (side column, page 58).

1. Record your reflections, questions, and insights from these daily Bible readings in your *My Witness Journal.*

   Day 1: Exodus 35:30–36:38 (the Spirit of creativity and giftedness)

   Day 2: 2 Corinthians 5 (the Spirit of the new creation)

   Day 3: John 16:1-15 (the Spirit as advocate for truth)

   Day 4: 1 Corinthians 2 (the Spirit and the mind of Christ)

   Day 5: Romans 8 (the Spirit of our new life)

   Day 6: 2 Corinthians 3 (the Spirit of the new covenant and freedom)

2. As you read the chapter for next week (pages 63–68), underline or highlight special thoughts and answer the questions in the Q boxes.

ACTION ASSIGNMENT

During the week prayerfully let the Spirit melt, mold, fill, and use you. Write down in your *My Witness Journal* notes about how these things can happen in your life. Are you ready for the surprises of the Spirit? Keep your eyes open.

Take a few minutes to hear any announcements; then close in prayer.

See you on the path!

Spirit of Creation and New Creation

Prayer

Sing to him in whom creation
    Found its shape and origin;
Spirit, moving on the waters
    Troubled by the God within;
Source of breath to all things breathing,
    Life in whom all lives begin....

Pray we, then, O Lord the Spirit,
    On our lives descend in might;
Let thy flame break out within us,
    Fire our hearts and clear our sight,
Till, white-hot in thy possession,
    We, too, set the world alight.

              Amen.

(Words by Michael Hewlett [born 1916]; from *English Praise.* © Oxford University Press. Used by permission. All rights reserved.)

Trail Talk

The Bible begins with the announcement that in the earliest moments of creation, the Spirit swept over chaos and beckoned it to rise up and dance to the tune of divine love. And it was good! It was beautiful! The Spirit of God is the Spirit of creation and creativity and goodness. There is wonder and awe and order and glory in creation.

As you have been hiking the trail, have you stopped to glimpse the glory? Have you rejoiced in a sunrise or the golden lining of clouds at sunset? Have you stooped to notice drops of dew on a rose or lost yourself in the Milky Way? Have you soaked in the sounds of a chorus and orchestra filling the earth with Beethoven's Ninth Symphony or caught yourself laughing with a jazz saxophone? Have you marveled at the movements of a hummingbird or a young athlete? Have you been blessed watching an older couple walk hand in hand? Have you held your firstborn or reached out to embrace an old friend? Life is a fragile yet wonder-filled gift. And the Spirit is Lord of the Dance.

Our goal in this camp time is to see the Spirit as the one who orchestrates the songs of creation and the new creation. There is a song that all creation sings, and the Spirit is behind and above and within the music. This camp is a songfest.

We are created in God's likeness, we bear His image. We should not only notice it but also love it and revel in it. But in our man-made world, we cut ourselves off from the created order.... God wants to be found through all creation.... I am trying to commune with God in my walk in solitude, and it is in my solitude that I am the least alone.

              Wadi

Make a joyful noise to the LORD,
    all the earth;
    break forth into joyous song
        and sing praises.
Sing praises to the LORD with the lyre,
    with the lyre and the sound of melody.
With trumpets and the sound of
    the horn
    make a joyful noise before the
        King, the LORD.

Let the sea roar, and all that fills it;
    the world and those who live in it.
Let the floods clap their hands;
    let the hills sing together for joy
at the presence of the LORD.

           (Psalm 98:4-9)

Camp Notes

Q1
When were some of those moments in your life when you caught a glimpse of God's glory in creation?

_____

_____

_____

_____

Q2
What aspect of God's creation has captured your fascination and led you to read about and explore more of the wonder it contains?

_____

_____

_____

Q3
Where have you most recently sensed a moment of wonder and delight in a gift of creativity shared?

_____

_____

_____

Did you recognize this as the activity of the Spirit and give thanks either to God or to the one employing the gift?

_____

_____

The Spirit of Creation

Although most of us recognize that the whole creation and what we call nature have God's fingerprint, many of us have not communed with God's world in a long time because we are caught in our world of Web pages and computer-enhanced virtual reality.

Paul reminds us that "ever since the creation of the world his eternal power and divine nature, invisible though they are, have been understood and seen through the things he has made" (Romans 1:20). The Spirit of God's presence in creation swirls around us, both in the awesome majesty of space and in the intricacies of life's tiniest stands of DNA. When the psalmist viewed the heavens, he declared:

> *What are human beings that you are mindful of them,*
> *mortals that you care for them?*
> *Yet you have made them a little lower than God,*
> *and crowned them with glory and honor....*
> *O LORD, our Sovereign,*
> *how majestic is your name in all the earth!*
> *(Psalm 8:4-5, 9)*

We are in danger of losing this sense of wonder and worship if we confine our spiritual disciplines only to reading and our own witnessing. The creation is part of God's witness, and the Spirit of creation lifts our spirits to "join the mighty chorus"[8] when we take time to soak in the "music of the spheres."[9]

The Spirit of Creativity

As you read the passage from Exodus 35–36 this week, did you notice that it is the Spirit who distributes gifts of artistry and creativity? Churches that use the arts as gifts of the Spirit to celebrate God's presence are churches that are reaching many we call seekers. But the arts can never be restricted to only a certain list sponsored by highbrows who head the local arts council. The creativity of the Spirit, whose love is displayed through gifts employed to honor God, is to be found everywhere!

Creation is not merely a big bang; it is an ever-unfolding revelation of God's awesome nature as Holy Trinity. The Spirit, like the wind, is always stirring the elements somewhere to bring forth manifestations of the playful beauty of divine love. Aren't you stirred by the Spirit's presence in refrigerator art from a child? by a bagpipe or harmonica sounding out "Amazing Grace"? by dancing hands and fingers signing out a song? by the colors woven into a crafted wooden table, a banner, a kente-cloth stole, or a floral arrangement? The Spirit is breathing out reminders of God's glory, grace, and generosity wherever gifts are displayed and recognized as being just that—gifts.

The witness we seek to offer is not merely to a set of religious doctrines or to a long-ago event, but to the eternal God of the heavens and the earth who is still creating life out of what might be called clay. Each of us is but clay, dust, and ashes, apart from the miracle of being swept up into the dance of life by the Spirit.

Twice now the activity of God in creation has been compared to a dance. There is more to this than may at first meet the eye. Gregory of Nazianzus, Bishop of Constantinople in the late fourth century, captured the mystery of dynamic, creative love at work in the Trinity by describing the relationship as a dance (in Greek, *perichoresis*). A choreographer is someone who creates the dance; a periscope is an instrument that allows one to look around. The Triune God *dances around* through time and space—Father, Son, and Sprit together, each moving in perfect harmony and inviting all of creation into the movement of eternally creative life.

C. S. Lewis used this image in his classic book *Mere Christianity*. He said of Christianity:

> *In Christianity God is not a static thing—not even a*
> *person—but a dynamic, pulsating activity, a life, almost*
> *a kind of drama. Almost, if you will not think me irreverent,*
> *a kind of dance.*

(From *Mere Christianity*, by C. S. Lewis; page 152. Copyright © C. S. Lewis Pte. Ltd. 1942, 1943, 1944, 1952. Extract reprinted by permission.)

Camp Notes

Q4

What would you add to your list of the Spirit's creative gifts that touch your heart and kindle praise in your soul?

_____

_____

_____

Lord of the Dance

I danced in the morning
when the world was begun,
and I danced in the moon
and the stars and the sun,
and I came down from heaven
and I danced on the earth.
At Bethlehem I had my birth.

Dance, then, wherever you may be;
I am the Lord of the Dance, said he.
And I'll lead you all wherever
*   you may be,*
and I'll lead you all in the dance,
*   said he.*

(Taken from "Lord of the Dance" by Sydney Carter. © 1963 Stainer & Bell Ltd. Admin. by Hope Publishing Co., Carol Stream, IL 60188. All rights reserved. Used by permission.)

Q5

What is your response to this ancient image describing the Holy Trinity as involved in a cosmic dance of love?

_____

_____

_____

_____

The Spirit of the New Creation

Camp Notes

Q6

Sin in the Bible has many descriptions: willful disobedience, missing the mark, lawlessness, trespass, debt, unrighteousness, and so forth. The consequences are the same. "The wages of sin is death" (Romans 6:23). How might you explain this to someone who asks, "Why?"

Sinners, Turn: Why Will You Die

Sinners, turn: why will you die?
God, the Spirit, asks you why;
he, who all your lives hath strove,
wooed you to embrace his love.
Will you not his grace receive?
Will you still refuse to live?
Why, you long-sought sinners, why
will you grieve your God, and die?…

You, whom he ordained to be
transcripts of the Trinity,
you, whom he in life doth hold,
you, for whom himself was sold,
you, on whom he still doth wait,
whom he would again create;
made by him, and purchased, why,
why will you forever die? [10]

God designed us and invites us to join in the dance of love that celebrates unity in diversity. This unity is God's nature—and our own. But made in the divine image, we have been given a will to choose to follow or not to follow the music and the leading of our host and maker. Sadly, dancing never works well when a rebellious partner decides to do it his or her own way.

Jesus the Son danced to the Spirit's song and followed the Father's will even when tempted to choose another way. "Therefore God also highly exalted him and gave him the name that is above every name" (Philippians 2:9). Humanity, however, did not choose to dance to the Spirit's song. We all "have gone astray; we have all turned to our own way" (Isaiah 53:6).

This turning away is sin. Sin ruins the dance. Sin sours the song. Sin distorts the beauty of creativity in the name of a false freedom.

> *Your iniquities have been barriers*
> *between you and your God,*
> *and your sins have hidden his face from you.*
> (Isaiah 59:2)

To describe our human predicament as resulting from a fall is truly appropriate. But through the faithfulness of Jesus, we have received the long-awaited promise and the power to be lifted up with him into a new creation. And as the Spirit first moved across chaos to bring the divine dance to the first creation, the Spirit moves again to help us hear and move to the glorious strains of a resurrection song.

The Spirit of creation is also the Spirit of truth, who convicts us of our lies and our sin (John 16:8-9) and reveals the glory of Jesus (John 16:14). The Spirit helps us understand that "he was wounded for our transgressions" and "by his bruises we are healed" (Isaiah 53:5). The Spirit clarifies that "our old self was crucified with him so that…we might no longer be enslaved to sin" (Romans 6:6), but rather "walk in newness of life" and be "alive to God in Christ Jesus" (Romans 6:4, 11).

It was indeed a *good* Friday for sinners saved by grace, because there is "now no condemnation for those who are in Christ Jesus" (Romans 8:1). "If anyone is in Christ, there is a new creation: everything old has passed away; see, everything has become new" (2 Corinthians 5:17). The Spirit who filled the life of Jesus is poured out now from heaven to fill our lives (Acts 2:38-39) and lead us in the dance as children of God (Romans 8:14-16).

With the Spirit in us, there is a recovery of true freedom (2 Corinthians 3:17), a freedom that all creation longs for: to "be set free from its bondage" and to "obtain the freedom of the glory of the children of God"

(Romans 8:21). This is a freedom that reveals the glory of God because it celebrates rather than rebels against the will of God. It is a liberty that follows the lead of perfect love. And nothing can "separate us from the love of God in Christ Jesus our Lord" (Romans 8:39).

The Spirit works in us to this end so that we might have "the mind of Christ" (1 Corinthians 2:9-16; Philippians 2:3-8). It has always been God's design that we "be conformed to the image of his Son, in order that he might be the firstborn within a large family" (Romans 8:29). We are being written as "a letter of Christ" for all the world to read, "written not with ink but with the Spirit of the living God, not on tablets of stone but on tablets of human hearts" (2 Corinthians 3:3).

One Last Image

As we examine images of the Holy Trinity and the special new creation wrought in us by the Spirit, we must finally look at an image Jesus himself supplies:

> *I am the vine, you are the branches. Those who abide in me and I in them bear much fruit, because apart from me you can do nothing…. My Father is glorified by this, that you bear much fruit.*
> *(John 15:5, 8)*

Tertullian of Carthage in North Africa (c. A.D. 160–220) was the first to actually use the word *Trinity* to describe the three-in-oneness of God. One of his analogies was "Root-Shoot-Fruit." The Root is the invisible God, who is Father, Source, and Creator. The Shoot is the visible manifestation: God Incarnate, God the Son, the True Vine. The Fruit of the Spirit is the wonderful result of divine life emerging on the branches.

With only minor adjustments, we might suggest an alternative image as Root-Vine-Sap. The life inherent in the Root (Father) grows up among us as the true Vine (Son). The divine essence of life from the Root (Father) that flows through the Vine (Son) also flows as holy Sap (Spirit) into the branches connected to the Vine. The resulting fruit brought forth by the Spirit is Christlikeness. God the Father is glorified as we bear much fruit. The Spirit's fruit in us contains the seeds of new life for others.

Our witness, then, is to this reality and to this possibility for every person. We invite all to come to Christ for cleansing (John 15:3) and to abide in him. Then his Spirit can flood through them, bearing fruit that glorifies the Father and fulfills Jesus' promise "that [his] joy may be in you, and that your joy may be complete" (John 15:11).

The fruit of the Spirit is love, joy, peace, patience, kindness, generosity, faithfulness, gentleness, and self-control.
(Galatians 5:22-23)

Camp Notes

Of All the Spirit's Gifts to Me

Of all the Spirit's gifts to me,
I pray that I may never cease
to take and treasure most these three:
love, joy, and peace.

The Spirit shows me love's the root
of every gift sent from above,
of every flower, of every fruit,
that God is love....

Though what's ahead is mystery,
and life itself is ours on lease,
each day the Spirit says to me,
"Go forth in peace!"

We go in peace, but made aware that,
in a needy world like this,
our clearest purpose is to share
love, joy, and peace.

(From "Of All the Spirit's Gifts to Me," words by Fred Pratt Green. © 1979 Hope Publishing Co., Carol Stream, IL 60188. All rights reserved. Used by permission. Permission to reproduce this text must be obtained from Hope Publishing Co., 800-323-1049.)

Moving On

The Spirit is the dynamic, creative presence of God at work as amazing grace. Next week we will examine in more detail how this grace grows in us "from one degree of glory to another" (2 Corinthians 3:18). We will explore grace as God's provision for every human need along the path. Take a moment to clarify next week's assignments.

READING ASSIGNMENTS

1. Record your reflections, questions, and insights from these daily Bible readings in your *My Witness Journal.*
   - **Day 1:** Isaiah 45 ("though you do not know me")
   - **Day 2:** Jeremiah 31 ("grace in the wilderness")
   - **Day 3:** Zechariah 3:1–4:7 (a vision of grace)
   - **Day 4:** Romans 2:29–3:26 (justified by his grace through faith)
   - **Day 5:** Galatians 2:15–3:14 ("the promise of the Spirit through faith")
   - **Day 6:** Galatians 5 (called by the Spirit, live by the Spirit)
2. As you read the chapter for next week (pages 69–74), underline or highlight special thoughts and answer the questions in the Q boxes.

ACTION ASSIGNMENT

During the week prayerfully review how the Spirit has been at work in your life. Make some notes in your *My Witness Journal* to describe the Spirit's work. Continue to identify people you will pray for and witness to.

Take time to pray, and keep singing.

Spirit of the Living God

Spirit of the living God,
fall afresh on me.
Spirit of the living God,
fall afresh on me.
Melt me, mold me, fill me, use me.
Spirit of the living God,
fall afresh on me.[11]

See you on the path!

Spirit of Amazing Grace

Prayer

Great God, your love has called us here,
as we, by love for love were made.
Your living likeness still we bear,
though marred, dishonoured, disobeyed.
    We come, with all our heart and mind
    your call to hear, your love to find....

Great God, in Christ you call our name
and then receive us as your own,
not through some merit, right or claim,
but by your gracious love alone.
    We strain to glimpse your mercy seat
    and find you kneeling at our feet....

Great God, in Christ you set us free
your life to live, your joy to share.
Give us your Spirit's liberty
to turn from guilt and dull despair
    and offer all that faith can do
    while love is making all things new.
              Amen.

(From "Great God, Your Love Has Called Us Here,"
words by Brian Wren. © 1975, 1995 Hope Publishing Co.,
Carol Stream, IL 60188. All rights reserved. Used by
permission. Permission to reproduce this text must be
obtained from Hope Publishing Co., 800-323-1049.)

Trail Talk

All that we call life, and especially that which we know as eternal life, is a
gift of amazing grace. God "makes his sun rise on the evil and on the
good, and sends rain on the righteous and on the unrighteous" (Matthew
5:45). We do not earn by some merit system any sunrise or shower. Neither
do we earn suffering or salvation, but both can be gifts of grace.

This seems incomprehensible to some: "Surely the good people on the
earth should get a better deal than those who aren't. Doesn't God pay
any attention to what's going on?" Yes, God does pay attention. And we all
will stand "before the judgment seat of Christ, so that each may receive
recompense for what has been done in the body, whether good or evil"
(2 Corinthians 5:10).

Camp Notes

However it be expressed, it is certain all true
faith, and the whole work of salvation, every
good thought, word, and work, is altogether
by the operation of the Spirit of God.[12]
                    John Wesley

Q1
Have you heard some people complain that
God is unjust because bad things happen to
good people? Do some also complain that
good things happen to bad people?

Q2
What grace can you glean
from these passages?

Romans 5:1-5

2 Corinthians 1:1-7

Philippians 4:6-7

Camp Notes

> ### Q3
> What are some memories you have of how God's Spirit was wooing you into a relationship with Christ even before you understood all that was happening?

I was nine years old and walking home from school with a friend when he asked me, "Are you a Christian?" I answered, "Are you?" Confidently he replied, "Yes!" I said, "Me, too."

"When were you baptized?" he asked. "When were you baptized?" I shot back. "Yesterday!" he boasted.

I was stuck. I couldn't say, "Me, too," so I mumbled, "I don't remember." He sprang back incredulously, "You don't remember! I'll bet you aren't baptized! And I'll bet you're not a Christian!"

The Spirit probed my young heart deeply with this prevenient grace. I immediately went inside to ask my mother when I had been baptized.

Baptism had not been high on the agenda of my unchurched family. But within a few months we began to attend Community Presbyterian Church in Flint, Michigan. A year later I was baptized.

Ron Crandall

But in this life, there is no simple answer to why good things or bad things happen to people. Even as I wrote those words the phone rang. It was an old friend who recounted his terrible auto accident four years ago and the resulting brain damage and battle with depression. The Bible doesn't offer a *because* answer to many of the *why* questions. Much is left a mystery, as Job discovered thousands of years ago.

There is much we don't know, but we do know with Paul that those who have tasted God's amazing grace can declare that "in all these things we are more than conquerors through him who loved us" (Romans 8:37). For more perspective on grace even in times of trial, read Romans 5:1-5; 2 Corinthians 1:1-7; and Philippians 4:6-7 **(Q2)**.

We look now at three facets or phases of amazing grace and examine how the Spirit makes them real for us.

The Spirit of Grace Before Salvation

In the passage read this week from Isaiah, Cyrus King of Babylon is named as God's chosen instrument to restore the Temple in Jerusalem. Jeremiah declares that though others do not know him (Isaiah 45:4), God knew him before he was formed in the womb (Jeremiah 1:5), and grace is to be found even in the wilderness (Jeremiah 31:2).

Long before we know God, God knows us and provides bridges of grace to draw us into a relationship. The Spirit moves from the heart of God toward each of us to woo us and help us hear and respond to the offer of life and hope and salvation.

Like others before him, John Wesley referred to this activity of the Holy Spirit as prevenient grace. Part of this activity is "prevent-ing" grace. Even though we are unaware of it at the time, the Spirit prevents us from wandering so far away from God that we can't one day turn around and head home (as the prodigal son did).

Notice the *pre* meaning "ahead of" or "in front of." God's prevenient grace means the Holy Spirit goes before us. We might compare the Spirit's work to that of a sweeper in the game of curling. The smooth stone fitted with a handle is launched on ice toward a circular target. The sweeper uses his broom to clear the ice in front of the stone to guide it to its destination.

God's Spirit is always just in front of us, guiding and clearing and preparing the way. "I know the plans I have for you, says the LORD, plans for your welfare and not for harm, to give you a future with hope" (Jeremiah 29:11). This is amazing grace.

Augustine (A.D. 354–430) was the first to use the expression *prevenient grace*. He knew it in part as the hounding of his Christian mother's faithful witness and prayers for his conversion in contrast to his own life of debauchery. One day he heard a voice like that of a child repeatedly saying, "Pick it up, read it." The Spirit used this to convict him to open a Bible. His eyes fell on Romans 13:13-14: "Let us live honorably as in the day, not in reveling and drunkenness, not in debauchery and licentiousness, not in quarreling and jealousy. Instead, put on the Lord Jesus Christ, and make no provision for the flesh, to gratify its desires." In a moment, Augustine was convicted and converted.

Martin Luther (1483–1546), who launched the Protestant Reformation, was led by fear of death during a thunderstorm to promise God he would become a monk instead of a lawyer. As an Augustinian monk (note the path of grace) and a professor of theology, he earnestly combed the Scripture trying to find how one could know for certain that he was forgiven and loved by God. In studying Romans, he discovered the secret: by grace, through faith.

Like Luther, John Wesley (1703–1791) was a troubled soul who earnestly sought assurance that he was a son and not just a servant of God. His strict family background, his efforts at holy living, his fear of death, and his failures as a parish priest and a missionary led him to the brink of despair. But friends from Germany (Moravians) bore witness to another possibility through their buoyant lives of faith, hope, and love.

And so, John Wesley, on the evening of May 24, 1738, followed an invitation "very unwillingly" to a small group meeting on Aldersgate Street in London. As someone was reading from Martin Luther's Preface to his Commentary on Romans, the Holy Spirit enabled John to hear the words he needed for his life in grace. He wrote:

> *About a quarter before nine, while he was describing the change which God works in the heart through faith in Christ, I felt my heart strangely warmed. I felt I did trust in Christ, Christ alone for salvation: And an assurance was given me that he had taken away my sins, even mine, and saved me from the law of sin and death.*[13]

John Wesley found the faith of a son.

Can you see the trail of grace that goes before our experience of salvation? The Spirit uses many tools—Augustine, Luther, Wesley, thunderstorms, fear, voices, memories, longings, readings, friends, Scripture—to nudge us and to sweep the path to bring us home to saving love.

Camp Notes

Q4

Can you see the Spirit's grace at work in the following instances?

The woman at the well (John 4)?

_____

_____

Cornelius and Peter (Acts 10)?

_____

_____

The prophets' warnings and Jesus speaking against hypocrisy?

_____

_____

Q5

God frequently uses people as instruments of prevenient grace. Who has told you that you were an instrument of God in his or her life?

_____

_____

_____

What can you learn from your answer?

_____

_____

_____

Camp Notes

I have suffered the loss of all things,…in order that I may gain Christ and be found in him, not having a righteousness of my own that comes from the law, but one that comes through faith in Christ.

(Philippians 3:8-9)

God made you alive together with him, when he forgave us all our trespasses, erasing the record that stood against us with its legal demands. He set this aside, nailing it to the cross. (Colossians 2:13-14)

———

Night and day I pondered… Then I grasped that the justice of God is that righteousness by which through grace and sheer mercy God justifies us through faith. Thereupon I felt myself to be reborn and to have gone through open doors into paradise. The whole of Scripture took on a new meaning.[14]

Martin Luther

———

Q6
If you can remember when you first realized that you trusted in Christ alone for salvation, describe some of the details. Where? When? Who? What?

The Spirit of Grace in Salvation

The Spirit's sweeping is only the beginning of amazing grace, not the end. This active love of God on our behalf (grace) is designed to prepare us to one day find the full embrace of our *Abba*, Father. Prevenient grace is God's way of getting our attention to remind us that although we are sinners, we are valued and loved. "God proves his love for us in that while we still were sinners Christ died for us" (Romans 5:8). When we realize the extent of this love, and our still-sinners status, we are ready for phase two of amazing grace.

For some of us many years of prevenient grace are needed before we are ready to surrender self-righteousness and accept the gift of being right with God through trusting in Christ alone for salvation. But in reality we have nothing to bring in our own defense.

Isaiah said, "We have all become like one who is unclean, and all our righteous deeds are like a filthy cloth" (Isaiah 64:6). Zechariah's vision reminds us that standing before God we should be ready to hear, "Take off his filthy clothes." Then stripped of our pitiful attempts to hide from the light of God's truth, we will be ready to hear the gospel: "And I will clothe you with festal apparel" (Zechariah 3:4). We are justified (made acceptable in God's holy presence) by being clothed in Christ's righteousness, not our own. Paul simply says, "Put on the Lord Jesus Christ" (Romans 13:14).

Justifying grace, phase two of the Spirit's work, begins as the Spirit convinces us that our cover-up isn't working. This is often a painful moment of being strip-searched deep in our souls. The Spirit of truth helps us recognize that the issue is not being better or more religious than someone else. The measuring stick is simply, "Are you guilty or not guilty? righteous or unrighteous?" There is no trick question, nor is eternal life the result of a final exam graded on a curve.

Have you ever stood before a judge? Justification is primarily a legal term. The scene is a court of law, and it is God's court and God's law. The Spirit helps us know we are lost if we try to defend ourselves. The Spirit is our Advocate (John 14:16), who advises us to face the facts, plead guilty, and accept the undeserved gift of life and freedom in Christ rather than defending our pride to the death. What strange justice! The Innocent dies, and the guilty go free!

> *But he was wounded for our transgressions,*
> *crushed for our iniquities;*
> *upon him was the punishment that made us whole,*
> *and by his bruises we are healed.*
>
> *(Isaiah 53:5)*

Previously, God's mercy made it look as if sin really wasn't a big deal: "He had passed over the sins previously committed" (Romans 3:25). But now Christ's atoning death has revealed sin's awful consequences as well as God's way through the dilemma. Christ is our "at-one-ment" (Romans 3:25), our way home through faith.

It may seem strange to us, but God has always counted faith toward righteousness (Romans 4:3). We sometimes see faith as a little thing, but faith in God and God's way is no small matter. It is the spiritual doorway through which we enter into God's life and God enters into ours. It is what attaches us to the Vine and opens the floodgates for all the amazing grace of the Holy Spirit to melt us, mold us, fill us, and use us.

The Spirit of Grace for Full Salvation

If prevenient grace leads us to the doorway of Christ, and justifying grace allows us to step by faith through the doorway to a new relationship with God, then sanctifying grace is the Spirit redecorating our lives into Christ-likeness, "from one degree of glory to another" (2 Corinthians 3:18). There is more to salvation than getting us into heaven. God desires also to get heaven into us. This is sanctification. The word means to be set apart wholly for God, or to be set apart as holy.

When John Wesley reflected on the nature of the new covenant described in 2 Corinthians 3, he boldly stated:

> *The incarnation, preaching, and death of Jesus Christ were designed to represent, proclaim, and purchase for us this gift of the Spirit.*[15]

In other words, God's whole design of Christ coming into the world was to open the way for the Holy Spirit to revolutionize our lives and to instill in us his own nature: holiness. Holiness looks like the fruit of the Spirit (Galatians 5:22), and its core is perfect love.

Some branches of Christianity have focused almost entirely on salvation as justifying grace. Others have emphasized holiness or justice or obedience, but mostly human endeavor. The gospel is that the Spirit of the Holy Trinity, who woos us and brings us to faith and new life in Christ, also fills us with power to be transformed.

Early Methodism was often criticized for fervently witnessing to this possibility for every human soul. In the small tract *The Character of a Methodist* (printed in 1742), Wesley describes a Methodist.

Camp Notes

By salvation I mean, not barely, according to the vulgar notion, deliverance from hell, or going to heaven; but a present deliverance from sin, a restoration of the soul to its primitive health, its original purity; a recovery of the divine nature; the renewal of our souls after the image of God, in righteousness and true holiness, in justice, mercy, and truth.[16]

John Wesley

Do not be conformed to this world, but be transformed by the renewing of your minds, so that you may discern what is the will of God—what is good and acceptable and perfect. (Romans 12:2)

Q7
Have you ever thought how strange the cross is as a religious symbol? If someone were to ask you why it is so important to Christians, what would you answer?

Camp Notes

Love Divine, All Loves Excelling

Love divine, all loves excelling,
joy of heaven, to earth come down;
fix in us thy humble dwelling;
all thy faithful mercies crown!
Jesus, thou art all compassion,
pure, unbounded love thou art;
visit us with thy salvation;
enter every trembling heart....

Finish, then, thy new creation;
pure and spotless let us be.
Let us see thy great salvation
perfectly restored in thee;
changed from glory into glory,
till in heaven we take our place,
till we cast our crowns before thee,
lost in wonder, love, and praise.[19]

"Who is a Methodist, according to your own account?" I answer: a Methodist is one who has "the love of God shed abroad in his heart by the Holy Ghost given unto him."... And he accordingly "loves his neighbour as himself"; he loves every man as his own soul. His heart is full of love to all mankind, to every child of "the Father of the spirits of all flesh."[17]

This character of holiness and love manifested itself in serving every social and human need these early Methodists could address. "But," wrote Wesley, "much more does he labour to do good to their souls, as of the ability which God giveth: to awaken those that sleep in death."[18]

Moving On

Our purpose as we walk this *Witness* trail is to focus on the task of doing "good to their souls." Next week we examine how the Spirit enables us to be more faithful and fruitful. Take a few minutes to review next week's assignments.

READING ASSIGNMENTS

1. Record your reflections, questions, and insights from these daily Bible readings in your *My Witness Journal.*

Day 1: 1 Corinthians 12–13 (many spiritual gifts, one body)
Day 2: Ephesians 4:1-16 (gifts to equip the saints for the work of ministry)
Day 3: Isaiah 51:1-11 ("The coastlands wait.")
Day 4: Matthew 5:1-16 ("You are the light of the world.")
Day 5: 1 Thessalonians 2:1-13 (entrusted with the gospel)
Day 6: Hebrews 12:1-13 (discipline for running the race)

2. As you read the chapter for next week (pages 75–80), underline or highlight special thoughts and answer the questions in the Q boxes.

ACTION ASSIGNMENT

Use the SHAPE outline in your *My Witness Journal* to guide you as you think again about how the Spirit has shaped your life. Remember to keep praying and witnessing to the people you have chosen to include on your list for special prayers.

Sing "Love Divine, All Loves Excelling." Then close with prayer.

See you on the path!

Spirit of Ministry and Witness

Prayer

Gracious Spirit, dwell with me;
I myself would gracious be,
And with words that help and heal
Would thy life in mine reveal,
And with actions bold and meek
Would for Christ my Saviour speak.

Truthful Spirit, dwell with me;
I myself would truthful be,
And with wisdom kind and clear
Let thy life in mine appear,
And with actions neighbourly
Speak my Lord's sincerity….

Holy Spirit, dwell with me;
I myself would holy be;
Separate from sin, I would
Choose and cherish all things good,
And, whatever I can be,
Give to him who gave me thee.[20]
                    Amen.

Trail Talk

We've come halfway on our *Witness* trail. How are you doing? Has the trail at times been steeper than you expected? Have you stumbled here or there? Have you found it hard to press on week after week out on the trail? Have you been surprised more than once by joy and awe? Have you sensed the Spirit teaching you things about the love of God and showing you day by day opportunities to offer this love to others? Have you grown? Have you enjoyed the company? Are you beginning to get in SHAPE? Take a little while here at the midway marker to reflect on and record some notes as you ponder these questions.

As we arrive at the end of Trail Three, we want to examine how the Spirit intends to use us as instruments of God's grace for others. Each of us occupies a unique place in the body of Christ, yet we are all called to be witnesses. How can we each contribute our part and together contribute to "the body's growth in building itself up in love" (Ephesians 4:16)?

We begin with a brief look at spiritual gifts. Then we will explore how the larger idea of SHAPE helps us discover and/or confirm our special callings and roles for ministry and witness.

Llama and I walked all day together, talking mostly about God and what I believe. She had been taught that to be a Christian and to go to heaven, you had to go to church each week, pray, be nice to everyone, be honest,… do this and do that…. An interactive relationship of love with God was something she had not heard of, but it was very appealing to her. A life of purpose and joy with the creator of the universe was something she wanted to understand better. My relationship with God amazed her because she did not know that kind of life could be lived, but she wanted it.

Wadi

Camp Notes

Q1
What spiritual gifts are listed in Romans 12; 1 Corinthians 12; and Ephesians 4?

The eye cannot say to the hand, "I have no need of you," nor again the head to the feet, "I have no need of you." On the contrary, the members of the body that seem to be weaker are indispensable.

(1 Corinthians 12:21-22)

A Word on Spiritual Gifts

A growing emphasis on discovering spiritual gifts for ministry has been emerging in the church for the last several decades. A variety of survey instruments have been created to help Christians identify which gifts of the Spirit (listed in Romans 12; 1 Corinthians 12; and Ephesians 4) might be theirs. Some of you may be familiar with these inventories already.

For those of us not familiar with this concept, identifying our spiritual gift or gifts might be difficult. We're not sure we know how to think in these terms. For many of us, it even sounds elitist to talk about having a special gift of the Spirit. But Paul begins his description of the gifts in 1 Corinthians 12 by saying:

> *There are varieties of gifts,…services,…activities, but it is the same God who activates all of them in everyone. To each is given the manifestation of the Spirit for the common good.*
> *(1 Corinthians 12:4-7)*

And Peter, speaking to all the ordinary Christians scattered across the land, advised them:

> *Like good stewards of the manifold grace of God, serve one another with whatever gift each of you has received. Whoever speaks must do so as one speaking the very words of God; whoever serves must do so with the strength that God supplies, so that God may be glorified in all things through Jesus Christ. To him belong the glory and the power forever and ever. Amen.* *(1 Peter 4:10-11)*

All the gifts are special. We all have at least one gift to invest in building up the Body. Our task is to "speak" our gift or "serve" our gift to the glory of God.

Some gifts of the Spirit may seem unusual to those unfamiliar with them (working miracles, healing, discernment of spirits, prophet, apostle, evangelist, and some might add speaking in tongues and interpreting tongues). Other gifts are more easily recognized (pastor, teacher, leadership, service, generosity, faith). But we are reminded that all are important, and each is to be exercised with humility and grace. After all, these are gifts (literally, graces) from the Spirit, not merit badges. It might also be important to realize that the three lists of gifts are not identical or exhaustive. Remember, for example, the gifts of the Spirit listed in the description of the building of the tabernacle in Exodus 35 (Session 11).

If you are interested in learning more about spiritual gifts, check with your pastor, church library, or local Christian bookstore for resources that can expand your thinking on this important subject.

What SHAPE Are You In?

The SHAPE program was created by Rick Warren at Saddleback Church in southern California to make the discovery of gifts for ministry more holistic. Its goal is to help every person become more excited about his or her unique contribution to the Kingdom. Too often churches have tried to fit right-shaped pegs into wrong-shaped holes, or vice versa. Many times our approach in the past was enlisting volunteers and getting the job done. But the Spirit has again helped us understand that there is a special ministry place for each person. What's more, when people discover their God-given fit, their SHAPE for ministry and witness, the work is energizing and rewarding as well as fruitful. The focus is not on the job but on the body of Christ.

Some people seem to know their fit intuitively. They have a deep sense of being called to a special arena of activity for the Lord's work. Some of us, however, have had a harder time of it, and have often ended up doing things at church just because…well, just because of lots of things, except a deep sense of leading by the Spirit. Usually, the Spirit leads us to be ourselves, our new selves created for freedom. We grow through discipline (or self-control, one of the fruits of the Spirit in Galatians 5:23), which means doing things that stretch us. But as we mature we discover that we can't live out our faith exactly the same way others do.

So, how do we follow the leading of the Spirit into ministry and witness? The key is to follow the Spirit. Where has the Spirit of creation and the new creation been at work in your life? SHAPE is designed to help answer that question.

Your **S**piritual gifts + **H**eart + **A**bilities + **P**ersonality + **E**xperiences all contribute. (Permission was granted for the use of SHAPE, written by Rick Warren, Saddleback Church, in this publication only. No further permission is given.) What have you learned this week by talking with others and taking inventory that has helped you begin to get a new feel for the unique and special *you* God has shaped for ministry and witness? We're looking for the whole picture, not just one part.

The Spirit and Your Ministry

Ministry is a word that sometimes has been used to describe only the work of those who have been trained and ordained to be clergy. These people do have a ministry, and most are gifted as pastors (shepherds), teachers, or pastor-teachers. They may or may not have other gifts, such as leadership, faith, or evangelism. Not all with the pastoral gift are ordained. It is important to remember that all of us have a ministry.

Many lay people might have the gift of feeding and caring for the sheep. In fact, more and more churches are making use of gifted and trained lay people to do much of the calling, tending, and pastoral caregiving.

Q2
What new things have you learned this week about your SHAPE?

S

H

A

P

E

For all who are led by the Spirit of God are children of God. (Romans 8:14)

Q3
What from your reading this week is still unclear to you?

Camp Notes

Q4
What ministries are you involved in that seem to fit your SHAPE?

Q5
Are there some things you are involved in that don't seem to fit your SHAPE?

Q6
What part of "building up the body of Christ" do you think might belong to you?

Some clergy may be more gifted and perhaps better trained in leadership than in sensitive pastoral caregiving. This can create problems for churches that want a pastor only to pastor and not to teach or lead or prophesy. Being aware ahead of time of the gift mix, SHAPE, and ministry priorities of our clergy could greatly reduce the tension that is sometimes created when they feel disallowed from their true ministry. But this is true for all of us.

Remember Paul's instruction to the church at Ephesus:

> *The gifts he gave were that some would be apostles, some prophets, some evangelists, some pastors and teachers, to equip the saints for the work of ministry, for building up the body of Christ, until all of us come to the unity of the faith and of the knowledge of the Son of God, to maturity, to the measure of the full stature of Christ.* (Ephesians 4:11-13)

Some of the gifts are to be used to equip all of us for ministry: building up the church, helping everyone find faith in Jesus as God's Son, and growing to maturity in Christlikeness. We all are called to a ministry.

Our goal through this brief orientation to spiritual gifts and the larger concept of SHAPE has been to help you begin to think in terms of your ministry, not just church work. Just as pastors are most effective and most energized when their unique SHAPE is used to the fullest, so are all of the other members of the body of Christ.

Let me illustrate the process. Suppose you feel your spiritual gift is helping others or giving assistance (1 Corinthians 12:28). You love to help out and find it refreshing to do whatever needs to be done, especially if no one else wants to do it. This is a gift! And suppose one of your abilities is auto mechanics. And suppose your heart is with "messed-up teens who never had a chance," because that is also part of your experience. And suppose your personality is quite comfortable around rough-edged people. What possible ministries and opportunities for witness might seem to fit this SHAPE?

If such a ministry is already in place, humbly offer yourself to those giving leadership. If such a ministry is not in place but the need is obvious, offer to help begin such a ministry. It may be that you can do this on your own, but it is always appropriate to prayerfully look for others who might feel a similar calling to serve in this way. "A threefold cord is not quickly broken" (Ecclesiastes 4:12). We are always Christ's body in ministry, not just individuals doing good. This is the Spirit's life at work.

The Spirit and Your Witness

The word *witness* used in the New Testament is the Greek word *martus*, from which we get the English word *martyr*. The ultimate witness is with one's whole life or, if necessary, through one's death. Few of us know much about this latter form of bearing witness. But through the centuries and even today in dozens of countries around the world, Christians bear witness under the constant threat of persecution and death. Indeed, we are "surrounded by so great a cloud of witnesses" (Hebrews 12:1).

Christian witnessing is not merely about an occasional act of friendship or generosity. From the beginning, Jesus told his disciples that they were going to be his witnesses and would need his Spirit to have the power necessary to be both faithful and fruitful. Our witness is ultimately about letting the Holy Spirit, the Spirit of Jesus, use our eyes and our hands and our voices to love people with Jesus' love and lead those we can to open themselves to Jesus as their Lord, their Savior, and their true Friend.

Has it ever really sunk in that "you are the salt of the earth,…the light of the world" (Matthew 5:13-14)? Can you imagine a more important calling or identity than to be salt and light? Each one of us is designed for and filled with the Spirit for this purpose. There is no other plan. Every human being is created to be a participant in this life. We are only going through the motions of living until we are led by the Spirit through faithful witnesses to find "the way, and the truth, and the life," whose name is Jesus (John 14:6).

The wonderful thing is that your witness is totally unique. No one else can give what you can to those in your arena of influence. But unless we abide and seek constantly to be led and empowered by the Spirit, we lose the vital connection that keeps the light on and the saltiness in our words and deeds.

But you will receive power when the Holy Spirit has come upon you; and you will be my witnesses in Jerusalem, in all Judea and Samaria, and to the ends of the earth.

(Acts 1:8)

I tell you, there is joy in the presence of the angels of God over one sinner who repents.

(Luke 15:10)

Q7
In what ways has your understanding of being a Christian witness changed as you have traveled these first three trails?

_____

_____

_____

_____

_____

Camp Notes

At Pine Grove Furnace General Store, there is a thru-hiker tradition of eating a half-gallon of ice cream to celebrate the completion of half the trail. I ate it in 40 minutes.

Wadi

Moving On

There's more to come on our *Witness* trail as we continue to learn how to help one another and our congregations reach out with the gospel. We're only halfway there, but it is hoped that you're feeling encouraged and strengthened by the fellowship and are ready to finish the course, "looking to Jesus the pioneer and perfecter of our faith" (Hebrews 12:2). Any day with him is a taste of heaven, and any day without him is a taste of hell. It's worth the hike, both for you and for those the Spirit leads you to as witnesses.

Take some time to review the assignments for next week.

READING ASSIGNMENTS

1. Review the notes in your *My Witness Journal* for the first three trails of your *Witness* journey. Decide which Bible passages and which action assignments were most helpful to you as you learned more about your Christian faith and about how to be a witness.
2. Make notes in your *My Witness Journal* to recall your journey so far.
3. Read the chapter for next week (pages 82–86). Underline or highlight special thoughts and answer the questions in the Q boxes.

ACTION ASSIGNMENT

Ask two or more people in your church (not members of your *Witness* group) what they think the purpose of the church is; that is, why the church exists. Write down in your *My Witness Journal* some notes about their answers.

Stay "salty" and "let your little light shine."

See you on the path!

Trail Four
The Church and Its Witness

I will build my church, and the gates of Hades
will not prevail against it.

(Matthew 16:18)

Biblical Images of the Church

Camp Notes

My 100th day on the trail and I still love it. For over a week now, my right foot has hurt, and it is giving me a little concern. I started thinking worst-case scenario: I would have to come off the trail if it was fractured. That would depress me, not because I didn't complete the trail (that would be a pride issue), but because I love how my life has adapted. I have grown to love life in the mountains.

Wadi

Pentecost was a Jewish feast day fifty days after the beginning of Passover and the barley harvest (Exodus 23:14-17; Deuteronomy 16:9). It was a day of joy and came to be known as the anniversary of the covenant of law established when God gave the stone tablets to Moses on Mount Sinai.

In Acts 2, the Holy Spirit breaks in on the Pentecost festival with a new covenant. The church of Jesus the Messiah is born.

Prayer

God of grace,
you sent the promised gift of the Holy Spirit
  upon the apostles and the women,
  upon Mary the mother of Jesus and upon his brothers.
Fill your church with power,
  kindle flaming hearts within us,
  and cause us to proclaim your mighty works in every tongue,
  that all may call on you and be saved;
through Jesus Christ our Lord. Amen.[21]

Trail Talk

Although Jesus always paid attention to individuals and their special needs, he maintained a focus on a larger goal for his ministry. When Peter said, "You are the Messiah, the Son of the living God," Jesus responded, "You are Peter, and on this rock I will build my church, and the gates of Hades will not prevail against it" (Matthew 16:16-18). Building his church was in Jesus' mind from his earliest days of revealing himself as the Messiah and Son of God.

This session begins a new trail that focuses on some of the images used by Jesus and the early Christians to clarify the nature and purpose of the church.

But first, how was your review of the first three trails? Did you find it easy or difficult to summarize the most meaningful images, texts, and experiences?

The Church Is Born

Pentecost Sunday is often referred to as the birthday of the church. Luke tells us that the resurrected Jesus instructed his disciples that they were to be his witnesses and were not to leave Jerusalem until they had received power for this task from the outpouring of the Holy Spirit (Luke 24:44-53). Before the Day of Pentecost, when the Spirit of God flooded out upon these disciples and wove their individual lives together into a new entity, Christ's church did not exist.

The word for church in the New Testament is *ekklesia,* which means "the called-out ones." The focus of the church is always on the people whom God has called out for service in the Kingdom, not on a building. Nevertheless, the church is often thought of as existing in particular places. Thus Luke tells us that after the martyrdom of Stephen, "a severe persecution began against the church in Jerusalem" (Acts 8:1). Paul helped lead that persecution, but later wrote to the many churches he established and called them "the church in such-and-such a place." Yet, in Romans 16:23, Paul speaks of "the whole church," and in 1 Corinthians 4:17, he writes: "I sent you Timothy, who is my beloved and faithful child in the Lord, to remind you of my ways in Christ Jesus, as I teach them everywhere in every church."

Our focus in this session is on biblical images for the whole church. These images are also appropriate for any local congregation of that total body. In the Old Testament, images of God's called-out people are God's: (1) bride or wife (Isaiah 62:4-5; Jeremiah 31:32), (2) vine or vineyard (Psalm 80:8; Isaiah 5:1-5), (3) child or household (Isaiah 8:14-18; Jeremiah 31:20; Hosea 11:1), (4) kingdom of priests or holy nation (Exodus 19:6), and (5) holy hill Zion, or holy city Jerusalem (Isaiah 3:8; 4:3-4).

Several of these images carry over into the New Testament: a holy nation, a royal priesthood, the new Jerusalem, the new Israel, and even branches of the true vine. We will look at three images: the church as the body of Christ, as the bride of Christ, and as God's temple of living stones.

The Body of Christ

We caught a glimpse of this image of the church in our last session. The expression "the body of Christ" is first encountered in Romans 7:4. Paul expands the image in Romans 12, but the most significant descriptions occur in 1 Corinthians 12; Ephesians 4; and Colossians 1.

It is interesting to note that the most commonly used metaphor for the Christian church is the human body. Some religions and even some Christians see the body as unimportant, or worse. They focus only on the soul or spirit. But Jesus came as God in a human body, beginning as a totally unformed single speck of DNA and growing in size and wisdom and in and favor with God and people (Luke 2:52). The human body is an amazing manifestation of God's creativity and, might we even say, genius. Each of its systems is a complete network of almost miraculously complex functions, yet we live most of our lives barely giving a thought to the whole organism or any of its parts—unless something goes wrong.

Perhaps Paul used the body image for Christ's church for these very reasons. Something had gone wrong with the body of Christ in Corinth. There was division and tension (1 Corinthians 1:11). The body was hurting. Paul reminded them that only when all systems and members of the body are of "the same mind and the same purpose" (1 Corinthians 1:10) can they truly represent Christ. They could not manifest the oneness of the glory of God if they allowed their diversity to reflect their old nature instead of their new nature. Didn't they remember that they were baptized by the one Spirit into Christ's one body (1 Corinthians 12:12-13), and that the controlling dynamic was now divine love (1 Corinthians 13)?

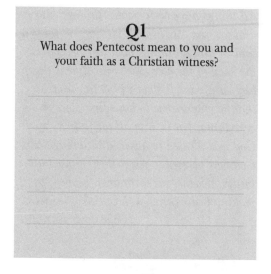

Q1

What does Pentecost mean to you and your faith as a Christian witness?

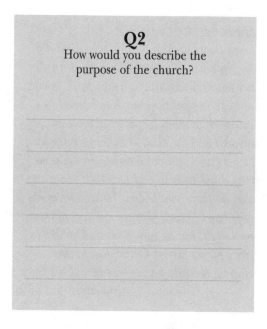

Q2

How would you describe the purpose of the church?

We must grow up in every way into him who is the head, into Christ, from whom the whole body, joined and knit together by every ligament with which it is equipped, as each part is working properly, promotes the body's growth in building itself up in love.
(Ephesians 4:15-16)

Camp Notes

All things have been created through him and for him. He himself is before all things, and in him all things hold together. He is the head of the body, the church; he is the beginning, the firstborn from the dead, so that he might come to have first place in everything. For in him all the fullness of God was pleased to dwell, and through him God was pleased to reconcile to himself all things, whether on earth or in heaven, by making peace through the blood of his cross.

(Colossians 1:16-20)

Husbands, love your wives, just as Christ loved the church and gave himself up for her, in order to make her holy by cleansing her with the washing of water by the word, so as to present the church to himself in splendor, without a spot or wrinkle or anything of the kind—yes, so that she may be holy and without blemish. In the same way, husbands should love their wives as they do their own bodies. He who loves his wife loves himself. For no one ever hates his own body, but he nourishes and tenderly cares for it, just as Christ does for the church, because we are members of his body.

(Ephesians 5:25-30)

*Let us rejoice and exult
   and give him the glory,
for the marriage of the Lamb has come,
   and his bride has made herself ready.*

(Revelation 19:7)

*The Spirit and the bride say, "Come."
And let everyone who hears say, "Come."
And let everyone who is thirsty come....
Come, Lord Jesus!*

(Revelation 22:17, 20)

Perhaps the best explanations of the church as the body of Christ are found in Ephesians 4:15-16 (side column, page 83) and Colossians 1:16-20 (side column, this page). The head of the body is Christ; there is no other. He holds all things together. He is at work in us as his body to reconcile (bring together again) all things and all people. His mission, and therefore the ministry of his body, is reconciliation through his cross, with the power of his resurrection, in the uniting love of the Holy Spirit. The church is the living, working hands and feet, eyes and ears, mouth and muscles of God for this planet and for all creation.

The Bride of Christ

The intimacy suggested by the idea of husband and wife or bride and groom is another hard-to-imagine metaphor used to describe the covenant love relationship between Almighty God and God's people. At times this relationship is strained to the limits, as depicted by Hosea's symbolic efforts to redeem and restore his unfaithful wife to a place of honor. And God's word from Jeremiah spoke of the old covenant, saying: "I took them by the hand to bring them out of the land of Egypt—a covenant that they broke, though I was their husband, says the LORD" (Jeremiah 31:32).

The new covenant is likewise depicted as a marriage. The church is the bride of Christ. The Gospels reveal that both John the Baptist (John 3:29) and Jesus (Matthew 9:15) delight in the wedding close at hand. Jesus enjoys it as the bridegroom, while John revels as the best man and dear friend of the bridegroom.

And here is where the images of marriage and body come close enough to touch. Paul reminds us in the passage from Ephesians 5 (side column, this page) that loving one's body and one's spouse are one and the same, for the two become one. Once more, here is the image of unity in diversity.

Actually, much of the bride and bridegroom imagery related to the church depicts a marriage anticipated but not yet fully accomplished. The plans are in place, the bridegroom and his court are waiting, the banquet is being prepared; but the bride is still being glorified for her radiant appearance. Then the bridegroom is unexpectedly taken away, and the bride now awaits his reappearance when they can be fully united.

The bride (Christ's church) is still being prepared. There are others to be invited into the joy of this holy union, and the bride is still being transformed in beauty, glorified to be pure and spotless dressed in her new righteousness. But the day is approaching, writes John in the Revelation, when the shout will be, "Come!" (Revelation 22:16-17).

The Temple of Living Stones

When we speak of our church, sometimes we are referring to a building made of wood or bricks or stones. But seldom, if ever, have we thought of the stones as living. Yet, living stones is the image Peter used to describe the church. The idea of living stones almost sounds like an animated movie. Can you see the faces and hear the voices as the living stones talk about the history of a place or a people? What would the stones on Easter Island or in Rome's Coliseum tell us if they could speak?

The Temple in Jerusalem was a magnificent stone structure that was known as the dwelling place of God on earth. As Jesus entered the city riding on a donkey on the day we now celebrate as Palm Sunday, the multitudes cried out, "Blessed is the king who comes in the name of the Lord!"

> *[But] some of the Pharisees in the crowd said to him, "Teacher, order your disciples to stop." He answered, "I tell you, if these were silent, the stones would shout out."*
>
> *(Luke 19:39-40)*

Jesus perceived that all of creation, even the stones of the Temple, understood more about this moment in time than did God's people.

After his grand entry, Jesus went directly to the Temple and cleansed it of the robbers who preyed on people instead of praying to God (Matthew 21:12-13). He taught in the Temple day after day, speaking about vineyards and marriage feasts and quoting Psalm 118 (Matthew 21:42). And he told them:

> *"Destroy this temple, and in three days I will raise it up." The Jews then said, "This temple has been under construction for forty-six years, and will you raise it up in three days?" But he was speaking of the temple of his body.*
>
> *(John 2:19-21)*

We are the living stones of God's temple and the body of Christ.

Camp Notes

Come to him, a living stone, though rejected by mortals yet chosen and precious in God's sight, and like living stones, let yourselves be built into a spiritual house... For it stands in scripture:
> *"See, I am laying in Zion a stone,*
> *a cornerstone chosen and precious;*
> *and whoever believes in him*
> *will not be put to shame."*
>
> *(1 Peter 2:4-6)*

The stone that the builders rejected
> *has become the chief cornerstone.*
This is the LORD's doing;
> *it is marvelous in our eyes.*
This is the day that the LORD has made;
> *let us rejoice and be glad in it.*
>
> *(Psalm 118:22-24)*

Q3
What would the stones that make up your church building say if they were to talk?

_____

_____

_____

_____

_____

_____

Camp Notes

Moving On

We are Christ's church, his body, his bride, and the living stones of his holy temple. His life is our life. His work is our work. As we continue with him on the trail, we will learn what all of this means for our witness.

Review the assignments for next week's reading and action on the trail.

READING ASSIGNMENTS

1. Record your reflections, questions, and insights from these daily Bible readings in your *My Witness Journal.*
    - **Day 1:** Isaiah 43:1-12 ("You are my witnesses.")
    - **Day 2:** Luke 5:1-11 (Follow me and catch people.)
    - **Day 3:** Matthew 9:35–10:32 (The disciples are sent out with instructions.)
    - **Day 4:** John 10:1-16 ("I have other sheep.")
    - **Day 5:** Acts 2 (All of us are witnesses.)
    - **Day 6:** 1 Thessalonians 1 ("The word of the Lord has sounded forth from you.")
2. As you read the chapter for next week (pages 87–92), underline or highlight special thoughts and answer the questions in the Q boxes.

ACTION ASSIGNMENT

Talk to at least two people in your church who are not members of your *Witness* group. Ask them two questions: (1) "What does our congregation do best in witnessing for Christ?" and (2) "Where does our congregation's witness need to be strengthened?" Write notes about their answers in your *My Witness Journal.*

See you on the path!

The Church as Evangelist

Prayer

> *O Spirit of the living God,*
> *thou light and fire divine,*
> *descend upon thy church once more,*
> *and make it truly thine.*
> *Fill it with love and joy and power,*
> *with righteousness and peace;*
> *till Christ shall dwell in human hearts,*
> *and sin and sorrow cease.*
>
> *Blow, wind of God! With wisdom blow*
> *until our minds are free*
> *from mists of error, clouds of doubt,*
> *which blind our eyes to thee.*
> *Burn, winged fire! Inspire our lips*
> *with flaming love and zeal,*
> *to preach to all thy great good news,*
> *God's glorious commonweal.*[22]

Trail Talk

The church is Christ's body filled with his Spirit; therefore, it stands to reason that the church must be about the same task that Jesus was committed to when he was here in his body. He came to bear witness to and inaugurate the kingdom of God, the new covenant, and eternal life. Our task is to reveal this new community of divine love and to invite all who would acknowledge Jesus as the Christ and Son of God to join with us as his beloved bride.

These actions mean that the church is God's ultimate evangelist. We, the church, are witnesses to more than just the message about God's saving love; we also *are* the message. If the church fails to live out its true identity, the gospel is seriously hindered, if not destroyed.

Gamaliel, "a teacher of the law, respected by all the people," told the Sanhedrin Council in Jerusalem as they interrogated and threatened those first apostles for openly speaking of Jesus as God's "Leader and Savior" (Acts 5:31-34):

> *Let them alone; because if this plan or this undertaking is of human origin, it will fail; but if it is of God, you will not be able to overthrow them—in that case you may even be found fighting against God!* (Acts 5:38-39)

People in every town I come to ask me, "Is this fun for you? I could think of many other things that would be more fun than that." I have been thinking about how to respond.... I love this not because it is continual fun and excitement but because it fulfills me. Because I have a vision or goal, I am finding passion and contentment. Because I am acting on my goal, I am finding joy and freedom. But the initial act was not searching for a goal or vision, but being obedient. Out of obedience I find peace.

Wadi

Q1

What do you consider the best ways your congregation serves as Christ's witness?

87

Camp Notes

Q2
What text was this?
(From now on, you will be asked
to find many of these key passages
for yourself. The practice will help you
build confidence in using the Bible.)

Q3
If you were to create a list from
Acts 2, what ingredients would
constitute the gospel message?

Q4
Why did Jesus pray we would be one?

Where is this prayer of his found?

Does the witness of the church today produce the same response? Do we create enough of a stir that society's lepers and leaders alike want to watch us to see if we will succeed or fail? What are people saying about us? What do they think we are about? What are we about?

The Evangelism of Pentecost

Since Pentecost is the birthday of the church, it shouldn't surprise us to look there first to get a glimpse of the church as evangelist.

Jesus told his disciples to wait in Jerusalem until they received power to be his witnesses (**Acts ___:___**) **(Q2)**. In an upstairs room, perhaps the same one provided for the Last Supper (Luke 22:7-12), the disciples waited, "constantly devoting themselves to prayer, together with certain women, including Mary the mother of Jesus, as well as his brothers" (Acts 1:14). Altogether "the crowd numbered about one hundred twenty persons" (Acts 1:15). Then the day of Pentecost arrived, and so did the Spirit.

It is obvious that from the beginning this church of one hundred twenty people, filled with the Holy Spirit, began to tell others in their own languages what God had been doing. Then Peter stood up and, in his first full-gospel sermon, clarified the whole story. After the audience heard the message, they asked what they needed to do. Peter told them, "Repent, and be baptized every one of you in the name of Jesus Christ so that your sins may be forgiven; and you will receive the gift of the Holy Spirit" (**Acts 2:___**). Three thousand responded, repented, were baptized, received the Spirit, and began to model for hundreds of generations to follow the day-to-day witness of the church. "They devoted themselves to the apostles' teaching and fellowship, to the breaking of bread and the prayers" (**Acts 2:___**).

The Church as Evangelist

If we take our clues from this earliest portrayal of the church's life, we could say that to be a healthy church means first of all that the church is alive in the Holy Spirit. Second, it announces the gospel of Jesus Christ to others in a language that they can understand. Third, it invites people by repentance and faith to come to Christ and welcomes them into his body. Fourth, it continues to practice the habits of the early church: learning Christian truth, enjoying fellowship, breaking bread in communion, praying, worshiping, sharing from their bounty with all who have need—always praising God with glad and generous hearts. When a church has this kind of life, it is God's evangelist; and day by day the Lord will add to their number those who are being saved (**Acts 2:___**).

What is an evangelist? An evangelist is one who offers the gospel to others. The one in this case is Christ's body, the one body he prayed for. Do you remember that prayer? Can you find it (**Q4**)? Can you see why the church is the ultimate evangelist in the world today?

The gospel is about belonging to God and God's people. It is not something that can be privatized or offered to individuals without inviting them into the reconciled and reconciling fellowship of the church. It is possible in the most unusual of circumstances for people to be saved without belonging to Christ's church, or at least not to any local congregation. The dying thief on the cross next to Jesus was offered mercy and a promise of being in paradise with Jesus (Luke 23:42-43). The Ethiopian eunuch led to Christ by Philip believed, was baptized, and went on his way (Acts 8:35-39). The tradition of the Christian church in Ethiopia indicates that he returned home and formed the first body of Christian believers in Africa. The design of God the Holy Trinity is that all who become Christian disciples will be bound together, in this life and in the life to come, as Christ's body.

We could say that although there may be evangelists who speak to individuals about the gospel, response to the gospel requires becoming one with Christ and his disciples in his body, the church. Only then is evangelism's word and work complete. Thus, there are no independent evangelists or independent Christians. All true evangelism is connected to the church as the source and the goal of our witness to Jesus as God's Son and Savior. Christ's church is central to the message and is itself the ultimate messenger.

The Evangelistic Work of the Church

Even people who are members of the church and regularly attend its functions do not always see the church as ultimately important. In addition, vast numbers of people think of themselves as Christians but not members of any local church. For them, the church is at best a building they visit on special occasions. Why has it become so easy to see the church as an optional religious club for those who are interested, rather than a central ingredient in the nature of Christianity?

There are probably many answers to this question, but most could be traced back to two or three important causes: (1) the gospel offered by Christian evangelists has failed to keep the church central to the message; (2) the church has failed to live and act like Christ's body; and/or (3) our modern culture's emphasis on individual freedom has made a commitment to membership unattractive. We will examine the third possibility later. For now, let's look at the first two, beginning with the second.

The church as evangelist has both work to do and a word to give as part of its witness. The work is to reveal the beauty of Christ's character in its daily life. In Acts 2:47, we are told that day by day God "added to their number those who were being saved." We are also told that the church had "the goodwill of all the people." In this passage, God's work of salvation appears to be connected to the witness of the church as a people who produce goodwill.

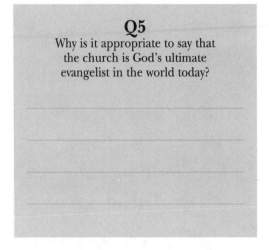

Q5

Why is it appropriate to say that the church is God's ultimate evangelist in the world today?

Q6

In your opinion, why do many people seem to believe they can be Christians without the church?

We see—and who does not?—the numberless follies and miseries of our fellow creatures. We see on every side either men of no religion at all or men of a lifeless, formal religion. We are grieved at the sight, and should greatly rejoice if by any means we might convince some that there is a better religion to be attained, a religion worthy of God that gave it. And this we conceive to be no other than love: the love of God and of all mankind… This love we believe to be the medicine of life, the never-failing remedy, for all the evils of a disordered world.[23]

John Wesley

Camp Notes

Q7

Use the space below to answer the questions in the text about the signs of goodwill.

How did the church in Acts 2 produce goodwill? First, the apostles did "many wonders and signs" (2:43). This was a continuation of the apostles' earlier ministry after Jesus gave them authority over unclean spirits and power to heal the sick and diseased (Matthew 10:1). Much debate has swirled around the question of whether or not this miraculous power for healing ceased after the first century. Some say yes; others say no. Whatever your answer, the challenge remains: How can the church today manifest Christ's compassionate concern and healing presence for broken lives within our arena of contact? What do we have to offer? Are we offering it?

Second, the believers shared a common life that was so strong "they would sell their possessions and goods and distribute the proceeds to all, as any had need" (Acts 2:44-45). What comes to your mind from the life and teachings of Jesus that helps you understand why they might have done this? This sort of generosity was no more common in Jesus' day than it is in ours. Is it dangerous to live like this? Do you think such radical self-sacrifice would drive many away rather than attract them to Jesus and his church? There is some indication that this rather ideal communal lifestyle was already breaking down by the fifth chapter of Acts. Read Acts 4:32–5:16 and record what you think. In what ways does the church today reveal some of this same spirit? In what ways could we do more?

Third, these early followers of the risen Jesus were highly visible. They walked through the streets together on their way to public worship in the Temple. They jammed into one another's homes to share meals, receive instruction and encouragement, remember the sacrifice of Jesus by eating together his communion meal, and recognize the presence of Jesus as they prayed and sang together for hours on end.

They were not a secret society, so there were no efforts on their part to keep a lid on things. All the people knew they were around and what they were up to, even those who wanted them silenced. Persecution was always just around the corner, but they couldn't hide the fact that they were full of the Spirit of Jesus. Is it obvious to people today that we Christians are around and thoroughly attentive to the presence of our Lord? What churches or programs are you aware of that seem to help communicate this bold public presence? Is there more we could do?

The early church as God's evangelist lived and acted like Christ's body. It also spoke an evangelistic word.

The Evangelistic Word of the Church

For the church to be faithful to its identity and calling as God's evangelist, it must help people hear and understand the gospel in their own language.

Pentecost was about more than just a loud wind and hovering tongues of fire. It was about more than just one hundred and twenty people getting high on God. It was about the prophet's word being fulfilled. The long-awaited gift had arrived. The Spirit of God was being poured out on all flesh, and the first manifestation of the Spirit's presence was the ability of each one to announce the things of God to "other sheep that do not belong to this fold" (John 10:16).

Was this a strange and wonderful miracle? Yes, and it still is. The Spirit gives Christ's people this power. It is not primarily a matter of a well-rehearsed speech. It is a combination of overflow from our living close to Jesus and the Spirit's sensitivity and love for all people. Have you been discovering more and more about how these two ingredients work together for your witness? Have you noticed any improvement in your ability to offer a meaningful word to others in their own language?

Has "the word of the Lord...sounded forth" from your church (**1 Thessalonians 1:___**)? Does your congregation sense that its word of witness is meant to be clearly understood by the other sheep who are still on the fringes of the gospel community? Does your worship in the Spirit speak their language or only your own?

If you get their attention, do you talk about Jesus in such a way that their concerns are addressed and his life, death, and resurrection all witness to his power to fulfill their lives? Does your congregation announce the "gift of the Holy Spirit" as the goal of your evangelism? Do you give people who want to know how this can happen to them a clear answer to the question, "What should we do?"

Q8
Which questions in the text are most important for your church to discuss? Why?

Camp Notes

Moving On

The church is God's evangelist. We each have a part to play; but unless the whole body of Christ recognizes the work and word of evangelism as central to its identity, we will more than likely end up investing more energy arguing over carpet colors than in reaching Christ's other sheep.

The goal of *Witness* is to help both individuals and congregations become more alive to this mission. Your part is to serve both in the world and in your church as salt and as light.

Next week we look at Jesus' description of this mission. Review the reading and action assignments for next week on the trail.

READING ASSIGNMENTS

1. Record your reflections, questions, and insights from these daily Bible readings in your *My Witness Journal*.
   Day 1: Matthew 28:16-20 ("Make disciples of all nations.")
   Day 2: Mark 16:14-20 ("Proclaim the good news to the whole creation.")
   Day 3: Luke 24:44-49 (Proclaim repentance and forgiveness of sins.)
   Day 4: John 20:19-23 ("As the Father has sent me, so I send you.")
   Day 5: Acts 1:1-8 ("You will be my witnesses.")
   Day 6: Ephesians 3 (Paul declares his commission to the Gentiles.)
2. As you read the chapter for next week (pages 93–98), underline or highlight special thoughts and answer the questions in the Q boxes.

ACTION ASSIGNMENT

Ask at least one person in your church (but not in your *Witness* group) and at least one person you are witnessing to what they think it means to be a disciple of Jesus today. Write notes about what they say in your *My Witness Journal*.

See you on the path!

Camp Notes

The Great Commission

Prayer

Lord, you give the great commission:
"Heal the sick and preach the word."
Lest the church neglect its mission,
and the gospel go unheard,
help us witness to your purpose
with renewed integrity.

Lord, you call us to your service:
"In my name baptize and teach."
That the world may trust your promise,
life abundant meant for each,
give us all new fervor,
draw us closer in community.

Amen.

(From "Lord, You Give the Great Commission," words by
Jeffery Rowthorn. © 1978 Hope Publishing Co., Carol
Stream, IL 60188. All rights reserved. Used by permission.
Permission to reproduce this text must be obtained from
Hope Publishing Co., 800-323-1049.)

Trail Talk

The body of Christ exists to glorify God, to enjoy the favor of God's grace,
and to carry out the mission given to it by its Lord. Sometimes that
mission seems lost in the everyday shuffle of committee minutes, Sunday
school papers, and choir robes. But this week we have been reviewing
Jesus' final instructions to his chosen disciples that are often referred to
as the Great Commission.

It's difficult to summarize the church's entire task in a few short
sentences. The prophet Micah asked, "What does the LORD require of
you but to do justice, and to love kindness, and to walk humbly with your
God?" (**Micah 6:___**). The two great commandments, summarized by our
Lord, are, "Love the Lord your God with all your heart, and with all your
soul, and with all your mind.... Love your neighbor as yourself" (**Matthew
22:___-___**). Jesus reminded his disciples that they were to feed the
hungry, welcome strangers, clothe the naked, and visit the sick and
imprisoned (**Matthew 25:___-___**). Thus, the larger mission of the
church involves more than the Great Commission; but without the Great
Commission, there is no church. The church was birthed for a mission: to
announce the gospel and make disciples.

What is a disciple? Would you know one if you saw one? Is it the same as or
different from being a Christian or a church member? What did you discover
through your reading and interviews? What are your own thoughts?

Llama and I were hiking again today and saw some of the most amazing views. Last night she told me she wanted to know God, but was still confused as to the how and why. So I prayed that God would reveal his love in a powerful, tangible way that she could not turn away from or rationalize away.

Around lunchtime we started talking, and she said she had broken down in tears recognizing how loved she is by others whom God has put in her life. She said she has also had a sense of peace within her and a quietness that has calmed her and sharpened her thoughts with clarity. She told me as we were eating lunch that she wants to give her life to God, but doesn't know how or what will happen.

So I told her how—tell God she accepts his gift of love for her, to know Jesus died

(continued on page 94)

Camp Notes

for her sins and then rose from the dead to give her freedom. She needs to lay her life before the feet of God and give up control of her life, to lay down pride and selfish ambition, to receive in return peace, purpose, and the joy of God's love. She just needs to say it to God from her heart.

She did, and she was changed instantly, forever.

Wadi

Q1
Which version of the Great Commission did you find most helpful? Why?

_____

_____

_____

_____

Which version did you find most challenging or difficult? Why?

_____

_____

_____

_____

_____

The Great Commission

To commission is to charge people with a particular task and grant the authority to carry it out. Jesus had already commissioned his disciples to go out two by two from village to village carrying on the same ministry he had been about (Matthew 9:35–10:15). So, why is the commissioning that appears toward the end of each Gospel the *Great* Commission?

There are two primary differences. First, this final commission is great because its scope is universal and not restricted only "to the lost sheep of the house of Israel" (Matthew 10:5-6). Second, it is great because the gospel message is now complete. When they were first sent out, it was to announce that the Kingdom had come near. Now it was to announce a complete gospel: fulfillment of the messianic promise, repentance and forgiveness of sins to all. This was indeed a *great* commission. For Jesus it was finished, but for his disciples it was really just beginning.

In addition to the four Gospel accounts of the Great Commission, we usually include the version in Acts 1:8. Each of these five versions has a different wording or emphasis, but all have the requirement of offering God's gift in Christ to the entire world.

Matthew 28	"Make disciples of all nations."
Mark 16	"Proclaim the good news to the whole creation."
Luke 24	"Repentance and forgiveness of sins is to be proclaimed…to all nations."
John 20	"If you forgive the sins of any, they are forgiven."
Acts 1	"Be my witnesses in Jerusalem, in all Judea and Samaria, and to the ends of the earth."

The first commission given to the twelve and later to seventy (Luke 10:1-20) was a mini-commission compared with this one. This is indeed a great commission.

It is also important to notice that this is a co-mission, a mission we are involved in together with the risen Christ and in the power of the Holy Spirit. This is not merely a commandment but a joint endeavor. This is God's work. Jesus' disciples are enlisted and authorized to be part of the means by which the following will happen:

> *The earth will be filled*
> *with the knowledge of the glory*
> *of the LORD,*
> *as the waters cover the sea.*
> **(Habakkuk 2:___)**

Matthew 28:16-20

Although the Great Commission involves receiving the Holy Spirit, being sent, forgiving, proclaiming, and witnessing, its best single summary is probably found in Matthew 28:16-20. Although they were not sure what to expect, the disciples went to the place in Galilee where Jesus had told them to meet him (28:10). Notice that even though they all worshiped him, "some doubted" (28:17). Yet, Jesus doesn't chastise the ones still struggling to understand and believe. Instead, he entrusts the commission to them all, knowing they all would grow in faith and in faithfulness.

Jesus' statement that "all authority in heaven and on earth has been given to me" (28:18) is important. Jesus knew what the disciples would face. In fact, each of these eleven and many others would pay with their lives for their witness (martyr). But this was a commissioning. We do not commission ourselves, but we are commissioned by someone in authority. The question is always, "How much authority?" They had seen his authority against wind and waves, against demons and diseases, and even against death. But at the end he seemed helpless against the powers of Rome and the Sanhedrin. How much authority did he really have? Some doubted.

Yet, Jesus had told the disciples exactly what was going to happen: his betrayal, his death, and that in three days he would rise from the dead. And now here he was, standing over them, alive, saying, "all authority...has been given to me"! If that were so, and surely now it seemed to them that it must be, how could they possibly resist giving all of themselves to obey the only one who ultimately mattered? So, here was the power behind them, and they were told to wait in Jerusalem for the power within them. Then they would be his witnesses to those nearby and to those as far away as the ends of the earth.

The Great Commission Plan

The last two verses of Matthew's Gospel contain an amazing account of the central mission of the church. In the first of these sentences, there is only one imperative verb, or command, in the Greek language of the New Testament ("make disciples"). Our English translations sometimes miss this distinction. The single mandate of the Great Commission is this mission. We are to do what Jesus did, make disciples.

How did Jesus do it? How are we to do it? Here is where the comprehensive strategy of this single sentence is astounding. Although there is only one true verb, *disciple* or *make disciples*, there are three participles, which are cousins to verbs and help clarify how to accomplish the mandate. Participles usually end in *ing* and are therefore fairly easy to spot. Of course, there are always exceptions, and the first participle in the Great Commission is one of the exceptions.

[16]*Now the eleven disciples went to Galilee, to the mountain to which Jesus had directed them.* [17]*When they saw him, they worshiped him; but some doubted.* [18]*And Jesus came and said to them, "All authority in heaven and on earth has been given to me.* [19]*Go therefore and make disciples of all nations, baptizing them in the name of the Father and of the Son and of the Holy Spirit,* [20]*and teaching them to obey everything that I have commanded you. And remember, I am with you always, to the end of the age.*
(Matthew 28:16-20)

Camp Notes

Q4

Where did Jesus take his disciples to help them get used to *going*?

Q5

What do you believe is the task of the total church community in *baptizing* people?

Q6

What areas need more attention if we are to make disciples by *teaching to obey*?

Usually translated as the strong verb *go,* the first action word could be translated "going" or "as you go." Disciples are made by *going.* We must move toward them, not wait for them to move toward us. This is the message of the Incarnation and of that first mini-commission, when Jesus sent the disciples from town to town. They had to move to help him make disciples. They had to follow him. And where was he going? He was going to places and peoples they could never have imagined. And if they thought following him was challenging before his death and resurrection, they would learn that it was all just a warm-up for the main event. Jesus had prepared them to be faithful "in a very little," so that now they could be faithful "in much" (Luke 16:10). They were to begin where they were (Jerusalem) and follow the Spirit outward in widening circles to Judea, Samaria, and finally to the ends of the earth. How well is your congregation doing at going to the people needing the gospel, rather than waiting for them to come to you?

The second participle, *baptizing,* should be more obvious. Disciples are made as people respond to the gift of divine grace by faith and are then incorporated into the fellowship of Christ. "No one can say 'Jesus is Lord' except by the Holy Spirit" (**1 Corinthians 12:___**), and in "one Spirit we were all baptized into one body" (**1 Corinthians 12:___**). Baptism is about water, but ultimately about being baptized by the Holy Spirit into the church. We all have a part to play in helping people new to the faith find their place in the body and feel that they belong. Baptism is into the name of the triune God: Father, Son, Spirit. Do we help those baptized into this name understand Whose they are and how this Holy Trinity equips them to be called out and gifted for their place of ministry in the Great Commission? How is your congregation doing at helping people of new faith become baptized into your body of Christ?

The third participle is *teaching.* Notice that Jesus did not say to teach them everything he commanded, but to teach them "to obey everything that I have commanded you" (verse 20). The method that Jesus used to make his disciples looked much more like mentoring than just teaching. Disciples are made as we help people actually begin to live by everything Jesus taught. A true Christian education can never be restricted to study, no matter what the resource or subject. The goal is to make disciples, not little professors. Disciples are made initially by going and baptizing, but disciples are only truly formed when their behavior is like their master's. This is a process "from one degree of glory to another" (**2 Corinthians ___:___**). But we have a part to play in bringing it to completion. How is your congregation doing at this third action, teaching them to obey what Jesus commanded?

Camp Notes

One mandate, three procedures, one audience—*all nations.* Actually, the expression used here is *all ethnics.* Jesus instructed them to make disciples of all different kinds of cultures and peoples. To some degree, this helped prepare them for what the Spirit was about to do. On Pentecost the nations had gathered in Jerusalem. But following Pentecost the disciples had to follow the Spirit's trails to peoples and lands and tongues they had never imagined. This was difficult for those early Jewish Christians. They had been taught, carefully taught, that they were God's children and that all others were less, sometimes much less. It may still be difficult today for us to understand all that Jesus has in mind for his church. But this is where the Spirit leads us, and this is how the church of Jesus Christ is faithful to the Great Commission. How is your congregation doing at reaching out to all peoples?

Finally, there is one ultimate reality: "I will be with you." These were God's words to Moses when God called him to go to Pharaoh **(Exodus 3:___)**, and they are the risen Lord's words to those he sends to make disciples of all the nations. If this were not true, how could we ever find the motivation to tackle such an enormous undertaking? We are not alone. The Lord is with us. In fact, it is his mission, his power, his gospel, his Spirit, his church, and his love for the lost that carries us. We are co-laborers and heirs with Christ. What a privilege! God has more invested in this endeavor than we do. No wonder we have not been left on our own. How is your congregation doing in recognizing the presence of the Lord in this place and in this mission?

**Matthew 28:18-20
The Great Commission**

One mandate

_____

Three procedures

_____

_____

_____

One audience

_____

One ultimate reality

_____

In Christ Jesus you are all children of God through faith. As many of you as were baptized into Christ have clothed yourselves with Christ. There is no longer Jew or Greek, there is no longer slave or free, there is no longer male and female; for all of you are one in Christ Jesus.

(Galatians 3:26-28)

Moving On

If our churches are to be communities of faithful disciples, they will need to be seriously engaged in the work of the Great Commission: making disciples of all peoples. Some churches have already given a good deal of effort and prayer to formulating a purpose or mission statement. If your church has such a document to guide your congregational mission and ministry, evaluate it in light of Jesus' final instructions to his disciples. If your church does not have such a statement, consider using Matthew 28:18-20 to help you formulate one.

When churches have a unifying vision of why they exist and what they are trying to do for the Kingdom, they are able to give all their energy to a common task. When this kind of vision is missing, the danger is always impotence and division.

Next week we will examine how the church can be a strong and united witnessing fellowship committed to making disciples of Jesus Christ.

Review your reading and action assignments for next week.

For the love of Christ urges us on, because we are convinced that one has died for all; therefore all have died. And he died for all, so that those who live might live no longer for themselves, but for him who died and was raised for them.

(2 Corinthians 5:14-15)

Camp Notes

Q7

What are some ways your church leaders have tried to focus congregational life around the Great Commission?

READING ASSIGNMENTS

1. Record your reflections, questions, and insights from these daily Bible readings in your *My Witness Journal.*

   Day 1: Romans 14 ("Let all be fully convinced in their own minds.")

   Day 2: 1 John 1:1–2:25 (Let all live in fellowship with God.)

   Day 3: John 13:1-35 (My disciples love one another.)

   Day 4: John 8:25-36 (My disciples "continue in my word.")

   Day 5: Luke 14:25-35 (My disciples count the cost and bear their cross.)

   Day 6: John 15:1-16 (My disciples "bear much fruit.")

2. As you read the chapter for next week (pages 99–104), underline or highlight special thoughts and answer the questions in the Q boxes.

ACTION ASSIGNMENT

Take some time to formulate your own description of what a disciple of Jesus looks like. Then ask at least one of the people you spoke to last week to listen to your ideas and to respond to your thinking. Write notes about their responses in your *My Witness Journal.*

See you on the path!

A Disciple-Making Fellowship

Prayer

O God, you have built your Church
 upon the foundation of the apostles and prophets,
 Jesus Christ himself being the chief cornerstone.
Save the community of your people
 from cowardly surrender to the world,
 from rendering unto Caesar what belongs to you,
 and from forgetting the eternal gospel
  amid the temporal pressures of our troubled days.
For the unity of the Church we pray,
 and for fellowship across the embittered lines
  of race and nation;
to growth in grace, building in love, enlargement in service,
 increase in wisdom, faith, charity, and power,
 we dedicate our lives;
through Jesus Christ our Savior.

Amen.

(Selection from prayer on page 21 (adapted version as it appears in *The United Methodist Hymnal*, 506) from *A Book of Public Prayers*, by Harry Emerson Fosdick. Copyright © 1959 by Harry Emerson Fosdick. Reprinted by permission of HarperCollins Publishers, Inc. Alteration used by permission of Abingdon Press.)

Trail Talk

According to the final words of Jesus before his ascension, the mission of the church is to make disciples of all peoples. Discipleship is another way of talking about all the purposes of God for humanity rolled up into one image. Jesus said, "A disciple is not above the teacher, but everyone who is fully qualified will be like the teacher" (Luke 6:40). A fully qualified Christian disciple is like the Teacher.

The church is a kingdom community of Christ's disciples who bear witness to God's amazing grace available to all through Jesus Christ. We witness as individuals to this reality, but the ultimate witness is that of the entire fellowship. How can the church as a whole and each congregation best manifest and offer to others the possibility of becoming disciples of Jesus? It starts with being clear about what disciples are and what they are not. Disciples are not perfect people, but they are becoming more-perfect people through Christ's Spirit alive in them. They are surrendered to the process of being fully formed or fully qualified. This session will examine some of the ways the Christian community can witness to this process and some of the marks of discipleship or signposts on the trail as we invite others to walk with us in the Spirit.

Let's start with what you found in your readings and action assignment.

Camp Notes

I asked Llama if anything was different in her life, if she could see a change over the past week. "Freedom" and "joy" are the words she used to describe the week, a joy that wells up within her and a freedom from the fear of life. I bought her the book "Hinds' Feet on High Places," by Hannah Hurnard, and she loves it. It is giving her a view of God who is deeply in love with us, and now she understands it. She knows she has flaws and problems in her life, but she is unafraid to approach God, because she knows acceptance for who she is, just as she is.

Wadi

Q1
What ingredients were used by others in your group to explain the meaning of being Christ's disciple?

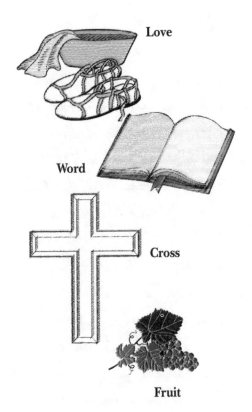

Love

Word

Cross

Fruit

Four Marks of Discipleship

Last week we learned that to make disciples we need to walk in the Spirit and work the threefold plan of going, baptizing, and teaching to obey. Our focus now is on the task of teaching to obey. But with all the areas of human life that need to be transformed into Christ's likeness, where do we begin and what do we emphasize as we are making disciples? According to the Gospels, Jesus uses the expression "my disciples" several times. On four of those occasions, Jesus describes a distinctive characteristic or mark of Christian discipleship. Together these four marks provide a framework for our own lives and for how we are to help others become fully qualified disciples.

The four marks of discipleship are found in the passages from the Gospels of Luke and John you read this week. We could summarize them with the words *love, word, cross,* and *fruit.* Different traditions of Christian history emphasize different starting points for how the gospel takes root in people's lives to make them into disciples of Jesus. Some would say that the starting place must always be the word. Others would say the starting point is love. I'm not sure we can resolve what ought to be, but we can say with assurance that most people are drawn into the possibility of becoming Christ's disciples because they see love for God and love for neighbor modeled in the lives of faithful witnesses. So, we'll begin with love.

Love

> *I give you a new commandment, that you love one another.*
> *Just as I have loved you, you also should love one another. By*
> *this everyone will know that you are my disciples, if you have*
> *love for one another.* (John 13:34-35)

John tells the story of Jesus and the disciples in the upper room preparing for Passover. In the course of the evening Jesus rises, takes off his robe, wraps himself in a towel, and begins to wash the disciples' feet. They are stunned. Foot washing was no task for the master! "You will never wash my feet," Peter protests loudly. But Jesus reminds him it is not an option; he must be washed. Grudgingly, Peter and all the disciples silently endure the embarrassment.

When Jesus finishes, he puts his robe back on and tells them that if they are to be his disciples, they will have to love one another just as he loves them. The other Gospel writers tell us of the jostling for position that had been taking place among the disciples (Matthew 20:20-28; Mark 10:35-45; Luke 22:24-27). Luke places this dispute over status right in the middle of the Passover meal.

Q2
Have you ever participated in a foot-washing ceremony? If so, what did you learn from it?

Jesus, knowing all that is to come, is grieved by the disciples' actions, so he intervenes in a dramatic way. He becomes their servant. None but a servant would be expected to perform such a degrading task as foot washing. And the love that Jesus wants the disciples to understand is that of a servant. They were not to be like others. For them, authority must be humble, serving love—not power *over* but power *under*. This kind of love would be the mark of the master on those who claimed to be his.

Have you ever felt the pain Jesus must still feel when members of his church act in self-interest, seeking to overthrow rather than undergird one another? Are you aware of how destructive this kind of conflict is to the witness of the church? The number-one reason given by those who stay away from churches and from becoming Christ's disciples is, "They're hypocrites. They're no better than we are."[24] If we are to be a witnessing fellowship of Christ's disciples, this mark of love is critical. Actions almost always speak louder than words. Christian leaders who don't understand this concept are not Christian leaders. Love is an area in which all of us must help one another grow. Is there an intentional effort in your church to address this mark of discipleship, this fruit of the Spirit? Is there teaching and training to help love become more and more a reality?

Word

> Then Jesus said to the Jews who had believed in him, "If you continue in my word, you are truly my disciples; and you will know the truth, and the truth will make you free."
> (John 8:31-32)

This passage was spoken to new believers, who had processed the information and made a choice about Jesus. But like seed falling on shallow soil or among the thorns, their faith was not yet rooted in the real Jesus.

Jesus' goal for the disciples was not just a quick, knee-jerk decision but a deep understanding of all that he had to offer them. Therefore, he told them there was more to come: Keep listening. Pay attention to all that I have for you, and you will find more than words. You will find truth and freedom.

A second mark of Christian discipleship is to "continue in [Christ's] word" (John 8:31). The old joke asks, "Why did the man fall out of bed?" And the answer is, "He stayed too close to where he got in." Too many approach their faith in Christ as a simple and surface-level religious decision, instead of a life investment. Near the end of his time with them, Jesus said to his disciples:

> I still have many things to say to you, but you cannot bear them now. When the Spirit of truth comes, he will guide you into all the truth.
> (John 16:12-13)

Q3
Where does your church best display this mark of foot-washing love?

Q4
How are we supposed to treat one another in Christ's body? Using a complete concordance or a computer version of the Bible (if either is available), see how many times the phrase *one another* occurs in the New Testament. The list of activities clarifies the meaning of foot washing.

Q5
How is your congregation helping believers become true disciples through "continuing in [Christ's] word" all the way to truth and freedom?

Camp Notes

The tempter came and said to him, "If you are the Son of God, command these stones to become loaves of bread." But he answered, "It is written,

*'One does not live by bread alone,
but by every word that comes
from the mouth of God.'"*

(Matthew 4:3-4)

Q6

As challenging as the disciplines of love and word are, they are not the end of discipleship. They are means of grace to lead us to the freedom needed if we are to carry our crosses. How is your witnessing fellowship helping Christ's disciples prioritize his agenda for their lives?

How do we continue to hear his word? At least three means are at our disposal: Bible study, prayer, and public worship. If our church is going to help each of us truly be disciples of Jesus Christ, we will be providing numerous opportunities for others to hear his word, know the truth, and find his freedom. The Spirit of truth and liberty is now leading in this endeavor. But as a witnessing community of Christ's disciples, we have a task: make disciples who continue in the word. How are you doing?

Cross

*Whoever comes to me and does not hate father and mother,
wife and children, brothers and sisters, yes, and even life itself,
cannot be my disciple. Whoever does not carry the cross and
follow me cannot be my disciple.... So therefore, none of you can
become my disciple if you do not give up all your possessions.*

(Luke 14:26-27, 33)

Jesus was continually manifesting a life in conflict with the values of his culture and its standard religious protocol. Nearly everyone was looking for an advantage in the categories of respectability and honor and were ignoring "the poor, the crippled, the lame, and the blind" **(Luke 14:___)**. But what are we to make of this third mark of discipleship?

Luke 14 ends with a reminder about saltiness. Jesus' disciples are to make a difference in the flavor of life around them, not blend into blandness. Matthew 10:37 helps clarify the hate language of Luke, saying: "Whoever loves father or mother more than me." But this still sounds like a harsh requirement from someone who taught love. The parable Jesus tells about the kingdom of God just before relaying these demands for discipleship sheds some more light on this mark of discipleship (Luke 14:15-24). The crowd invited to a great banquet all began to make excuses about family obligations, land purchases, and possessions. Jesus is making it clear that if anyone or anything gets in the way of following him, they cannot be his disciples.

In fact, his disciples need to see themselves as already having picked up their crosses. They are walking with one so radically different from nice and normal that they ought to be ready like their master to be misunderstood and even sacrificed by those who protect the system. I believe we can summarize this mark of discipleship with the word *cross*.

We must understand, however, that a cross for a Christian is not merely a painful burden to bear. It is not an illness, an accident, or any other unavoidable suffering. A disciple's cross is a choice made in radical obedience to God on behalf of the gospel and "the poor, the crippled, the lame, and the blind" (Luke 14:13). Jesus said of his cross, "No one takes [my life] from me, but I lay it down of my own accord" (John 10:18). What Jesus did for all of us who were broken (Romans 5:8), he invites us to do: count the cost and then follow him into the fray with a special concern for those who have "need of a physician" (Luke 5:31). How is your church doing at helping disciples prioritize the Kingdom rather than the world? at turning the love experienced in the body out to sinners and to all those in need?

Fruit

If you abide in me, and my words abide in you, ask for whatever you wish, and it will be done for you. My Father is glorified by this, that you bear much fruit and become my disciples.
(*John 15:7-8*)

In Session 11, we examined the image of the vine and the branches and the goal of bearing much fruit. Everything that *Witness* is about is tied to this ultimate purpose of God the Holy Trinity through Jesus, the true Vine. Disciples glorify God and prove their identity by bearing much fruit. They don't settle for none or some; they long for, pray for, work for, and endure the pruning for much fruit.

The Spirit flowing into our lives creates a qualitative change. As we abide in the Vine, we bear the Spirit's fruit: "love, joy, peace, patience, kindness, generosity, faithfulness, gentleness, and self-control" (**Galatians 5:___-___**). But Jesus came to call disciples who would also be *fruitful* in making disciples. The fruitfulness of a Christian community is both quality and quantity. If we neglect either, we fail. How well has your congregation prioritized through evangelistic witness the mark of discipleship called fruit?

Q7
In addition to offering this *Witness* experience, what is your church doing to "bear much fruit"? Is any pruning needed?

Camp Notes

Moving On

These marks of discipleship are appropriate guideposts for each of us to use as we evaluate our own growth toward maturity. But they can also serve as an evaluative tool for your entire congregation.

As new people join our fellowship, are we able to clearly explain what it means for us to be a body of Christ's disciples? Do we provide resources and opportunities for becoming more like Jesus, through foot washing love, attending to his word, taking up our cross, and bearing much fruit?

Next, we will explore how to make our witness more effective in our own community. Effective witness begins with knowing Whose we are and what we are about. But it is only fruitful if we plant seeds and prepare for the harvest.

Keep sowing and watering and cultivating. Review your reading and action assignments for next week.

READING ASSIGNMENTS

1. Record your reflections, questions, and insights from these daily Bible readings in your *My Witness Journal.*
   Day 1: Mark 10:13-16 (the children)
   Day 2: Matthew 9 (the broken, sick, and sorrowing)
   Day 3: Matthew 8:5-13; John 19:31-42 (leaders open to faith)
   Day 4: Mark 6:31-44 (the crowds)
   Day 5: Acts 16:6-15 (seekers and their households)
   Day 6: Acts 17 (the curious and receptive)
2. As you read the chapter for next week (pages 105–10), underline or highlight special thoughts and answer the questions in the Q boxes.

ACTION ASSIGNMENT

Select one or more people who are knowledgeable about your community (those who work in schools, social service organizations, volunteers, medical personnel, real estate people, and so forth). Ask them two questions: (1) What are the biggest problems you see in our community today? and (2) What could a church that wanted to help do? Write notes about their responses in your *My Witness Journal.*

See you on the path!

Our Witness in Our Community

Prayer

Where cross the crowded ways of life,
where sound the cries of race and clan,
above the noise of selfish strife,
we hear your voice, O Son of man.

In haunts of wretchedness and need,
on shadowed thresholds dark with fears,
from paths where hide the lures of greed,
we catch the vision of your tears.

From tender childhood's helplessness,
from woman's grief, man's burdened toil,
from famished souls, from sorrow's stress,
your heart has never known recoil....

O Master, from the mountainside
make haste to heal these hearts of pain;
among these restless throngs abide;
O tread the city's streets again.[25]

Amen.

Trail Talk

Read Wadi's journal entry. Surely you have been there—the end of your rope. It's so easy when everything is going great to think life is a snap. But when something happens, even those of us who know the blessings of amazing grace can lose it in moments of desperation. "So if you think you are standing, watch out that you do not fall," counsels Paul (1 Corinthians 10:12).

In troubled waters every soul needs an angel on the trail, a friend, and a lift from someone who knows that "nobody should be out walking on a day like this." Kindness is a fruit of the Spirit and its own witness. How is your church doing at offering hope to those in trouble?

The Bible, from beginning to end, reveals a special concern for the small, the weak, the sick, the abandoned, and the abused. Read again Isaiah 58:1-12, our text on Day 3 of Session 2. The light of our witness is directly connected to how well we care for those who are in desperate need and are suffering. The gospel is "good news to the poor" (**Luke 4:___**), especially when the Spirit who anointed Jesus inspires us to act like him.

What did your action assignment help you discover about community needs and how a church that really wants to could make a difference?

Camp Notes

I was feeling so proud of myself. People were dropping like flies, but I was untouched. I was feeling great until about 9:30 in the morning. At first I thought it was just the heat, until the diarrhea started up. My steps slowed to a labored crawl. I came up over a ridge and saw a valley leading to another monstrous mountain. I lost it emotionally. I started to curse and let out the longest stream of colorful metaphors in anger and depression. I knew I couldn't make it over another mountain. My strength was quickly leaving my body to fight whatever was afflicting me. I questioned God, my strength, and my ability to make my toilet paper last four more miles.

Then the trail turned left, away from the dark mountain, and I came across a hiker who told me I was almost to the road, safety. Joy

(continued on page 106)

105

Camp Notes

overwhelmed me, and I wanted to cry and shout out my thanks to God.

I dragged myself off the mountain, with sunken eyes and a growing fever.... I tried to get a hitch, but nobody liked the look of me, I guess. I threw up alongside the road several times before a wonderful woman picked me up. "Nobody should be out walking on a day like this," she said four times. I was so overwhelmed that my chin quivered and I started to cry. Her kindness touched me deeply, and I was very tired.

Wadi

Q1

If you were to make a list of the special needs calling out from your Jerusalem, how would it read?

_____

_____

_____

_____

_____

Jerusalem and Judea

When Jesus told his disciples they would receive power to be his witnesses (Acts 1:8), he also told them where their witness would begin: first in Jerusalem and then in Judea. Jerusalem was not home in the sense that it was where they grew up and were from, but it was where Jesus had led them and where they were now. Jerusalem was the home of their new family, Christ's church born on Pentecost. Their witness as the body of Christ was to begin at home in Jerusalem.

Although the church is a universal family, each of its local manifestations has a unique responsibility to bear witness to the community where it is. Even if three other congregations are on your corner, your church has its own Jerusalem. Your networks with people and your special gifts and graces for being Christ's witnesses are identical to no other Christian fellowship. You have an opportunity and a sacred responsibility that no other church can fulfill.

No single session can possibly clarify all that your church's witness in your community might mean, but consider these questions:

1. What do you know about the people in your witness arena (age and gender distributions, family compositions, economic conditions, housing patterns, education levels, employment opportunities, ethnic diversity, and so forth)? A good start for finding answers is census data, but much more is available through conference or district offices and ministry-area profiles secured from church-related organizations. Where can you find a demographic study or ministry area profile of your community? Check these reports and look at the fields to see the harvest (John 4:35).
2. What are some of the pressing needs that you have been aware of for a long time or have just uncovered this week?
3. What gifts, resources, and contacts in the community have been uniquely arranged by the Spirit in your congregation to help you reach out to address one or more of these needs?
4. Which of these needs are already being met by your congregation or another group, and which ones are still waiting for a witness of hope?
5. What has the Spirit been saying to your own heart out of your SHAPE survey, your prayers, and your experiences in *Witness* that might help guide your church in expanding its witness in your community?

If people like you in every congregation would seek answers to these questions and pray for the Spirit's guidance and power, our witness in our Jerusalem would look more like the early church's witness in their Jerusalem.

When Jesus told his disciples to begin as his witnesses in Jerusalem and then move out to Judea, he was mostly only expanding their geography. Acts 5:16 tells us that many people from these surrounding towns were in fact coming into Jerusalem, "bringing the sick and those tormented by unclean spirits, and they were all cured."

Judea was the mostly rural region surrounding the city of Jerusalem and was part of the territory under the Roman rule of Pontius Pilate. Its roughly two thousand square miles included a swath about forty miles wide running from the Jordan River to the Mediterranean. Judea was the geographical and cultural extended family of Jerusalem. Your congregation's Judea may be your larger metropolitan area, your county, your state, or even your region of the country. In United Methodism it may include your district, your conference, or even your jurisdiction. Your Judea is where people are pretty much like you are and face many of the same issues.

As you carry on your Spirit-filled witness in the primary ministry area for your church, news will travel. Opportunities will arise for you both to learn from and to offer insights to neighbors in your Judea. We are called to a larger world than just those who are close by, but we always begin where we are. Next week we will look at Samaria and the ends of the earth, but for now let's focus a bit more on our witness close to home.

Seeing the People

From the Bible readings and exercises this week, you can probably identify several audiences needing your congregational witness.

THE CHILDREN AND YOUTH

It doesn't take long for most of us to see the children, even though Jesus' disciples seemed to miss them. Most of our churches have Sunday school programs and other special opportunities for children and young people; but if we aren't careful, we will see these offerings as almost entirely for our own children—that is, for the children of our members. But disciples are made by *going*. It is critical to ask to what degree we have intentionally reached out to the children and youth in our community. Vacation Bible schools, daycare programs, and youth ministries are often the most natural ways our churches reach out to these groups. Yet, even in these ministries, we sometimes fail to focus beyond the programs themselves to the young people and the families they represent.

Childhood is a critical season of life to be touched by faith, hope, and love. Certainly our own children need all that the ministry of Christ's body can offer to help them form their own identities and prepare them for adolescence. But what about the children who are not part of our faith family? Who is serving as their advocate in our praying and our planning?

Q2
What opportunities are there to join with others in your Judea to witness for Christ? What do you need help with? What do you have to offer?

Q3
What efforts are we making through our witness to "let the little children come" to Jesus (Matthew 19:14)?

What needs have been identified that could lead us to expand our existing witness to children, youth, and their families?

Camp Notes

Checklist for Children and Youth

- ❑ Choirs and music programs
- ❑ Puppets and drama ministries
- ❑ Athletic teams
- ❑ Tutoring
- ❑ VBS and/or summer camps
- ❑ Afterschool recreation and Bible study
- ❑ Parenting classes
- ❑ Parents' days (or nights) out
- ❑ Drug, alcohol, tobacco, sex education and support
- ❑ Scouting and other skill development programs

- ❑ Other _____
- ❑ Other _____

Checklist for the Troubled

- ❑ Twelve-step recovery programs
- ❑ The hungry and homeless
- ❑ Unwed mothers and their babies
- ❑ The unemployed
- ❑ Those confined to home, hospital, and nursing home
- ❑ The mentally and physically challenged
- ❑ GED and reading programs
- ❑ English as a Second Language
- ❑ Habitat for Humanity
- ❑ Jail and prison ministries
- ❑ Providing meals and support at funerals
- ❑ Migrant workers' advocacy
- ❑ Budgeting and financial planning
- ❑ Auto repair assistance
- ❑ Clothing resources
- ❑ Working with the Salvation Army

- ❑ Other _____
- ❑ Other _____

What is our witness to them? How are we reaching out to offer them God's love, Jesus' friendship, and eternal life? Is this ministry truly a priority for us?

Take a moment to look through the short list in the "Checklist for Children and Youth" box. Consider ministries you might begin. Children and youth are on the top of God's list. Where are they on yours?

THE TROUBLED

Openness to God's intervention in our lives often comes in times of trouble. Think back on your own story of faith and see if some of the most important turning points came when you were restless, or worse.

The ministry of Jesus and his disciples to troubled people, sinners, and outcasts made many of the respectably religious people uncomfortable. Once when I was preaching a spiritual renewal weekend in a small town, the host pastor took me early Sunday morning to the jail for a worship service and follow-up conversations with some of the inmates. The pastor and a small witnessing team from the church had been doing this weekly for months. I was deeply touched by their loving witness. But later that day the pastor told me that many in the church were trying to get rid of him. They didn't want "that kind of people" coming to their church after they got out of jail. This same story with a hundred variations is told again and again.

How can the church be a safe haven from life's troubles and at the same time a hospital for broken people who need healing, hope, forgiveness, and a living Savior? The tension of living between these two worlds will always be with us, but we can't be Christ's body, faithful as his witnesses, unless we risk our safety for the sake of others. Cross-bearing has its dangers, but for Christians it is more dangerous not to follow Christ's commands.

Take a moment to look through the "Checklist for the Troubled." What witness ministries are you offering to the troubled in your community? What needs did you discover this week? Where might the Spirit be anointing and leading your church to bring good news to the poor and freedom for the oppressed?

THE SEEKERS

Jesus paid attention to every person interested in what he was doing and saying. Some of those who came to him seemed out of place. Nicodemus was a Pharisee, and most of his colleagues were seeking to get rid of Jesus (John 7:45-52). But Nicodemus took time to seek Jesus out (John 3) and became one of his followers (John 19:38-39). So did a Roman centurion, though Roman soldiers crucified Jesus. (Read about Cornelius in Matthew 27:54.)

Seekers come in many guises. In fact, many Christians might be utterly surprised to discover seekers among groups that often seem disinterested in God. But God promised "those who seek me diligently find me" (Proverbs 8:17), and Jesus said, "Ask, and it will be given you; search, and you will find; knock, and the door will be opened for you" (**Matthew 7:___**). Because the Spirit of God speaks in ways beyond our comprehension to the hearts of all people through prevenient grace, receptive people may always be only a single act or word away.

We all were created to be filled with God's divine love and presence. Therefore, every human being is a seeker sooner or later. Seekers are everywhere. Have you been discovering some as you have been witnessing? What is your church doing to help those who are curious and willing to seek after God? Are you doing all you can to find them, invite them, assist them, and patiently wait for them to discover how the mystery comes together in Jesus. Or are you still seeing them as unlikely, undeserving, and uninterested? Look at the "Checklist for Seekers" and see which practices are already in place in your church and which might still be added.

Seekers are people God loves, even though most of them still don't know that God loves them. But with the help of your loving witness, they can be encouraged to explore new possibilities if they don't feel they are pressured to decide too much too soon. Does your church manifest patient, thoughtful, caring love for seekers? Are you seeking seekers? Are you offering them the gospel in a way they can understand. Or are you requiring them first to get "churched" and then to find Jesus later if they can?

Moving On

It is impossible to offer in a single session like this all the wealth of information that is available to churches that really want to be centers of Christian witness in their communities. Many books and training programs are available to lead congregations through the steps that will make them more effective in reaching out to those whom God is preparing. The most important thing, though, is to help cultivate the spirit of openness on our part. Do we above all things long to be fruitful and faithful as witnesses of Jesus in our Jerusalem and Judea? If this is our most earnest desire, God will provide.

Churches faithful to the Great Commission remember that the Spirit leads them first to be witnesses to Jerusalem and Judea, but after that on to Samaria and the ends of the earth (Acts 1:8). Next week we head out to the fringes of the trail to explore how we can be part of God's glory filling the whole earth. Review your reading and action assignments.

Checklist for Seekers

We...
- ❏ Pray regularly for God to make us useful for the Kingdom.
- ❏ Follow up every visit by a new person with personal contact.
- ❏ Design special worship services for seekers and bring them.
- ❏ Offer nonthreatening classes to explain the Christian message.
- ❏ Have pleasant greeters and sometimes wear nametags.
- ❏ Provide refreshments and always talk to new people.
- ❏ Design our bulletin for those who aren't "churched."
- ❏ Invite all people to respond to Jesus Christ with new levels of faith every time we meet.
- ❏ Place a witness in every group that meets in our church.
- ❏ Study and then offer ministries to reach younger generations.
- ❏ Start a variety of new groups to help new people feel at home.
- ❏ Read, attend training, and make changes to be better witnesses.
- ❏ Don't have a dress code and aren't easily shocked.
- ❏ Have a wonderfully clean and attractive nursery.
- ❏ Encourage all questions and aren't defensive.
- ❏ Use multimedia presentations.
- ❏ Talk more about God and Jesus than we do about church.
- ❏ Are comfortable with people who are not coming every week.

- ❏ Other _____
- ❏ Other _____

Camp Notes

READING ASSIGNMENTS

1. Record your reflections, questions, and insights from these daily Bible readings in your *My Witness Journal.*
    - **Day 1:** Psalm 67 ("Let the nations be glad.")
    - **Day 2:** Acts 6:1-7 (Unity overcomes cultural distance.)
    - **Day 3:** Acts 8 (out to the Samaritans—Who?)
    - **Day 4:** Acts 10 (the great conversion of the big fisherman—What?)
    - **Day 5:** Acts 15 (the first missionary council—Why?)
    - **Day 6:** 1 Corinthians 9:1-22 (that I might save some—How?)
2. As you read the chapter for next week (pages 111–16), underline or highlight special thoughts and answer the questions in the Q boxes.

ACTION ASSIGNMENT

Choose at least one of these options:

1. Find someone in your church or community who can tell you what new people or groups who speak another language or come from another culture are moving into your area. Learn all you can about your Judea.
2. Find someone from a cultural group or generation with whom you have little familiarity. Have a good conversation and learn as much as you can.
3. Become familiar with the work of a specific missionary. Pray daily for Christ to be glorified in that person's work and in yours.

Record some new learnings or insights in your *My Witness Journal.*

See you on the path!

Our Witness in Today's World

Prayer

Wind who makes all winds that blow,
gusts that bend the sapling low,
gales that heave the sea in waves,
stirrings in the mind's deep caves;
aim your breath with steady power
on your church, this day, this hour.
Raise, renew the life we've lost,
Spirit God of Pentecost….

Holy Spirit, wind and flame,
move within our mortal frame;
make our hearts an altar pyre;
kindle them with your own fire.
Breathe and blow upon that blaze
till our lives, our deeds, and ways
speak that tongue which every land
by your grace shall understand.

Amen.

(Text by Thomas H. Troeger [born 1945]; from *Borrowed Light.* © 1994 Oxford University Press, Inc. Used by permission. All rights reserved.)

Trail Talk

Why do we need to talk about today's world? Because it is not the same as yesterday's world. It never has been, but this truism is more important to realize now than ever before. In fact, changes are taking place so fast in today's world that as soon as we think we've caught up, we're still one generation behind. Some of our most loyal church members still think that today's world is the one they fondly remember from the 1950's, the 1970's, or even the 1990's. But this is not true!

Think of the major shifts in technology, medicine, politics, and religion in the past ten years. Will you ever again own an up-to-date map of the world? How long is a new computer good for? Where are you supposed to watch movies? What is a phone for? What is the latest gene therapy? Why can't we get America back the way it was originally? When did interfaith marriages change to Christian and Buddhist instead of Methodist and Catholic? How can a nineteen-year-old become a multimillionaire in his first year of business? Why isn't anyone interested in rules anymore? If you've ever wondered about any of these questions, you know that this isn't your father's world.

How can we be faithful as Christ's witnesses in today's world? First, we have to see it with new eyes. Then, we have to follow the Spirit where we would not normally go on our own. Come on, it's fun!

I have much freedom in the woods. Social barriers are taken away, so people of all levels of life are introduced to the same new struggles and find support and community through one another. Doctors, farmers, TV producers, cooks, students, military, authors, artists, journalists, biologists, divorced, widowed, diseased, introverted, extroverted, wealthy, and poor all come together without regard to status. Character is the main issue, and the trail network communicates rapidly those of earned stature.

Wadi

Q1
What changes in the world around you have been the most difficult for you to deal with over the past ten years?

_____

_____

Which changes in the past ten years have been most wonderful and welcomed by you?

_____

_____

Camp Notes

The answer to the problems of culture is not to run away to the mountains and become separate from it. For me it is only reinforcing the knowledge that this world is not my home. But I am responsible to bring Kingdom values to it. My awareness of this need is being heightened to realize that, moment by moment and day by day, I am dependent on God Almighty and responsible for the lessons learned. How is culture to be restored to its knees before God? How hard it is for me to remain there with such stubborn knees.

Wadi

Q2

How easily do new people who don't value the old culture and traditions find a home in your church?
Or is it those who do value the old traditions who will have trouble feeling at home in your church?

Hebrews and Hellenists

For Christ's disciples, being witnesses in Jerusalem and Judea was just the beginning. Yet even in this fairly homogeneous context, there were seeds of what was yet to come. The Spirit on Pentecost Sunday brought all kinds of believers together in the new church, but they weren't all immediately cozy with one another. Hebrews had to learn how to open the doors of their hearts to Hellenists. Hebrews were the loyalists and purists who had kept the old language and the old culture of Judaism. They were conservative protectors of God's holy place and language. The Hellenists were Jews who had been influenced by Greek culture, spoke the Greek language openly, and enjoyed the benefits of the larger world of their day. Both groups were drawn into the early church by the power of the Holy Spirit. But the groups remained distanced from each other not by faith but by culture.

When there was only so much to go around, who got it? The ones who deserved it. And who were they? The age-old faithful of God, the ones in control, the Hebrews. But the apostles knew that this bickering and division could not continue, and under the Spirit's guidance they suggested that seven Hellenists (note that all are Greek names) with servant hearts be appointed to help break down the barriers. The apostles had played the "Who is the greatest?" game, and Jesus had painfully reminded them that there was no room for this attitude among his disciples. Notice that after the church solved this problem of cultural distance, even some of the religious skeptics (priests) saw these followers of the Way as filled with divine favor and joined them. The church continued to grow.

Does the church of today still have to face this problem? Do some get sidelined because they are too much a part of today's world instead of yesterday's?

Samaritans

Perhaps in God's design for the mission of the church, this early bit of cultural conflict was only preparation for the real journey out of their comfort zone. Geographically, Samaria was closer to Jerusalem than some parts of Judea. The distance to Samaria had nothing to do with miles and everything to do with history and culture.

Jews in Jesus' day at best saw Samaritans as distant cousins with bad blood. Several centuries earlier the Samaritans had intermarried with people who were "not their kind." In addition, their Bible contained only the Law (Genesis through Deuteronomy). Moses was their only prophet and their only link to a possible messiah. They were not considered unclean like the Gentiles, but they were despised and looked upon as ignorant and impure.

Human nature in every culture tends to protect itself from those who are considered not their kind of people. But Jesus represented and purchased with his blood a new nature and a new creation for a new world. Earlier he had made his disciples uncomfortable by taking them through Samaria on the way to Galilee (the shortest route); and he had shocked them when he took time to offer living water to the woman at Jacob's well in Sychar (**John 4:___-___**). But Jesus believed in her as a child of God and a person of worth. She believed in Jesus as the Messiah and became his witness.

The early church didn't go naturally or immediately to Samaria and the ends of the earth. Actually, they were forced out of Jerusalem (Acts 8:1). It was one of those dual-culture Hellenists (Philip) who first took the gospel to Samaria (Acts 8:5). After the apostles heard what was happening, they sent Peter and John to see if it was true that God was bringing Samaritans into the church. Sure enough, the Spirit was fulfilling the Great Commission.

Do some in our churches today still find it difficult to accept "Hellenists" or "Samaritans"? Probably, but the Holy Spirit is always leading us out past traditional human barriers to become a new kind of humanity. How much support is there in your church for following the Spirit and reaching out to people who are geographically close but culturally distant?

The Ends of the Earth

God had been blessing all the efforts of the church to faithfully bear witness to the risen Lord. Thus, Luke tells us:

> *The church throughout Judea, Galilee, and Samaria had peace and was built up. Living in the fear of the Lord and in the comfort of the Holy Spirit, it increased in numbers.*
>
> (Acts 9:31)

It's quite amazing that Philip, who is almost unknown to us except in Acts 8 and Acts 21:8, was God's first witness to Samaria and also to the ends of the earth through the Ethiopian eunuch (Acts 8:26-39). But one lay evangelist's actions didn't immediately convince the whole church to become witnesses to all the world. In fact, some other kinds of conversions were needed first.

Peter was in the forefront of this exciting season of growth and had adjusted fairly well to following the Spirit to the Hellenists and Samaritans. But he was on the verge of one of the most radical conversions of his life. Tired and hungry from his faithful labors, he was relaxing on a rooftop. When in a vision God revealed emphatically that Peter's thinking had to change about traditional boundaries. He thought like a good Jew, but God was doing "a new thing" (Isaiah 43:19) and shaping a new humanity. No longer was it appropriate to categorize things or people as unclean when God was declaring them to be clean (Acts 10).

Q3

How is your church involved in reaching out directly or with other congregations to people of diverse social and cultural backgrounds?

_____

_____

What steps are you taking to participate jointly with these people in Christian worship and witness?

_____

_____

Camp Notes

Even though I am free of the demands and expectations of everyone, I have voluntarily become a servant to any and all in order to reach a wide range of people: religious, nonreligious, meticulous moralists, loose-living immoralists, the defeated, the demoralized—whoever. I didn't take on their way of life. I kept my bearings in Christ—but I entered their world and tried to experience things from their point of view. I've become just about every sort of servant there is in my attempts to lead those I meet into a God-saved life. I did all this because of the Message. I didn't just want to talk about it; I wanted to be in *on it!*

(1 Corinthians 9:19-23, The Message*)*

Q4
What differences would it make in your congregation if you adopted Paul's approach to servant evangelism (1 Corinthians 9:19-23) so that as many as possible might find the "God-saved life"?

We would...

_____

_____

_____

_____

_____

_____

_____

Even nominal Jews felt totally uneasy around Gentiles who were considered and often even referred to as unclean dogs. Jesus had tried to help Peter get ready for this conversion earlier (Luke 15:10-28), but now the Spirit was taking him beyond possibilities to a place he had never been before: inside the house of a Gentile.

Cornelius, though a good and God-fearing man, was a Gentile and off limits. What a powerful moment in history this was! Most of us would not be Christians were it not for this courageous crossover. Peter, following his faith in the love of God revealed in Jesus, was finally forced totally outside of his cultural box all the way to the ends of the earth.

Can you feel the discomfort Peter must have felt? What would you compare it with in your way of thinking about being Christ's witness? Have you ever been this uncomfortable and realized it was something God was doing to make you grow up "to the measure of the full stature of Christ" **(Ephesians 4:___)**? If we were all more sensitive to the Spirit's leading, would we find ourselves all the way to the end of our comfort zone in order to be witnesses to the ends of the earth?

The early church struggled with all that the conversion of Cornelius—not to mention the conversion of Peter—was to mean. The gospel began to spread like wildfire. The Spirit poured out grace upon more Gentiles, and the fire spread up the coast three hundred miles to Antioch, a Roman cultural center. Here Jewish and Gentile believers participated openly in the church together and were first known by the Latin expression *Christians* (Acts 11:26), meaning something like Christ's people. I like that, don't you? But think what it would look like today if Christians could unite folks from hostile backgrounds and diverse cultures into a new humanity of love and faith utterly dependent on the Spirit of God.

Paul met the risen Lord on the road to Damascus. His conversion and commissioning to be the apostle to the Gentiles is another unlikely twist in how Jesus was building his church. And what did Paul have to learn in order to share in the ever-expanding witness of the Spirit? Read again the text from 1 Corinthians 9 (side column, this page).

Peter's transforming experience with Cornelius and Paul's missionary success led the church in Jerusalem to become something it never could have imagined. The Messiah's people were no longer a little Jewish sect. The people of Christ were becoming a worldwide movement attracting attention and helping people come to Christ everywhere they went.

Marcus Aurelius, emperor of Rome from A.D. 161 to A.D. 180, ruthlessly persecuted Christians, as many before him had. Their rapid spread across the empire and their unbending resistance to acknowledge the emperor as "Lord" made them scapegoats to be blamed by Rome for every ill fortune. Diognetus, Marcus Aurelius' tutor, received a letter offering the emperor an alternative perspective (side column, this page).

For two thousand years now, Christians have been both persecuted and praised. But they have no other option when they are faithful to their Lord, Jesus, than to be witnesses to his risen presence and transforming power. Every land on the face of the earth has a Christian witness. One-third of the world's population today would claim that they were Christians. In some lands the church is strong and Christ's people are still paying with their lives for their witness. In other lands where once the church was strong, it is drying up, dying, and seldom if ever is described as the soul of the world. What happened? Is there always a danger that Christ's disciples might gain the world and lose their soul?

What does your congregation do to be part of Christ's witness to the ends of the earth? Use the "Checklist for Worldwide Witness" (side column, this page) to evaluate your congregation's witness.

Witnessing in Today's World

The challenges facing Christ's witnesses today are great, but for most of us the challenges are no greater than those our brothers and sisters have faced through the ages. The critical need is to recognize that we are part of the witnessing stream of the Spirit stretching through time and across nations. Are we intentionally trying to follow the Spirit to those in our world who are both nearby and distant? Are we willing to let the Spirit lead us and change us as we seek to find the joy that faithfulness to Christ's calling brings? Do we manifest in our churches our deep belief that Christian witnessing must always include intimate involvement with congregations, missionaries, and denominations among peoples distinctively different in culture yet wonderfully similar in their need for God's divine gift in Jesus? Will we continually be open to those who remind us that adjusting our agenda and comfort zone to the Spirit's work is the only way to be truly alive in Christ? These are the questions and issues of being Christ's people in today's world.

Camp Notes

The Epistle to Diognetus

Christians are not distinguished from the rest of mankind by country, or by speech, or by dress. For they do not dwell in cities of their own, or use a different language, or practise a peculiar life.... But while they dwell in Greek or barbarian cities according as each man's lot has been cast, and follow the customs of the land in clothing and food, and other matters of daily life, yet the condition of citizenship which they exhibit is wonderful, and admittedly strange.... They love all men, and are persecuted by all. They are unknown, and they are condemned; they are put to death, and they gain new life. They are poor, and make many rich; they lack everything, and in everything they abound. They are dishonoured, and their dishonour becomes their glory; they are reviled, and are justified. They are abused, and they bless; they are insulted, and repay insult with honour.... In a word, what the soul is in the body Christians are in the world.[26]

Checklist for Worldwide Witness

We...

❑ Pray regularly for God's work among other peoples. (Who? Where?)

_____

❑ Support missionaries with prayer, finances, and regular correspondence. (Who? Where?)

_____

❑ Host an annual Church in Mission conference to keep us focused on our larger task.

❑ Send work and witness teams to serve in other lands.

❑ Receive work and witness teams from other lands.

❑ Other _____

❑ Other _____

Camp Notes

Moving On

The greatest Christian witness is the one we make together as the body of Christ. For six weeks now you have hiked a trail asking you to be salt and light for your entire congregation. What have you learned? How can you help your church become more faithful to its calling?

From here we press on to finish the final leg of the *Witness* journey: living out our own personal witness in the world.

Review your reading and action assignments for next week as you begin the final trail, where you will look even more closely at your own life as a witness for Jesus Christ.

READING ASSIGNMENTS

1. Record your reflections, questions, and insights from these daily Bible readings in your *My Witness Journal*.

   Day 1: 1 Peter 3:15-16a (sanctifying Christ in your heart—Memorize these verses.)

   Day 2: John 15:5-11 (abiding in Christ—Memorize verse 5.)

   Day 3: Galatians 2:20 (Christ living in you—Memorize this verse.)

   Day 4: Philippians 3:8-17 (our highest priority: knowing Christ)

   Day 5: Ephesians 3:14-21 (our ultimate goal: "the fullness of God")

   Day 6: Romans 12:1-2 (our ongoing need: the renewing of our minds)

2. As you read the chapter for next week (pages 118–22), underline or highlight special thoughts and answer the questions in the Q boxes.

ACTION ASSIGNMENT

There are two assignments this week.

1. Each day this week spend some time in quiet meditation. Picture yourself in the presence of Christ. Listen to what he says to you about your life in him and his life in you. Record your thoughts, insights, and responses in your *My Witness Journal*.

2. Listen prayerfully to the Spirit's leading this week and do one or both of these things: (1) invite someone to come to church and offer to provide a ride, or (2) seek to have a meaningful conversation with someone about his or her spiritual life and your discoveries of the new life in Christ. Write notes in your *My Witness Journal* about the conversation.

See you on the path!

Trail Five
My Life as Christ's Witness

In your hearts set apart Christ as Lord. Always be prepared to give
an answer to everyone who asks you to give the reason for the
hope that you have. But do this with gentleness and respect.

(1 Peter 3:15, New International Version)

My Witness and Christ's Presence

Camp Notes

We crossed the Housatonic River, meaning "place beyond the mountains," and climbed a mountain filled with red pine, white birch, and many sturdy oaks.

To the Celts, oaks were... synonymous with wisdom. The word druid means "men of oak." The Druids were lovers of nature, searching out and finding the answers to life there. They would find a place of solitude and memorize history, law, poetry, and other things.... They made a fast to draw closer to the God of creation. To become a full Druid, the disciples would go through a long training.... They would be the counselors to kings, the wise men, and historians of the land.

Then when the Druids converted to Christianity, the largest mass conversion without a martyr began. The Druids believed Christianity completed the answers for which they had been searching.

Wadi

Prayer

Write a prayer about your relationship with Christ and your desire to live as his witness.

_____

_____

_____

_____

_____

_____

_____

Amen.

Trail Talk

Can you believe that we are on our last trail? Congratulations!

In five more weeks we will arrive at the end of our journey together. These may be the most challenging and important weeks of the whole trek. We will need to draw on every lesson already learned and help one another if we are all going to become more-confident witnesses.

The name of this last trail is "My Life as Christ's Witness." Our challenge is discovering how to "lay aside every weight and the sin that clings so closely, and...run with perseverance the race that is set before us" **(Hebrews 12:___)**. Our goal is to find the confidence, the power, and the freedom we need to be contagious witnesses for Christ in our world. Our starting point is learning how to maintain and continually renew our personal relationship with Christ.

The Scriptures we read and memorized for this week all emphasized the priority of our own relationship with Christ. True Christian witness flows from a contagious relationship with Christ. Therefore, how can the prayer you have written for your own life in Christ become an ever-expanding reality? What disciplines and practices on our part can help the Spirit of Christ become more fully present in our lives and easier to recognize in our service to others? These are the steps we take as we begin our last trail on this part of our journey.

Staying Contagious

We have noted several times that those who intend to bear witness to the power of God to forgive, liberate, and transform human lives need to be alive in that power themselves, not just talk about it.

> *For the kingdom of God depends not on talk but on power.*
> *(1 Corinthians 4:20)*

> *To all who received him, who believed in his name, he gave power to become children of God.*   *(John 1:12)*

If we are going be useful in God's mission to bring this power of redeeming love to the world, we must be contagiously alive in the source of this love, Jesus Christ. Sometimes people have summarized the nature of this relationship with Christ by drawing a central seat of authority inside a circle representing each human life. (See the drawing in the side column.) The question is then asked, "Who is in charge here?" or "Who is on the throne of your life?" Sometimes we Christians seem to live as though we own and manage our lives, and consider ourselves generous because we offer a little corner to Christ. Or we believe we are faithful because we carry out certain obligations and duties. But the contagious Christian life is Christ alive in us. What did Paul say in Galatians 2:20?

_____

_____

And what does Jesus say in John 15:5?

_____

_____

To acknowledge that Christ is Lord of my life means I have entrusted him with sovereignty over my whole being. I live in him for my joy, and he lives in me for his glory. This kind of Christian life is contagious because Christ is truly shining through us to reach others with his offer of forgiveness, love, power, and righteousness. Some years ago Henri Nouwen, a Catholic priest, missionary, and professor of pastoral theology at Yale Divinity School, said:

> *When we no longer walk in the presence of the Lord, we cannot be living reminders of his divine presence in our lives. We then quickly become strangers in an alien land who have forgotten where we come from and where we are going. Then we are no longer the way to the experience of God, but rather in the way of the experience of God.*[27]

Q1
What disciplines are needed to help Christ's disciples today grow in faithfulness to him?

_____

_____

_____

_____

_____

How would you complete the drawing to illustrate where Christ is in your life? What or who occupies the driver's seat? Mark where you (Y) are and where Christ (C) is in the picture.

Christ in Your Life

Q2
Are there some memories, habits, or arenas you need to surrender to Jesus' lordship instead of hoarding as off limits?

_____

_____

_____

Camp Notes

Q3

We are all still in the process of being changed into Jesus' likeness (**2 Corinthians 3:___**). What are some areas in your life that still need more healing or work or discipline?

_____

_____

_____

Q4

What ingredients of Paul's formula for knowing Christ can you identify in Philippians 3:8-17?

_____

_____

_____

_____

_____

_____

Whether we speak of "walking in the presence," "abiding," or "Christ at the center," we are acknowledging the same reality.

Recall once again the verse you memorized from 1 Peter 3:15. I like the New International Version translation:

> *In your hearts set apart Christ as Lord. Always be prepared to give an answer to everyone who asks you to give the reason for the hope that you have. But do this with gentleness and respect.*
> *(1 Peter 3:15, New International Version)*

The start of our witnessing for Christ must always be to allow him to be Lord, set apart or sanctified in our hearts. This is our first and most important preparation. Then we can with confidence and freedom offer to others "the reason for the hope" that is within us. But how do we continue to grow in our understanding and experience of Christ as Lord of our lives? How do we "walk in his presence"?

Knowing Christ

Paul helps us realize that our highest goal is knowing Christ himself (Philippians 3:8-17). How does he say it?

Philippians 3:8

_____

_____

Philippians 3:10

_____

_____

And how does Paul intend to arrive at this end? Read again Philippians 3:8-17 and answer **Q4.** Almost every verse has something in it describing Paul's strategy. There are things to leave behind, things to take hold of, and an earnest spirit of pressing forward for the prize.

Knowing Christ is not something left to chance. It is accomplished by many of the same methods we would use to know anyone: watching, listening, speaking from the mind and heart, clarifying, and learning the deepest values held in the heart. And we are told to "observe those who live according to the example you have in us" (Philippians 3:17). Paul is saying that others have already become models for you. Pay attention!

Through the ages Christians have learned from Scripture, from the Spirit, and from one another how to know Christ. Some have called these lessons spiritual disciplines; others have referred to them as means of grace. Whatever the terminology, we grow in our knowledge of Christ by using the following gifts:

Scripture (study, memorization, meditation)
Prayer (praise, petition, confession, intercession)
Fasting (focusing on Christ through abstinence)
Sacraments (especially Communion)
Worship (personal and corporate)
Fellowship (especially in small groups)
Serving (ministries of mercy, justice, and witness)

Two Priorities

It is not our intention here to examine each of the disciplines listed above. Many wonderful resources are available to help you grow in Christ through these means of grace.[28] But two of the disciplines are of particular importance to us as his witnesses: Scripture and prayer.

Scripture—You may have already noticed how central the Bible is to our growth in faith and our ability to clarify the "hope we have." Indeed, with the psalmist we all have to say, "Your word is a lamp to my feet and a light to my path" (Psalm 119:105). Reading the Bible, studying it, memorizing it, treasuring it, discussing it, and living it are all part of how we know Christ and how we bear witness to him and share his gospel with others. We will continue to explore how to let Christ's words abide in us (John 15:7) and how to offer them to others in the weeks to come. But every effort we make to hear and do the word of God bears fruit.

Prayer—Next week we will give additional attention to this gift of God. Often, we see prayer as a duty, but it is an enormous privilege. As we read, memorize, and meditate on God's word, we are involved in a conversation with the Almighty. In prayer we continue the conversation. Notice how closely these two—our study of Scripture and our communion with God—are related in Jesus' instructions in John 15:7. Prayer is the doorway through which the Holy Spirit enters to accomplish in us the prayer in Ephesians 3:14-19. To be "filled with all the fullness of God" is not only our goal but also our gospel.

Through daily prayer and meditation on God's word, we open ourselves to the renewing power of the Holy Spirit, who enables us to be worthy representatives of amazing grace and to accomplish the following admonition:

Do not be conformed to this world, but be transformed by the renewing of your minds, so that you may discern what is the will of God—what is good and acceptable and perfect.
(Romans 12:___)

Camp Notes

Q5
Which of the gifts for knowing Christ are you already making good use of?

_____

_____

_____

Which ones still need more attention?

_____

_____

_____

I treasure your word in my heart,
so that I may not sin against you.
(Psalm 119:11)

If you abide in me, and my words abide in you, ask for whatever you wish, and it will be done for you. *(John 15:7)*

Let the word of Christ dwell in you richly; teach and admonish one another in all wisdom; and with gratitude in your hearts sing psalms, hymns, and spiritual songs to God. And whatever you do, in word or deed, do everything in the name of the Lord Jesus, giving thanks to God the Father through him. *(Colossians 3:16-17)*

Camp Notes

Moving On

Disciples have disciplines. But the amazing thing about disciplines is that in time they bring freedom and joy to living. Successful athletes, musicians, students, and artists harness their dream to the disciplined work of foundational exercises before they find what they are looking for, "what is good and acceptable and perfect" (Romans 12:2).

Next week we will explore in more detail how to "renew our minds" and how prayer serves both as a means of grace for us and for others. Keep the lamp burning.

READING ASSIGNMENTS

1. Record your reflections, questions, and insights from these daily Bible readings in your *My Witness Journal.*
   > **Day 1:** Matthew 7:7-11 (Prayer is asking, seeking, knocking.—Memorize verses 7-8.)
   > **Day 2:** 1 Thessalonians 5:16-25 ("Pray without ceasing."— Memorize verses 16-18.)
   > **Day 3:** Romans 10:1-15 (Pray for the salvation of others.— Memorize verse 1.)
   > **Day 4:** Matthew 9:37-38 (Pray for laborers in the harvest.)
   > **Day 5:** 2 Corinthians 13:9b; 2 Thessalonians 1:11-12 (Pray for the ultimate objective.)
   > **Day 6:** Philemon 1:6 (Pray for one another as witnesses.)
2. As you read the chapter for next week (pages 123–28), underline or highlight special thoughts and answer the questions in the Q boxes.

ACTION ASSIGNMENT

There are two assignments this week:
   (1) Pray Ephesians 3:18-19 daily for all on your prayer list this week. Pray without ceasing (1 Thessalonians 5:17). Listen carefully to Christ's word for you as his witness. Record your thoughts and learnings in your *My Witness Journal.*
   (2) Follow the Spirit's leading and do one of the following:
   - Have a follow-up conversation with the one who came to church with you. Write a summary in your *My Witness Journal.*
   - If you have not already invited someone to come to church, invite someone now.
   - Tell someone about one or more of the verses you have memorized, and explain the implications for how you are living in this world. Make some notes about your conversation in your *My Witness Journal.*

See you on the path!

My Witness and Prayer

Prayer

Drawing on Scripture and your own life experiences, write a one-sentence prayer you might offer daily for all those you lift before God.

_____

_____

_____

_____

_____

Amen.

Trail Talk

The Bible is full of examples of people praying and of encouragements for us to pray. In the Gospels we frequently see and hear Jesus praying. He teaches his disciples to pray and urges them to pray for specific concerns. The apostles fill their letters with their own prayers and with instructions for how those who are Christ's disciples should pray. Prayer saturates the pages of the Bible. Does prayer saturate the days of our lives?

Prayer is both a means to keep us "walking in the presence" of God and a way for us to participate in the plan of God for others. During this session we will give some attention to each of these, with emphasis on participating in God's plan.

Before we look at more of what the Bible has to say, think about your own experience with prayer. When did you first learn to pray? What occasions can you remember that made prayer an urgent necessity rather than something you were supposed to do? Have you experienced times when it seemed almost impossible for you to pray? Have you experienced others praying for you in a way that made a profound difference in your life? What have you learned about prayer in the last few days, weeks, or months?

In School With Jesus

There's an old gospel song that says, "If Jesus had to pray, what about me?" Asked another way, the question is, "If the Son of God while on earth had to spend time in prayer to be faithful and effective in his task, doesn't it make sense that the rest of us would have to follow his example?" Obviously, the answer required is yes, but many of us try to get by with as little investment in prayer as possible. I have. What about you? What would we learn about prayer if we spent a little time in school with Jesus?

Hiking for five months has shown me many beautiful wonders of God's hand. But even more importantly, I have been sensitized to the voices around me....

My faith in God has been increased and in some areas renewed. It has not been easy to pick my pack up every day, but it has been something I have felt compelled to do. Thoreau said, "I went to the woods because I wished to live deliberately, to front only the essential facts of life, and see if I could not learn what it had to teach, and not, when I came to die, discover that I had not lived."[29]

Wadi

Camp Notes

Pray in the Spirit at all times in every prayer and supplication. To that end keep alert and always persevere in supplication for all the saints. Pray also for me, so that when I speak, a message may be given to me to make known with boldness the mystery of the gospel. *(Ephesians 6:18-19)*

Q1
What resources have been most helpful in keeping you in a spirit of praise to God?

_____

_____

_____

_____

_____

_____

_____

Jesus was praying when the Holy Spirit came upon him at his baptism (Luke 3:21-22). The disciples experienced a similar connection between the filling of the Holy Spirit and prayer **(Acts 4:___)**, which enabled them to speak "the word of God with boldness." Frequently, especially when facing important decisions, Jesus withdrew for special extended times of prayer (Matthew 14:23; 26:36; Luke 5:15-16; 6:12; 9:28). Thus, James counsels us, "If any of you is lacking in wisdom, ask God" **(James 1:___)**.

Sometimes we think the Lord's Prayer **(Matthew 6:___-___; Luke 11:___-___)** was the most important lesson Jesus taught the disciples about prayer. But his *example* of praying far surpassed the wonderful summary of prayer emphases contained in those few words. Jesus lived a life of prayer, and thus his disciples learned that prayer was the doorway into the presence of God, the channel through which living water flows. He told his disciples "to pray always and not to lose heart" **(Luke 18:___)**, and this emphasis is passed on in the writings of the apostles.

> *Rejoice always,*
> *pray without ceasing,*
> *give thanks in all circumstances;*
> *for this is the will of God*
> *in Christ Jesus for you.*
> *Do not quench the Spirit.*
> **(1 Thessalonians ___:___-___)**

Notice the relationship between constant prayer and the Holy Spirit, who fills us with joy and thanksgiving—two ingredients in a wellspring of contagious witness.

> *Beloved, build yourselves up on your most holy faith; pray in the Holy Spirit; keep yourselves in the love of God.*
> *(Jude 1:20-21)*

As was mentioned last week, prayer consists of several ingredients, including praise, petition, confession, and intercession. When we pay attention to the Lord and to his word, we find ourselves filled with **praise**.

> *Hallowed be thy name.*

We long for and **petition** (ask) for God's will to be done and for our needs to be met.

> *Thy kingdom come, thy will be done...*
> *Give us this day our daily bread.*

We recognize and **confess** our own sin and shortcomings, ready to receive forgiveness and offer it to others.

> *Forgive us our trespasses,*
> *as we forgive those who trespass against us.*[30]

And we **intercede** (pray) for one another—for loved ones (John 17:9), for our enemies (Luke 6:27-28), for those needing to be saved (**Romans 10:___**), for laborers in the harvest field (**Matthew 9:___-___**), and for those offering the gospel to others (2 Thessalonians 3:1). We should bring everything and everyone to God in prayer (1 Timothy 2:1-4), but especially that all would find God's ultimate purpose for their lives in Christ.

Ephesians 3:18-19

_____

_____

_____

2 Corinthians 13:9b

_____

_____

_____

2 Thessalonians 1:11-12

_____

_____

_____

Praying Without Ceasing

Some might respond to this counsel from Paul by saying, "How is such a thing possible?"

Most of us have at one time or another experienced the difficulty of remaining faithful to keeping a time for prayer early in the morning or at night. To pray without ceasing sounds crazy. We have to sleep. And eat. And go to work. We aren't monks.

True. But the emphasis here is to remain aware of God's presence all through the day, and to let the Spirit guide us to prayer whenever the thought comes to us. Such prayer might be praise, confession, petition, or intercession. For example, what do you do when an ambulance or other emergency vehicle rushes by? What do you do when you get a phone call with some bad news? What do you do when someone on your prayer list crowds into your thoughts or your busy schedule? Why not pray? This kind of prayer, whether silent or out loud, whether two or three words or two or three sentences, is a reminder to ourselves and to others that we _live_ in Christ, not just believe in him.

Camp Notes

Q2

We have used _praise, petition, confession,_ and _intercession_ as a model for prayer. What other approaches or experiences have helped you learn to pray and open more of your life to God's presence?

_____

_____

_____

_____

_____

_____

_____

Q3

What new insights came to you this week as you prayed Ephesians 3:18-19 for each person on your prayer list?

_____

_____

_____

_____

_____

_____

_____

The secret of the Christian life and of being an effective witness is to become more and more aware of the Holy Spirit's presence and to bring every situation before God in prayer.

Camp Notes

On my six-month hike, I have noticed that...with each day fears once hidden become revealed. I don't have to be afraid once they are brought out into the open. I find dark thoughts in my mind, and I'm learning how to heal from their origins. I have been able to throw my prayers into the sky to God, both the wheat and the chaff. God listens to them both and knows what is important and lets the wind carry away the rest.

Wadi

One way to prepare ourselves for this kind of living in the Spirit of Christ is to find ways to move our personal home altar (wherever you regularly read Scripture and pray at home) out into the world where we live. Paul's word to us about the "renewing of [our] minds" (Romans 12:2) fits here. Without looking it up, see how well you can remember Paul's words.

_____

_____

_____

_____

Do you listen to a CD or tape of hymns or praise music as you drive? Are you reading literature to help you better understand the Bible; church history; societal changes; contemporary views and values; how to answer questions unchurched people and pre-Christians have about Jesus, God, and the Bible? Do you have a favorite framed Scripture verse or prayer hanging on the wall or sitting on your desk at work? Do you keep a Bible or devotional book you are reading out in plain sight on a table? Do you carry in your pocket a cross or other special reminder of your relationship to Christ? Is there a group you meet with every week in your office, in a dorm room, or at a restaurant to tell your prayer concerns to and discuss how to live better as Christ's witnesses? These are just a few of the ways to prime the pray-without-ceasing pump in the world you live in day after day.

Jan Wood has written a wonderful little book on how to make the place we work an arena for healing and Christian witness. In *Christians at Work,*[31] Wood uses her own experiences and those of others to tackle head on both the challenges and the opportunities presented by our day-to-day relationships in the marketplace of life. Each chapter concludes with a list of discussion questions. It might make an ideal discussion book for a small group, either at the office or as a follow-up to *Witness.*

But the heart of the issue is how to remind ourselves hour by hour, day by day, that we are Christ's ambassadors in every context of life. Prayer in its many and varied forms is our lifeline to effective Christian witness. And we need to remember that there is One who is always interceding for us as we faithfully pray for others.

> *God, who searches the heart, knows what is the mind of the Spirit, because the Spirit intercedes for the saints according to the will of God.* **(Romans 8:___)**

Q4
What methods have you found most helpful to remind you day in and day out that you live for Christ and desire to be his witness?

_____

_____

_____

_____

_____

_____

Interceding for Others

Our witness is fueled by an ever-growing ability to see others as Jesus himself would see them. Following the lead of Paul (**1 Corinthians 2:___**), John Wesley called this goal "having the mind of Christ." The closer we draw to this divine perspective, the more we find ourselves praying without ceasing and ready to be instruments of God in others' lives. In the weeks to come, we will talk more about how to speak to others for God, but first let's look at how to speak to God for others.

Throughout these weeks on the *Witness* trail, you have been praying regularly for special people in your life. Maybe you have created a list of people you pray for daily, which probably includes family members, friends, colleagues, neighbors, people involved in groups or activities you attend, and one another. I have found it helpful to record these names on a small card I can carry in my wallet. I also have them on a page in my journal or as a bookmark in my Bible or devotional book.

Exactly how praying for others impacts their lives we may never completely understand this side of heaven, but every now and then God shows us that it does. Some years ago I was preaching in a small town in Kansas. At the conclusion of my sermon, I read a poem written by a young man who had renewed his faith in Christ while sitting in my car in Nashville, Tennessee. Two or three months had passed between these two events. At the end of my sermon, a woman ran to the front of the little church and, full of joy and excitement, told me she knew the young man and his family. She said they had been praying for him for six years. We both were filled with awe at how God uses all of us in the divine plan, and that people who pray are as important as those who share the gospel.[32]

This is Paul's perspective when he continually asks others to "pray for us, so that the word of the Lord may spread rapidly and be glorified everywhere, just as it is among you" (2 Thessalonians 3:1). Often, intercession is something we do quietly and alone. Sometimes we join in prayer with others in a group. And occasionally we pray for people when we are with them.

I had been witnessing to and praying for my neighbor for eight years. Then, after his mother's death and his young son's strange experience of seeing his grandmother (who was one thousand miles away) come into his room early on the morning she died, my friend invited me over for coffee. After conversing for more than an hour, I said, "You know you're in my prayers, but would you like me to pray for you and for God's wisdom before I leave?" He eagerly agreed. More happened to change his openness to Christ in one brief minute of prayer with him than in eight years of praying for him; yet both forms of intercession were equally important in God's economy. Many people have never heard another human being pray for them by name. There is a wonderful power in intercessory prayer.

Q5
What methods have you discovered that help you pray for those on your list?

Q6
What special experiences have helped you to know that God truly does honor and answer our prayers?

Q7
Have you ever prayed aloud for someone over the telephone or in a public setting away from church? If so, what was your experience?

Camp Notes

Q8
What thoughts have you had about additional things you could do to live more openly as Christ's witness?

Moving On

When we abide in Christ and live a life that is always being renewed through prayer for ourselves and others, we will find a multitude of opportunities to bear witness to the hope that is within us.

Every testimony of this hope is unique in the details of how and when and where we found our way into vital faith, but the heart of the message of hope remains the same. This coming week on the trail, we will focus on learning how to tell our own unique stories of coming to Christ. In the two weeks that follow, we will concentrate on learning how to tell others the gospel story that can clarify for them how Jesus Christ is "the way, and the truth, and the life" (**John 14:___**).

READING ASSIGNMENTS

1. Record your reflections, questions, and insights from these daily Bible readings in your *My Witness Journal.*
   Day 1: Psalm 77 (Sometimes God seems silent and far away.—Memorize verse 2.)
   Day 2: Psalm 107 ("Let the redeemed of the LORD say so."—Memorize verse 2.)
   Day 3: John 8:2-11 (Sometimes we can't believe God could forgive us.—Memorize verses 10-11.)
   Day 4: John 9:1-38 (No one else can tell our story.—Memorize verse 25b.)
   Day 5: 2 Timothy 1:1-14 (Sometimes our story involves generations.—Memorize verses 5-7.)
   Day 6: Acts 25:1–26:29 (Our story is part of God's story.—Note 26:16-18.)
2. As you read the chapter for next week (pages 129–34), underline or highlight special thoughts and answer the questions in the Q boxes.

ACTION ASSIGNMENT

Imagine that a publisher has contacted you about publishing your spiritual autobiography. Prepare an outline on a single sheet of paper, including:
   1. Your **title** (be creative; stimulate interest);
   2. A **dedication** (one paragraph acknowledging special people who have contributed to your faith);
   3. A list of 6 to 8 **chapter titles** important to your story;
   4. A **closing word of encouragement** (one paragraph) for others like you who sometimes struggle with faith and faithfulness.

Prayerfully follow the Spirit's leading for (1) follow-up conversations, (2) inviting someone to church, and (3) telling your story to another person. Summarize your experiences in your *My Witness Journal.*

See you on the path!

My Witness as My Story

Prayer

Write a prayer giving thanks to God for your own unique story of faith and the events and people the Holy Spirit has used to lead you to where you are now.

_____

_____

_____

_____

_____

_____

_____

Amen.

I remember my thoughts of walking through a forest before. It was all surface, like the view of the ocean. Inside is life that has amazed me and put me at awe. I have met people of all walks of life on the trip who have done the same thing. The heart is just below the surface.

Wadi

Q1
What are some of your favorite kinds of stories (movies, books, and so forth)? Why?

Trail Talk

The gospel is a story, God's story of interaction with people over the course of time and with a view toward eternity. The Bible includes moral instruction, religious responsibilities, and proverbs of wisdom; but it is primarily a story. It is an accounting of what happened, where, when, and how people telling the story experienced God's presence both for correction and for salvation.

Telling our personal stories as part of God's story is indeed biblical and a powerful way to make the gospel story as up-to-date as today. Paul illustrates this several times in his writings. It is also illustrated in the Book of Acts. Listening to others tell their stories of life's journey and telling our own is perhaps the most human of all activities.

There is a special power in story because, as Wadi says, "the heart is just below the surface." This is why many of us find ourselves moved when invited (either face to face or vicariously through television, movies, or books) into the deep stories of others—stories of love, bravery, dedication, sacrifice, rejection, survival, generosity, kindness, and just plain life. Even soap operas and commercials get to us. Human beings are created for story. Your story and mine are marvelous and powerful gifts to the heart when offered to others in love and as expressions of trust and concern for their stories. So let's begin with a few stories.

Q2
What stories of personal witness do you remember that impacted your life and your desire to live for Christ?

Camp Notes

The Bible as Story

We've spent several weeks examining the Bible story, and we will work more next week to try to summarize it for others. Our purpose this week, however, is to recognize that story is God's idea and to rehearse our own stories as part of the gospel's impact on the lives of others. First, let's look at story as God's idea.

It is important to realize that the Bible is a bit unusual as a religious holy book. Unlike the Koran, for example, which is a random collection of teachings and mandates, the Bible is a story. It has a beginning and an end and what we would call a plot. It is mostly about what happened and what is going to happen, not about principles and abstract concepts. God speaks to individuals and to nations within a context of history (his story). There are dates, places, names, and numbers. Almost every important truth the Bible contains is revealed as part of an encounter with particular problems and people who are in conversation with one another and with the God who is both above and within our day-to-day stories.

What's more, the Bible is full of unlikely heroes. The prophets and saints are certainly not perfect people. They at times struggle to find how to be faithful and even to have faith. Have you ever wanted to cry out like this psalmist?

> *I cry aloud to God,*
> *   aloud to God, that he may hear me.*
> *In the day of my trouble I seek the Lord;*
> *   in the night my hand is stretched out*
> *   without wearying;*
> *   my soul refuses to be comforted.*
> *I think of God, and I moan;*
> *   I meditate, and my spirit faints....*
>
> *Has his steadfast love ceased forever?*
> *   Are his promises at an end*
> *   for all time?*
> *Has God forgotten to be gracious?*
> *   Has he in anger shut up his compassion?*
>   **(Psalm ___:___-___, ___-___)**

I have. I remember once, when I was trying to follow God's leading for my life, feeling really angry with God and confused about the way that my prayers were being answered. I sat on a large rock at Lake Tahoe, California, and I stumbled upon this psalm as I read my Bible. I thought to myself, *Wow! If someone who actually wrote the Bible could talk like this to God, maybe I can be honest about my feelings.* But note what the psalmist goes on to say.

Q3
Which story (or stories) in the Bible do you most identify with? Why?

I will call to mind the deeds of the LORD;
I will remember your wonders of old.
I will meditate on all your work,
and muse on your mighty deeds.
Your way, O God, is holy.
What god is so great as our God?
(Psalm ___:___-___)

Because the psalmist had a real relationship with God, he was able to express his current sense of being abandoned and still draw on his memory of God's mercy.

This combination of honestly acknowledging our present troubles and remembering God's intervention in the past offers all of us a way through the "darkest valley" (Psalm 23). What's more, being real in recounting our stories enables others who are not yet in touch with God to trust us when we speak of the hope we have. It's a bit like being at a Twelve-Step meeting where everyone introduces him or herself as, "Hi. I'm ___, and I'm an addict." We all "fall short of the glory of God" (Romans 3:23) and need to guard against sugar-coating our stories or God's grace. The Bible reminds us we can tell it like it is.

The Bible is real, and it allows us to be real. It also allows us to listen and understand at least part of what others struggle with as they try to find their way to the real and living God, who encounters us with saving and transforming grace through faith in Jesus Christ.

Your Story as Christian Witness

I grew up with only limited exposure to Christian witnesses and no clear presentation of the gospel. Nevertheless, a hunger to discover God's reality drew me through family and friends toward Christ and his church. I had several significant turning points, more than one effort at surrender, and one special moment of discovering the power of "Christ in [me], the hope of glory" (Colossians 1:27).

My story is not my wife's story. Bonnie grew up a preacher's kid, and she doesn't remember a time when she didn't believe in God and Jesus. Much of her understanding of being a Christian, however, was about keeping the rules. She remembers a time when as a child she felt close to Jesus as her special friend, and yet in college (a Christian college) she went through a period of doubt and confusion. She tells others that I was one of the people who helped her discover God's amazing grace. One of the most significant faith moments in her life came later when she was home after surgery. Through a single Bible verse (Matthew 5:44: "Love your enemies...") she discovered a whole new freedom to love others without worrying about their response.

Camp Notes

Q4
Which autobiographical stories told by other members of your group today most encouraged you? Why?

Exercise

Sometimes we don't have a good feel for how our stories come across to others. We may think they are too something (nice, churchy, plain, unusual, nasty, or whatever).

Take a few minutes to tell your story to someone in your group. Ask that person for honest evaluation and, if appropriate, some suggestions.

Camp Notes

Q5

Does your story easily divide into "before coming to Christ," "when I came to Christ," and "since coming to Christ"?

If not, can you talk about special moments, decisions, or events along the way when you owned your faith in new ways? Name those you think of as most important.

Q6

Which people on your prayer list might you best approach with a Bridge story? What part of your own story might help you connect?

Our stories are all different. No one else can tell my story or your story (see John 9). No story of God's work in a human life is void of power to touch another person's life. Some people think they don't have much of a witness because their story is a response to gentle nurture (**2 Timothy 1:___**) rather than a dramatic encounter (**John 8:___-___**). But each of us has a story to tell of how God has worked with us (**Psalm 107:___-___**). And our stories have different angles, even if the facts don't change. So let's look at a variety of ways we can tell our stories. We will examine three approaches to telling a personal story of faith, which we will label as A, B, and C (Autobiography, Bridge, and Confession).

AUTOBIOGRAPHY

An autobiography is a self-written life story, usually told from the perspective of the passing of time. In a sense, both my story and Bonnie's (page 131) were told this way. They started with our childhood and moved through to our adult lives, stopping briefly along the way to point out special moments or seasons of encountering challenges or trouble and discovering God's mercy and grace. Often, these two kinds of encounters (our limitations and God's intervention) are closely connected.

Probably many of you told the assigned spiritual autobiography as a chronological story. Perhaps the chapter titles were even clearly labeled with an age or season of life. This kind of Christian testimony is much like Paul's story in Acts 25–26 and Luke's telling of the story of Jesus in Luke 1:1-4. It gives most of us a chance to tell about our lives (1) before we really came to Christ, (2) when we came to Christ, and (3) the difference Christ has made. This is a natural way to tell your story, especially if someone asks, "Well, how did you become so sure of your faith?" But it's not the only way to tell your story or to offer your witness.

BRIDGE

A bridge is something constructed to make a connection between two points or places. When we think of offering our Christian story as a bridge, the goal is to identify something in our own story with an experience, problem, or transition going on in the other person's life. In other words, your Christian story is told by focusing on one facet in more detail rather than by trying to give a summary of the whole thing. It is a way of helping to eliminate the distance or the gap some people feel when they talk to us about life's deeper issues.

Sometimes people get the impression that we Christians live in a world very different from the one they see and experience. They don't know how to get to where we are; they can't build a bridge to our side. So, we build a bridge to where they are. This is incarnational storytelling. We enter their world and carefully listen to their story; then we tell of a time in our own lives when we remember feeling much the same way.

We need to approach this kind of story-witness with care. Let's not tell someone who just lost a job or a loved one, "I know how you must feel" unless we really do! Sometimes the connection is better made by saying, "I have no idea what you must be going through. I've never experienced that before, but I have felt alone and abandoned." If they wish to hear about when you experienced this distancing in your life, it gives you a chance to tell a portion of your story and perhaps to tell how this experience helped lead you to the One who said, "I will never leave you or forsake you" **(Hebrews 13:___).**

CONFESSION

A confession is a self-revelation of one's own sins or shortcomings, or a declaration of one's faith. Isn't it interesting that both kinds of confessing take us into the presence of God. We talked a while ago about the special power of confessional storytelling. The recovering addict who says up front, "I'm an addict" disarms those who might be thinking, *I can't believe this guy.* Storytelling that openly acknowledges our own experiences with failure and pain set us all on common ground.

The confession approach to telling a witness story does not mean hanging out all of our dirty laundry. It means using expressions such as: "I have really struggled for a long time with _____"; or "There was time in my life when _____"; or "I remember when I really blew it with _____"; or "I don't know how I would make it through if it weren't for _____." Such a statement might come after discussing a problem in the news; an issue raised by a movie or television show; or something your friend is facing at work, at home, or in school. A simple statement of confession invites the other person to ask you questions, and may give you a chance to say, "But my faith in and relationship with God has made all the difference."

Witness as storytelling is not antagonistic. It doesn't lead to debate or foster tension, because it is not primarily a matter of opinions or beliefs. It is a recounting of experience. It is not preaching or telling others what they should think or do. It is offering an alternative perspective through personal experience. It has amazing power to touch the heart and open the door for a new possibility.

Q7
What opportunities have you had when you have used, or could have used, a Confession model?

Q8
What are the most helpful insights you have gained this week from our emphasis on witness as Christian stories?

Camp Notes

Moving On

For all the power of personal storytelling, there is even more power in telling God's story. When we decide to love faithfully, listen to, pray for, and share our witness with others, the Holy Spirit sooner or later will provide the opportunity for us to explain to them how Christ can become real in their lives, bringing God's love, forgiveness, a new start, wonderful new meaning, and power for living.

Telling the gospel story is no more difficult than telling your own story. Do you remember everything that happened in your life? Of course not. Do you need to know everything about God's story to tell it? Of course not. Will you know how to answer every question others may ask? Of course not. But no one expects that from you, including God. What is expected is that you give the reason "for the hope that is within you" (1 Peter 3:15). Our job is to explain, as best we can (being faithful to Scripture), what God has done for the world in Jesus Christ, and how the reality of eternal life can become theirs. Get ready for next week, when we will concentrate on God's story.

READING ASSIGNMENTS

1. Record your reflections, questions, and insights from these daily Bible readings in your *My Witness Journal*.

    Day 1: Micah 6:6-8 (what God requires of us—Memorize verse 8.)

    Day 2: Romans 6:21-23 (life or death? wages or free gift?—Memorize verse 23.)

    Day 3: John 10 (why Jesus came—Memorize verse 10b.)

    Day 4: John 3:16-17 (the gospel in two verses—Memorize these verses.)

    Day 5: Ephesians 2:1-10 (It's all about grace.—Memorize verses 8-10.)

    Day 6: Acts 2:36-39 (What must we do?—Memorize verses 38-39.)

2. As you read the chapter for next week (pages 135–40), underline or highlight special thoughts and answer the questions in the Q boxes.

ACTION ASSIGNMENT

During the week review the content of God's story. Review the Scripture passages (especially from Sessions 2 through 13). Name some of the texts that best help you clarify God's purpose, our problem (sin), God's provision, and our response. Record those passages in your *My Witness Journal*.

Continue your interviews. Talk with at least one person who is not in your *Witness* group. Ask for his or her thoughts about the four foundational elements of the gospel that you have been working with: God's purpose, our problem (sin), God's provision, and our response.

Ready? Let's go.

My Witness as God's Story

VISTA ONE

Prayer

Write a prayer giving thanks to God for the gospel. Include the ingredients that have special meaning for your own life and thankfulness for the privilege of offering such wonderful news to others.

_____

_____

_____

_____

_____

_____

Amen.

Trail Talk

"I Love to Tell the Story"—How often have you sung that song? Some of us may not be as familiar with it as others, but it's usually considered one of the old favorites. It has appeared in every Methodist hymnal since 1878. The author, Katherine Hankey (1834–1911), originally composed it as a poem of more than one hundred verses while recovering from a serious illness. The daughter of a wealthy and devout English banker, Kate invested her whole life and all her gifts in organizing Sunday school classes and trying to reach both the rich and the poor with God's wonderful story.[33]

Kate Hankey loved to tell the story. Millions of worshipers over a century and half have loved to sing her song. Why, then, do so few who love to sing it actually love to do it?

Of all the ways we witness, telling "the old, old story" seems to be the most difficult. Why? There are probably many reasons; but when we know deep in our own hearts that "it did so much for me," we want to tell it to others. In this session, we will explore how to enable that desire to become more of a reality. We will examine the story and learn some ways to tell it.

I Love to Tell the Story

*I love to tell the story
    of unseen things above,
of Jesus and his glory,
    of Jesus and his love.
I love to tell the story,
    because I know 'tis true;
It satisfies my longings
    as nothing else can do.*

*I love to tell the story,
    'twill be my theme in glory,
to tell the old, old story
    of Jesus and his love.*

*I love to tell the story;
    more wonderful it seems
than all the golden fancies
    of all our golden dreams.
I love to tell the story,
    it did so much for me;
and that is just the reason
    I tell it now to thee.[34]*

Camp Notes

Q1

Do you remember how Wadi summarized God's story in his conversation with Llama (Session 17)? What points did he make?

_____

_____

_____

_____

_____

Q2

What are some of the key points in God's story, as summarized in the Nicene Creed (Sessions 7 and 10)?

_____

_____

_____

_____

_____

_____

_____

The Story

Telling God's story to others follows many of the same guidelines we discovered for telling our own stories. The task is to listen with love and then to offer a new option that helps people connect their own life with God's life through the gospel story. Ultimately, we entrust the connecting to the Holy Spirit, but we've been given the privilege of speaking on behalf of the living God.

God's story is about God and God's love for the world (_____). It is about a tough love that holds us accountable (_____), confronts us with justice and truth (_____), and provides through Jesus Christ the only way out of sin's judgment and death (_____) and into the abundant life God intends us to enjoy forever (_____). (Fill in the Scripture references for these ideas.)

The story is found in the best-selling book of all time, the Bible. It is a story full of power to leap out of pages and into the deepest recesses of the human soul because the Spirit of God is active in the story and writes it on human hearts (**2 Corinthians 3:___-___**). Every person who has ever heard the story and experienced the Spirit's penmanship can't help but want others to hear it, understand it, and be forever changed by it.

So what's the story? Let's look at it from the perspective of the plot. The story tells us first about the one eternal God who is the creator of all that exists—"and…it was very good" (**Genesis 1:___**). We human beings were fashioned by God to be the crowning jewel of creation and to reflect the very likeness of God (**Genesis 1:___**). Our purpose is to enjoy and care for the earth and one another (Genesis 1:26; 2:24-25) and to experience God's blessings and presence (Genesis 1:28; 3:8).

As stewards of God's masterpiece and God's image, we received instructions and the precious gift of freedom. But temptation lurks near human freedom, and, like Adam and Eve, we all have fallen short of God's glorious purpose (**Romans 3:___**) and turned like stubborn sheep to our own way (Isaiah 53:6). In fact, in our sinful rejection of God's guidance, we have wandered off and are lost. It is our own doing, and yet we are undone. There is no way back unless a good and brave shepherd comes to find and save us (Luke 19:10).

God's only eternal Son, Jesus, who is one with the Father (**John 10:___-___**), is that Good Shepherd (**John 10:___-___**). He has come from heaven's riches into our poverty to rescue lost sheep (2 Corinthians 8:9). In his love for the lost, he even sacrificed his own life so that we might live (**John 10:___-___**). But to show the power of God available for our salvation and to confirm the unique identity of Jesus as the Christ, God raised him from the dead (Acts 2:32-36). The risen Lord appeared to many of his disciples and instructed them to tell everyone the full story as soon as they received the gift of God's Holy Spirit.

Disciples of Jesus have been passing on this story for two thousand years. When those who long for God's restoration hear this offer of amazing grace and place their faith in Christ as Savior and Lord, they are forgiven and cleansed of the ravages of sin (**1 John 1:___**), filled with the Holy Spirit (**Acts 2:___**), and enabled to walk in fellowship with God manifesting the beauty of God's nature revealed in the fruit of the Spirit (**Galatians 5:___**). This new humanity is the beginning of God's new creation, which will one day be completed with the return of Christ and the final establishment of God's heavenly reign over the earth (Matthew 25:31).

Is this the only way to summarize the story? By no means. It's a big story, with lots of details that can't be summarized in three or four short paragraphs. In Scripture, the story is told in many different ways using many different metaphors. But it is a story with a beginning and an end, which invites every lost child of God to hear the Shepherd's voice, turn around, and come home.

The Ingredients

Let's take some time to examine various ways that God's story could be told in its most basic form. I chose to use the images of lost sheep and the good shepherd to carry the visual imagery of the story. But most of us don't live in an agrarian society. Do you think this image still works for people you know? From the texts you examined this week, how would you prefer to describe the following?

God's Purpose: _____

_____

    Source texts: _____ _____

Our Problem: _____

_____

    Source texts: _____ _____

God's Provision: _____

_____

    Source texts: _____ _____

Our Response: _____

_____

    Source texts: _____ _____

Q3
What are some ingredients you think are missing from or need to be strengthened in the story as told, using the images of lost sheep and a shepherd?

Q4
How did the person you interviewed describe each of the ingredients in God's story?

Camp Notes

For the wages of sin is death, but the free gift of God is eternal life in Christ Jesus our Lord.   *(Romans 6:23)*

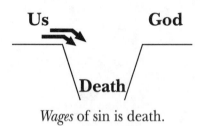

Wages of sin is death.

Free *gift* is life through Christ Jesus.

Q5

What do you see as the advantages of the Bridge model of presenting the gospel?

Disadvantages?

Some Models

Many people have found it helpful to tell the gospel story using a diagram or a summary list of key ingredients. Probably hundreds of these models exist, but we will look at only three.

The Bridge is a diagram that explains the story usually using Romans 6:23 as its text.[35] The good news is that we are created to live in intimate fellowship with God. But the bad news is that we all experience a deep chasm between ourselves and God. Why? Because we all have sinned (Romans 3:23), and sin separates us from God. In fact, this separation, whether in this life or the next, is what sin earns (wages) and is death not life. We cannot by our own will or good deeds, or even religious devotion, cross over to connect with God. All such efforts fall short. (Note the diagram in the side column.) God is holy and those who come into God's presence must be holy and clean from sin (Isaiah 59:1-3). But how can we be clean and holy before God and cross over?

This is the good news. God has done through Jesus Christ what we could not do. Jesus is God's bridge to enable us to pass over from death to life, from separation to fellowship, from brokenness to wholeness and holiness. How? It is totally a gift of grace. Jesus took upon himself our death (sins) through his cross, so that we might share in his eternal life. But we must choose to cross over the bridge through faith. The bridge is available to the whole world, but only truly effective for those who step out in faith and put all their trust in Jesus. When we do that, we experience the fellowship with God for which we were made, and God's Spirit confirms that we are forgiven and embraced in perfect love (Romans 8:15-16, 38-39).

The final question asked with this model is, Where are you in this diagram (or story)? Are you trying to find a way across the divide but failing, or have you truly accepted the gift of eternal life through trusting Christ as your personal Savior and Lord and come home to God?

Some people like to draw this diagram step by step as a way of showing and telling the gospel. Others, like a friend of mine, always carry a little metal or wooden cross in their pocket and offer it to the person to whom they told the gospel. What do you think of this model?

The Offer of new life in Christ is another diagram model of presenting the gospel and has many variations. Sometimes the offer is made by tracing a hand on a sheet of paper or drawing a five-pointed star and saying, "God offers us perfect friendship and a wonderful new life that is spelled G.R.A.C.E." (Ephesians 2:3-10, especially 8-10).

G = God's love and new life is a *gift* of *grace*, not something we can achieve or earn.

R = To experience the reality of God's grace, we must begin by *recognizing* and *repenting* of our sin.

A = Repentance allows us to *acknowledge* Christ and *accept* him as Savior and Lord.

C = As we *confess* our faith in Christ, we also *commit* ourselves to walking with him.

E = And we *enter* God's family, the church, and become *engaged* with others in God's mission in the world.

The Circle of Life diagram (with the throne in the center), which we looked at in Session 20, has been helpful to many witnesses. This model might be especially helpful for those who think of themselves as Christian but have no deep acquaintance with the gospel or the reality of "Christ in you, the hope of glory" (Colossians 1:27). Here the basic story is told as it is with the other models, but with an emphasis on these questions: Where are you in your relationship with Christ? Is he in your life? Have you received him (John 1:12; Revelation 3:20)? Is he the center of your life, or are you trying the impossible—living a double life (Matthew 6:24; James 4:1-8)?

The details of any of these models can be fleshed out by other passages of Scripture and by personal illustrations. These are only the basics. It is hard to beat the nugget of the gospel contained in John 3:16-17. Some simply use the football stadium advertisement as a starting point, and then write out those two verses and explain God's purpose, our problem, God's provision, our response. Others like to go with an outline like the ABC's of the gospel or a metamorphosis image (caterpillar—chrysalis—butterfly) to explain the meaning of baptism and the way through death to our old life and freedom in our new life. I like to use the Vine and the Branches model that we talked about in Session 11 (page 67).

Can you see that some models might work better in one situation, while others might work better in another? Has this been helpful to you, or do you prefer another approach entirely? If you had the chance tomorrow to explain in ten minutes the heart of God's story, how would you do it?

Moving On

This week we have tried to become more comfortable with the basics of God's story and to look at a few models of how to tell that story to others. We will continue this discussion next week, but with a different emphasis. The goal will be to learn how to tell the gospel story through narrative stories in the Bible. In other words, as we love and listen to others in such a way that we begin to understand what they are struggling with, we try to show them how someone in the Bible dealt with that same problem.

Q6

What do you see as some of the advantages of the G.R.A.C.E. model when presenting the gospel?

Disadvantages?

Q7

Which of these models do you like best? Why?

Which do you like least?

Camp Notes

READING ASSIGNMENTS

1. Record your reflections, questions, and insights from these daily Bible readings in your *My Witness Journal.*

   Day 1: 1 Peter 2:24-25 (the gospel summary—Memorize these verses.)

   Day 2: Matthew 6:19-21 (the heart check—Memorize these verses.)

   Day 3: Romans 5:1-5 (grace for the journey—Memorize these verses.)

   Day 4: 2 Corinthians 3:17-18 (the Spirit's transforming work—Memorize these verses.)

   Day 5: 1 John 3:14-24 (signs of new life—Memorize verse 14.)

   Day 6: Philemon 1:6 (motivation for effective faith sharing—Memorize this verse.)

2. As you read the chapter for next week (pages 141–46), underline or highlight special thoughts and answer the questions in the Q boxes.

ACTION ASSIGNMENT

1. Be prepared to roleplay telling God's story at the next session. Choose one of the models in Session 23, or use a model of your own. Use at least two verses from Scripture as the source of the gospel in the story you tell. Write in your *My Witness Journal* notes about the model and Scripture you will use.

2. Read one of these Bible stories each day. Tell others who face similar challenges about the truth and hope each story illustrates.

   David—Grace is real, even in the face of deceit, murder, and adultery (2 Samuel 11:1–12:25; Psalm 51).

   The Astrologers—God can use all of creation to lead true seekers to Christ (Matthew 2:1-12).

   The Woman at the Well—Hearts broken by repeated failure in relationships can find hope (John 4:1-42).

   Mary and Martha—The good can get in the way of the best (Luke 10:38-42; John 11:1–12:8).

   Zacchaeus—Jesus loves and restores those who step on people to get to the top (Luke 19:1-10).

   The Adulteress—When we are most vulnerable, our sins made public, Jesus forgives (John 8:1-11).

Keep looking for opportunities. They are everywhere.

My Witness as God's Story

VISTA TWO

Prayer

Write a prayer asking God to grant wisdom and courage to you and to all who witness for Christ. Emphasize especially your desire to listen carefully and understand the pain and longings of others, and to be able to help them see in the stories of the Bible glimpses of hope that can lead to faith.

_____

_____

_____

_____

_____

_____

_____

Amen.

Trail Talk and Roleplay

As Wadi says, there is "joy in the journey," and the one we are on with God never ends. Yet, there is also a destination not only for us but also for those with whom we are investing our time and love and witness. Our goal and the goal of God the Holy Trinity is for all of us to reach the top of the mountain and stand with Jesus Christ observing new vistas of glory and wonder and grace.

Many of the people in today's world who long for the gusto and want to find all that life has to offer are not particularly interested in religion or Bible verses. Instead, some force within them prompts them to have it all and live it up. But which way is up? As important as this question is, it may not even be asked until we find ourselves tumbling head over heels. A swimmer caught in the undertow is desperately interested in the way up.

Sometimes our best witness comes when we have the opportunity to be lifeguards who patiently hang around until we are needed. Then, because we are ready (**1 Peter 3:___-___**), we reach into the turmoil and pull with all our might toward "the way, and the truth, and the life" (**John 14:___**). Often, the best way to pull is through a story that connects the one in need to the power of God to address such a need.

Camp Notes

All I have left to hike is the mountain.... I guess I should be excited, but I am far from it. The life I've grown accustomed to is about to end.... I know I have always said I am to take just the joy in the journey and not the destination, but that was before I got to within five miles of the end. Katahdin is 13 feet shy of being a mile high. Now that I am here, it is hard to give it up. I am going to make a run for it in two days, but the mountain may turn me back before I reach the summit.... Blizzard conditions are on the mountain. I may not get to hike it this year.

Wadi

Camp Notes

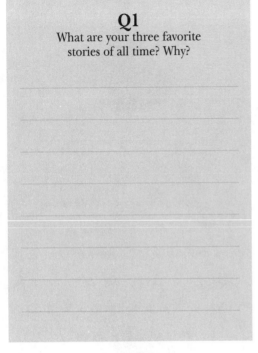

The Power of Story

Many of us are familiar with the name Garrison Keillor, one of America's premier storytellers. Perhaps no other spinner of yarns has had the weekly audience captured by Mr. Keillor and his tales of Lake Wobegon. He makes us laugh, remember, and see others and ourselves in a new light. He critiques our values, tells his own, and talks of God—but as a storyteller not a preacher. And people listen.

Perhaps you've never heard of Garrison Keillor; but every society, every culture, every age has its storytellers. Some are singers of ballads or actors on a stage. Others write novels or create amazing movies with digital surround sound that take us forward into space or backward into history or cull up the deep feelings associated with romance or war. But no doubt the most common setting for telling stories through the ages has been at night around a campfire. People love a good story. They always have.

Why? What is the power of story? I'm not sure any single answer is adequate, but some of the reasons that a story is so close to our hearts as humans might include the following.

A story

- presses past the mere information questions of what and when, trying to answer the more uniquely human questions of who and why.
- moves in a direction from seemingly unconnected happenings to final purpose.
- strives to clarify meaning in the midst of the human struggle to make difficult choices.
- creates new possibilities by expanding our experience and thus our view of the world and reality.
- allows us to evaluate our own values and motivations by giving us a virtual tour inside the lives of others.
- reveals that we are much more like one another than we sometimes could ever imagine.
- touches deep feelings, often hidden below the surface until stirred by imagery.
- provides an opportunity for making sense out of life.

No wonder Jesus used stories to carry much of the message he wanted to get across. I believe Jesus understood that humans learn some things best by the discovery process involved in hearing a story. Every story offers the possibility of adding something, perhaps even the keystone piece of the puzzle, to the quest we all began as young children—the quest to know "Why?" Telling gospel stories and *the* gospel story are God's way of inviting us as children of creation to find life's most important piece of the puzzle: Jesus Christ, God's Son, our Savior.

Telling Gospel Stories as Witness

To some degree we have already explored the meaning of telling the gospel as story, our story and God's story. The new twist here is how to let some folks in on the Bible as a source of insight for living rather than a dusty book of old-fashioned religion and morality.

Many people with whom we interact today have at best a limited appreciation of the Bible as a source of practical and contemporary wisdom. If we are regularly soaking in the wisdom of Scripture and asking, "How might this story or this passage help someone else?" we will have opportunities to offer a witness that can be helpful to others.

Here's an example of what that might look like. Picture yourself with a friend whose child is going through a season of lying or rebellion. In addition to your own witness (which for many of us could very well begin with empathy and confession), you might draw on several points of contact from Scripture. For example, suppose you had been reading Proverbs regularly as part of your devotions. You might say,

> *You know, just the other day I got some help from something I read in the Bible. Have you ever heard of the part of the Bible called Proverbs? A lot of it is aimed at trying to teach children how to live. A couple of sayings really helped me. One says: "Whoever winks the eye causes trouble, but the one who rebukes boldly makes peace" (Proverbs 10:10). I realized I'm the kind that doesn't like to get into conflict with my kids. But in a sense that's my job if I'm really going to help them. Another verse says: "Train children in the right way, and when old, they will not stray" (Proverbs 22:6). We all stray, but foundations are really important. So we've decided to be our children's parents, not just their friends. It's given us a lot more freedom, and we've found we can approach things with more love and less anger.*

Or you might choose to tell a story about a youth.

> *You know, this challenge of raising kids is as old as family life itself. There's a story Jesus tells in the Bible that has helped me. It's about a family that has two kids. The oldest is no trouble and all business; the youngest is determined to find his own way and escape his family's restrictions. He takes off with all the money he can squeeze out of his dad and heads out to have a good time....*

Q3

What kinds of problems are some of your friends facing?

Can you think of any stories in the Bible that might relate to your friends' needs? Do others in your group have suggestions?

Camp Notes

Exercise

For each of the texts below (read this week) indicate the kind of situation and/or the kind of people for whom each story might be helpful.

David (2 Samuel 11:1–12:25; Psalm 51)

_____

The Astrologers (Matthew 2:1-12)

_____

The Woman at the Well (John 4:1-42)

_____

Mary and Martha (Luke 10:38-42; John 11:1–12:8)

_____

Zacchaeus (Luke 19:1-10)

_____

The Adulteress (John 8:1-11)

_____

Q4
What kinds of people in what kinds of situations might best be candidates for Nick's story?

_____

_____

_____

_____

_____

_____

Could you tell the rest of the story? Could you draw some helpful insights? Could you tell part of your own story and, without belittling the problem, suggest prayer, love, patience, and forgiveness? Could you say, "Do you know the reason Jesus told that story in the first place? He was reminding us that we are like one or the other of those children when it comes to God." If appropriate, could you go on and explain which child you were? Could you ask your friend which one he or she identified with in relationship with God? Stories have a lot to offer. Being familiar with them is a wonderful way to be prepared to tell good news to people we encounter.

Some Other Gospel Stories

Your reading assignments this week prepared you for some other gospel stories. Take some time to talk with one another about situations in which these stories might be told.

In addition, let's look at some other stories in the Bible that could be helpful in our witnessing.

Nicodemus—In John 3:1-21, the story is told of a highly respected and respectable teacher, Nicodemus, who was curious about Jesus. But the social circles he was part of had already written off Jesus as just one more troubled person. Nevertheless, Nick saw enough in Jesus and the impact he was having on others that Nick's honesty required a personal investigation. So, he went to Jesus by night when no one would notice.

Nick had rehearsed all of his questions ahead of time, but Jesus surprised him in the middle of his polite niceties and said, "Nick, the heart of the matter is far more radical than you seem to know. If you want to understand what I'm doing and get in on it, you must experience a brand-new beginning, a new birth from above. It's not about mere ideas and respectability. God's kingdom is about connecting with the Spirit's transforming power at work in the world."

Obviously, I've taken a little liberty with an exact word-for-word presentation of the biblical text. But isn't this what Jesus was saying? Can we tell the story accurately and yet in a language that connects with people today? As we tell it, can we discuss with them the implications it has for our lives and for theirs? And then can we answer their questions—like Nick's question—"What do you mean? How can this happen?" It might even lead to other conversations, maybe even an informal appointment, a Bible study group, or just to the suggestion that they read the story themselves and see if it helps or stimulates any other questions they would like to explore. Can you think of any types of people who might fit this story?

Rich Young Ruler—This story shows up with slight variations in Matthew 19:16-30; Mark 10:17-31; and Luke 18:18-30. The rich young ruler is from an influential family, doesn't lack for much in life, and has some degree of spiritual sensitivity. But Jesus reminds him that his perspective of what is good is quite shallow. Even the young man's question, "Teacher, what good deed must I do to have eternal life?" reveals that he believes some form of doing good will earn him eternal life. Maybe he could provide an endowment, set up a hospital, or contribute to a special project?

Jesus clarifies that goodness begins with how we live in relationship to God and others. The rich young ruler replies that he has done that since he was a kid. Looking at him with great love (Mark 10:21), Jesus reveals the real barrier between the young man and God: money. Will he let go of what he really worships to find the One who alone is worth having? The young man had the chance of a lifetime, but he decided to forego the possession of eternal life, choosing instead the possessions of a good life.

Are eternal life and a good life here on earth mutually exclusive? Maybe not, but we cannot serve both. Which life is more important to you? Jesus tells his disciples after the young man leaves, "How hard it will be for those who have wealth to enter the kingdom of God!" (Mark 10:23). What situations or people come to mind as you reflect on this story?

Stories for Every Occasion—As we read the Bible, looking for ways we might be more engaging and effective as witnesses, stories jump out at us page after page. There's the story of the paralytic whose friends stopped at nothing to give him an opportunity to be healed by Jesus (Luke 5:17-26). And immediately following is the story of Jesus' encounter with Matthew and his friends (Luke 5:27-39). What about the man who had been ill for thirty-eight years and complained that no one would help him when he really needed it (John 5:1-15). Jesus asks him, "Do you want to be made well?" I like the short story about Joanna, who is mentioned in only two verses (Luke 8:3 and 24:10), but think of all that lies behind her story. She is the wife of an influential man (King Herod's treasurer), but she leaves her easy life and follows Jesus all the way.

The Bible is filled with stories of all kinds of people encountering the holy presence of God and being called on to make choices. Our privilege as witnesses is to help clarify the story of God's love and saving grace for those we encounter along the trail and to point them to Jesus, who helps them make the ultimate choice of life.

Q5
What kinds of people in what kinds of situations might best be candidates for the story of the rich young ruler?

_____

_____

_____

_____

_____

_____

_____

_____

_____

_____

Our ultimate aim is to help seekers understand that their problems in life, whatever they may be, cannot be solved unless they first resolve their bigger problem: getting their relationship with God right. But if we don't first listen carefully to their story, it will be difficult to draw their attention toward hearing God's story.[36]

Rebecca Pippert

Camp Notes

Moving On

We're almost there. One week to go. It's hard to believe, but in the next few days we'll reach the summit. It's time to look back over all the ground we've covered and evaluate the things that have happened and the lessons we've learned. Then we'll gather at the top, enjoy the view, and think about where we are to go from there. Have a great week.

READING ASSIGNMENTS

1. Review the notes in your *My Witness Journal* for Trails Four and Five. Decide which Bible passages and which action assignments will be most helpful to you as you continue to learn more about your Christian faith and about being a witness.
2. Make some notes in your *My Witness Journal* to recall your *Witness* journey. What have you discovered about God and the gospel? What new things have you discovered about being a witness? What changes would you like to help bring about in your church to make your church a more effective witness? What do you still need help with as you become a more effective witness?
3. Read the chapter for next week (pages 147–51). Underline or highlight special thoughts and answer the questions in the Q boxes.

ACTION ASSIGNMENT

Listen for God's voice. Think about what commitments God is calling you to make that demonstrate that you are ready to follow the Spirit's lead as a living witness.

See you on top.

Partners With God

Prayer

Lord, make me an instrument of thy peace;
where there is hatred, let me sow love;
where there is injury, pardon;
where there is doubt, faith;
where there is despair, hope;
where there is darkness, light;
and where there is sadness, joy.

O Divine Master,
grant that I may not so much seek
to be consoled as to console;
to be understood, as to understand;
to be loved, as to love;
for it is in giving that we receive,
it is in pardoning that we are pardoned,
and it is in dying that we are born to eternal life.[37]
                                    Francis of Assisi

Trail Talk

Twenty-four weeks ago we began an adventure together in what for many of us seemed like a journey into the wilderness. God led Abraham and Sarah from their comfortable and long-established home into the wilderness. Jacob met the God of Abraham and Isaac in the wilderness. And the God of Abraham, Isaac, and Jacob spoke to Moses out of a burning bush in the wilderness. Elijah encountered God in the wilderness. Jesus, led by the Holy Spirit, entered the wilderness to prepare for his work as God's ultimate witness, the Messiah, the Christ.

Wadi suggests to us that the wilderness is a place of power, hope, and grace, a place where a future can be given and God calls our name. How would you describe what has happened to you over these weeks on the *Witness* journey? Have you found new strength? Have you discovered a new future? Have you sensed the presence and power of God?

This is our last campfire on this phase of our journey as witnesses. The months of discipline and determination have paid off. I hope you feel a sense of accomplishment; but more than that, I hope you are aware that in many ways you are not the same person who picked up the workbook and journal six months ago. It is my prayer that you have found new heights and depths in your faith and have grown closer to God and to those on your team. But most importantly, I pray that as you move beyond this *Witness* experience, you will have a greater sense of excitement and confidence. I pray that what you have experienced and learned will help you become living witnesses to the God of love in your everday world.

The wilderness is a place of power, hope, and grace. It is a place where the past can be erased and a future given. In the wilderness a burning-bush experience can take place where God calls our names, fulfilling our deepest desires and bringing life to a cracked and dry soul.

Bright and early I got up for the drive to Katahdin, the last mountain. When our shuttle to the mountain reached the Baxter State Park front gate, a park ranger stuck her head in the van and said, "You do know that the mountain is closed, don't you?"

When we were all out of the van with packs on, another ranger pulled up to tell us again that the mountain was closed and that a rescue operation started at $3,400 an hour just for the

(continued on page 148)

Camp Notes

helicopter..., but it was our only weather window before more snow was to come in.

Perma-Grin said she had hiked several mountains in Colorado, and that this was tougher by far. It took the full body to get up this mountain. This was my final exam to see what I had learned. I can see why the rangers were stern with us.

Wadi

Exercise 1

Talk about your reflections over Trails Four and Five. Note what others found helpful.

_____

_____

_____

_____

Exercise 2

Talk about the most important things you have learned about God and the gospel. Note others' answers.

_____

_____

_____

_____

Remembering

The Bible is full of reminders to God's people to remember.
— "Remember the sabbath day, and keep it holy" (Exodus 20:8).
— "When the LORD your God has brought you into the land that he swore to your ancestors,…take care that you do not forget the LORD, who brought you out of the land of Egypt, out of the house of slavery" (Deuteronomy 6:10, 12).
— "He is the LORD our God; his judgments are in all the earth. Remember his covenant forever, the word that he commanded, for a thousand generations" (1 Chronicles 16:14-15).
— "The steadfast love of the LORD is from everlasting to everlasting on those who fear him, and his righteousness to children's children, to those who keep his covenant and remember to do his commandments" (Psalm 103:17-18).
— "Then he took a loaf of bread, and when he had given thanks, he broke it and gave it to them, saying, 'This is my body, which is given for you. Do this in remembrance of me'" (Luke 22:19).
— "Go therefore and make disciples of all nations, baptizing them in the name of the Father and of the Son and of the Holy Spirit, and teaching them to obey everything that I have commanded you. And remember, I am with you always, to the end of the age" (Matthew 28:19-20).

To remember means to attach again our experience to an event in the past. Sometimes this can be painful and even destructive. God therefore promises in the new covenant not to remember our sins of the past (Jeremiah 31:34). Neither should we, for in Christ they have been forgiven and nailed to the cross (1 Peter 2:24). "There is therefore now no condemnation for those who are in Christ Jesus" (Romans 8:1).

But there are many things we must remember. To forget is to live without the benefit of what it means to be fully human. Any of us who have lived with Alzheimer's patients, or others who have lost their ability to remember, know how much our whole identity is wrapped up in memory. Thus we are told that to be God's faithful children, we must **remember**.

This week has been a week for remembering all that God has been teaching us by the Spirit and the word. What have you been remembering?

Refocusing

I have discovered a couple things about vision as I've gotten older. First, even if you have had good eyes for the first forty years of your life, there comes a time when if you want to see the details up close, you need to take advantage of the enormous benefit of glasses. And even with good eyes or glasses, some form of magnification is wonderful if you want to enjoy the game on the field from the top row of a seventy-thousand-seat stadium.

These weeks on the *Witness* journey have been for many of you a time of discovering that there were things to see that you had never imagined. Perhaps you weren't even aware that your sight was less than twenty-twenty. Or maybe everything you could see was in perfect focus, but now it's like someone has just given you your first pair of binoculars.

Regardless of the metaphor, the result is that you can now see many things previously beyond your view. You have already told about some of the most important things you've learned about God and the gospel; now tell what you've discovered about being Christ's witness.

Second, I've learned that as I get older it takes longer for my eyes to adjust as I move from one focusing context to another. This adjusting seems especially noticeable after spending hours reading a book or in front of a computer screen and then trying to read the signs down the hall or out the window. (Of course, as we grow older all kinds of things we used to take for granted require a few more adjustments.)

This process of regaining my long-distance focus after hours of close-up work is particularly challenging when I'm driving the highway. It's not that I'm in any real danger, but it requires more effort to read signs that I can easily read when my eyes are rested and not in the near-sighted mode.

Something akin to this may be happening to you in the weeks ahead. You've been part of a group focusing on the up-close and personal. Week after week you've had the support of your group as you've talked and prayed and read both the lines and between the lines. Now you're about ready to head out onto the highway, and your vision will need to refocus. It may require a little adjusting.

For example, as you reflect on your own growth as Christ's witness, you may realize that it's going to be different without the workbook assignments and the group meeting every week. Likewise, you may have discovered some things as an individual or as a group that could help strengthen your congregation's witness in your community or in the world. But knowing how, where, when, and to whom to tell these things may take some more thought and prayer. Refocusing for the highway view can feel awfully intimidating. Surely the disciples must have felt some of this when Jesus told them, "It is to your advantage that I go away, for if I do not go away, the Advocate will not come to you; but if I go, I will send him to you" (John 16:7).

Remembering the reality of "I am with you always" is part of our refocusing. And realizing that we are members one of another in the body of Christ means we ought always to feel free to call on one another for prayer, for counsel, and for encouragement. In fact, some of you may already see one another regularly in another group. Or you may decide to continue to meet as part of this group in some regular fashion to study and pray. These are some of the decisions involved in refocusing.

Talk about what you have learned about being a witness. Note others' answers.

Talk about what you still need help with as a witness. Note others' answers. Would you like to meet again to maintain the momentum?

Talk about the changes you want to help bring to your church. Look for patterns and partners as you listen to others. Do you want to plan a time to meet with your pastor to discuss these things?

Camp Notes

I talked with several people on the way up who came to me saying, "I hear you went to a seminary. Are you going to be a priest?" I don't know how my secret got out, but I thought it was funny that people wanted to talk with me about God, even while going up the last mountain.

Wadi

Exercise 6

List one or more refuturing commitments you are ready to make as you leave this *Witness* experience behind and move ahead with the Holy Spirit to more boldly and joyfully be Christ's disciple.

_____

_____

_____

_____

_____

_____

_____

Refuturing

Refuturing is a strange word; but in light of what we've been exploring, this *Witness* trek has been an exercise in refuturing. Perhaps we could use the term *revisioning*. But to revise or to undergo revision usually means changing something already in place. And it's my guess that you are beginning to see future options for your life and your congregation that were not in place before we started.

All of us have a certain frame of reference we think of as our future. Most of us expect things to turn out well. Therefore, we don't feel a great need to invest much energy in the proverbial ounce of prevention, or in planning. But occasionally things happen—an illness, an unexpected blessing, or a setback—that make us pause and take stock. You might say these are moments for *re*-futuring.

What has been happening during these weeks that has moved you to reconsider how you are going to invest in your future as Christ's witness? What new resolves or commitments are you going to make as you reflect on the last six months of your life? The end of the trail we have called *Witness* is upon us, but our whole reason for this investment has been to become better equipped for the real journey—day by day, week by week, year by year faithfulness and fruitfulness as living witnesses for God and the gospel.

What have you learned (1) about daily Bible reading, prayer, and journaling that you want to invest in your future? (2) about being bolder in deeds of grace-filled love and in conversations with family, friends, and even strangers? (3) about being a good listener and offering a word of hope and the gospel of salvation? (4) about your unique SHAPE and place in the body of Christ? (5) about the needs of your world and God's mission around the corner and across the seas? Your answers to these questions are gifts of the Spirit for a new future for you and for your congregation.

All of us have been called to be Christ's witnesses today. As Jesus reminded his early disciples when he was speaking to them at their last evening together:

> *I am the true vine, and my Father is the vinegrower.... Every branch that bears fruit he prunes to make it bear more fruit. You have already been cleansed by the word that I have spoken to you. Abide in me as I abide in you. Just as the branch cannot bear fruit by itself unless it abides in the vine, neither can you unless you abide in me.... I have said these things to you so that my joy may be in you, and that your joy may be complete.... You did not choose me but I chose you. And I appointed you to go and bear fruit, fruit that will last.*
> *(John 15:1-4, 11, 16)*

Moving On

On August 6, 1755, John Wesley recorded the following in his journal:

> *I mentioned to our congregation in London a means of increasing serious religion, which had been frequently practised by our fore-fathers, the joining in a covenant to serve God with all our heart and with all our soul.... On Monday at six in the evening we met for that purpose... All the people stood up, in token of assent, to the number of about eighteen hundred. Such a night I scarce ever knew before. Surely the fruit of it shall remain for ever.*[38]

Wesley's Covenant Renewal Service has been kept in churches around the world for about 250 years. May the words of this covenant prayer in the Wesleyan tradition always be yours.

> *I am no longer my own, but thine.*
> *Put me to what thou wilt, rank me with whom thou wilt.*
> *Put me to doing, put me to suffering.*
> *Let me be employed by thee or laid aside for thee,*
> *exalted for thee or brought low for thee.*
> *Let me be full, let me be empty.*
> *Let me have all things, let me have nothing.*
> *I freely and heartily yield all things*
> *to thy pleasure and disposal.*
> *And now, O glorious and blessed God,*
> *Father, Son, and Holy Spirit,*
> *thou art mine, and I am thine. So be it.*
> *And the covenant which I have made on earth,*
> *let it be ratified in heaven.*[39]
>
> *Amen.*

Stay on the trail. Bear witness. Be fruitful. Live in joy.

When I got to within one mile of the summit, I hit the flatland, which made the end feel like a sprint. There was a crowd of people getting pictures taken with the summit sign...and lots of cheers and congratulations. I am done. I am ready for something new and the time to reflect on this journey. Distance will help me see the whole picture, and that will possibly help me understand the next step God wants me to take. God was always faithful to me, and I was faithful to stay on the trail. I pray that I may always have the obedience to follow God's leading, an open heart and mind to learn, and ears to hear his voice.

Ken (Wadi)

Endnotes

1 From *The Unshakable Kingdom and the Unchanging Person*, by E. Stanley Jones; page 75. © 1972 Abingdon Press. Used by permission.

2 From "A Plain Account of the People Called Methodists," in *The Works of John Wesley*, Volume 9, edited by Rupert E. Davies; page 254. © 1989 Abingdon Press. Used by permission.

3 From "O For a Thousand Tongues to Sing," words by Charles Wesley, in *The United Methodist Hymnal*, 57. Used by permission.

4 From "The Lord's Prayer" (from The Ritual of the Former Methodist Church), in *The United Methodist Hymnal*, 895. Used by permission.

5 From Baptismal Covenant II, in *The United Methodist Hymnal*, 40. © 1976, 1980, 1985, 1989 The United Methodist Publishing House. Used by permission.

6 From "What a Friend We Have in Jesus," words by Joseph M. Scriven, in *The United Methodist Hymnal*, 526. Used by permission.

7 From "Spirit of the Living God," words by Daniel Iverson. © 1935, 1963 Birdwing Music. All rights administered by EMI Christian Music Publishing. Used by permission.

8 From "Joyful, Joyful, We Adore Thee," words by Henry Van Dyke, in *The United Methodist Hymnal*, 89. Used by permission.

9 From "This Is My Father's World," words by Maltbie D. Babcock, in *The United Methodist Hymnal*, 144. Used by permission.

10 From "Sinners, Turn: Why Will You Die," words by Charles Wesley, in *The United Methodist Hymnal*, 346. Used by permission.

11 From "Spirit of the Living God," words by Daniel Iverson. © 1935, 1963 Birdwing Music. All rights administered by EMI Christian Music Publishing. Used by permission.

12 From "A Farther Appeal to Men of Reason and Religion," in *The Works of John Wesley*, Volume 11, edited by Gerald R. Cragg; page 108. © 1975 Oxford University Press. Used by permission of Abingdon Press.

13 From "Journal From February 1, 1738, to August 12, 1738," journal entry on May 24, 1738, by John Wesley.

14 From *Here I Stand: A Life of Martin Luther*, by Roland H. Bainton; page 65. © 1950 Abingdon Press. Used by permission.

15 From Sermon 141, "On the Holy Spirit," by John Wesley. Used by permission.

16 From "A Farther Appeal to Men of Reason and Religion," by John Wesley. Used by permission.

17 From "The Character of a Methodist," in *The Works of John Wesley*, Volume 9, edited by Rupert E. Davies; pages 35, 37. © 1989 Abingdon Press. Used by permission.

18 From "The Character of a Methodist," in *The Works of John Wesley*, Volume 9, edited by Rupert E. Davies; page 41. © 1989 Abingdon Press. Used by permission.

19 From "Love Divine, All Loves Excelling," words by Charles Wesley, in *The United Methodist Hymnal*, 384. Used by permission.

20 Words by Thomas Toke Lynch, in *Hymns and Psalms: A Methodist and Ecumenical Hymn Book* (London: Methodist Publishing House, 1983). Used by permission.

21 From "Day of Pentecost," words by Laurence Hull Stookey, in *The United Methodist Hymnal*, 542. © 1989 The United Methodist Publishing House. Used by permission.

22 From "O Spirit of the Living God," words by Henry H. Tweedy, in *The United Methodist Hymnal*, 539. Used by permission.

23 From "An Earnest Appeal to Men of Reason and Religion," in *The Works of John Wesley*, Volume 11, edited by Gerald R. Cragg; page 45. © 1975 Oxford University Press. Used by permission of Abingdon Press.

24 From *The Unchurched: Who They Are and Why They Stay Away*, by J. Russell Hale; pages 156–59. © 1980 by J. Russell Hale. Used by permission of HarperCollins Publishers, Inc.

25 From "Where Cross the Crowded Ways of Life," words by Frank Mason North, in *The United Methodist Hymnal*, 427. Used by permission.

26 From *A New Eusebius: Documents Illustrative of the History of the Church to A.D. 337*, edited by J. Stevenson; pages 58–59. © 1963 SPCK, London. Used by permission.

27 From *The Living Reminder: Service and Prayer in Memory of Jesus Christ*, by Henri J.M. Nouwen; page 29. © 1977 The Seabury Press. Used by permission of HarperCollins Publishers, Inc.

28 Both Discipleship Resources and The Upper Room have a wide variety of books and resources as well as staff available to assist you in learning to employ these disciplines for Christian growth and service. Discipleship Resources: 800-685-4370 or http://www.discipleshipresources.org. The Upper Room: 800-972-0433 or http://bookstore.upperroom.org.

29 From *Walden*, by Henry David Thoreau. Used by permission.

30 From "The Lord's Prayer" (from The Ritual of the Former Methodist Church), in *The United Methodist Hymnal*, 895. Used by permission.

31 *Christians at Work: Not Business as Usual,* by Jan Wood (Scottdale, PA: Herald Press, 1999).

32 This story is told in more detail in *The Contagious Witness: Exploring Christian Conversion,* by Ron Crandall (Nashville: Abingdon Press, 1999), pages 101–2, 145–46.

33 See *101 Hymn Stories,* by Kenneth Osbeck (Grand Rapids, MI: Kregel Publishers, 1982), pages 109–10.

34 From "I Love to Tell the Story," words by Katherine Hankey, in *The United Methodist Hymnal,* 156. Used by permission.

35 Reprinted from *Bridge to Life,* © 1956 by The Navigators. Used by permission of NavPress, Colorado Springs, CO. All rights reserved.

36 From *Out of the Salt Shaker and Into the World: Evangelism as a Way of Life,* by Rebecca Manley Pippert; page 213. © 1999 InterVarsity Press. Used by permission.

37 From "The Prayer of Saint Francis," by Francis of Assisi, in *The United Methodist Hymnal,* 481. Used by permission.

38 From "A Short History of the People Called Methodists," in *The Works of John Wesley,* Volume 9, edited by Rupert E. Davies; page 461. © 1989 Abingdon Press. Used by permission.

39 From "A Covenant Prayer in the Wesleyan Tradition," in *The United Methodist Hymnal,* 607. Used by permission.

Trail Guide for Leaders

Welcome *to a great adventure, and thank you for accepting the responsibility of being a trail guide and group leader for **Witness: Exploring and Sharing Your Christian Faith.***

We have looked forward to this moment for a long time, and we hope you have too. Our goal in this "Trail Guide for Leaders" is to provide all you will need to successfully help your *Witness* group and your whole congregation find a new sense of excitement and effectiveness in living as Christ's witnesses today.

You may be feeling less than fully qualified as a trail guide in such an undertaking. Maybe you are thinking, *I'm not the witness I want to be, so how can I lead a group on this challenging adventure?*

Well, welcome to the team. Probably none of us feels completely qualified to be an instrument of God for the calling that is ours as witnesses. With Moses we say, "Who am I that I should go?" (Exodus 3:11). But the Lord's answer to Moses is one for us as well, and it is the same promise Jesus gave his disciples: "I will be with you" (Exodus 3:12; Matthew 28:20). In fact, we believe you will sense God's presence and guidance over the next few months in ways you may never have experienced before. We also trust that those in your group and others in your congregation will have a new experience of God's presence as well.

So, again, welcome to a great adventure and a time of growth in discipleship. The Lord himself has selected you and will be with you as you walk this trail and guide others in the weekly group sessions we call Trail Talk.

The Trail

As you have already noticed, the overarching theme of *Witness* is being thru-hikers, like those on the Appalachian Trail. This image is clarified for the entire group in the Orientation Session. There are many similarities between the twenty-four weeks that follow the Orientation on the adventure called *Witness* and the long-term commitment required from those who would succeed as thru-hikers on our nation's longest hiking trail. If you are interested in gathering more background information on hiking or on the Appalachian Trail, check with your local library or bookstore. You can also find information on the Internet by searching for "Appalachian Trail" or by going to the Appalachian Trail Home Page (http://www.fred.net/kathy/at.html) or to the special site for thru-hikers (http://www.trailplace.com). Finally, you might consider inviting someone familiar with hiking to come and speak briefly to your group during the Orientation Session. Any or all of these resources can help set the stage for the adventure and remind your *Witness* group that discoveries are around every bend for those who will gear up and set out as thru-hikers with the Lord.

Getting Ready to Lead

All who are invited to consider this adventure deserve an opportunity to fully understand what lies ahead before embarking on the trail. The first group meeting, the Orientation Session, is designed to present this overview. It gives potential group members a chance to decide if they are ready to get started or if they would rather wait for another group. Certainly most who attend this hikers' Orientation will be interested enough to make a commitment to begin the journey. However, it is important to remind everyone that the commitment to the *Witness* experience is to being a thru-hiker, not a day-hiker.

Participants need to know that anyone is permitted to drop out along the way, but we would ask them to tell the group their decision and be sent off on their new path with a prayer and the blessing of the group.

As you prepare to lead the Orientation Session, turn the page to find some suggestions about things you will need to do.

1. **Have an adequate ratio of trail guides to group members.** *Witness*, like any small-group format, is best experienced with about four to ten people in each group. If twelve or more people are interested in committing to the experience, plan for two groups. This decision will provide for the most rewarding level of interaction during the weekly Trail Talk meetings.

2. **Read through the Orientation Session in the workbook.** In order to be familiar with the content and the flow of this first session, read through the material at least twice. You will also want to be familiar with the basic format of the whole program and generally what is required weekly regarding Bible readings, prayer, and action assignments.

3. **Prepare the room where you will meet.** You may wish to have light refreshments—coffee, tea, cookies, and so forth—as people arrive or during a break. If all who gather will not know one another, provide nametags.

Arrange the chairs so that all will be in a circle or as visible to one another as possible.

4. **Prepare the materials needed.** You will need a workbook and a *My Witness Journal* for each person and extra pens or pencils. Plan to have marking pens and nametags if they are needed, at least one Bible, the *Witness* video and the equipment needed to use it, and any materials on hiking or the Appalachian Trail you wish to display.

5. **Prepare yourself in prayer.** Pray for each person who will be attending, by name if you know who will be coming. Pray that each one will sense God's Spirit leading him or her to be thoroughly committed to this undertaking. Pray that there will be a sense of excitement and that your own leadership will be directed and inspired by God. Pray that the presence of Jesus, who promised to join wherever two or three gathered in his name, will be recognized; and that his name and purpose will be honored in this endeavor.

The Orientation Session

(Following the flexible time allotments indicated for a group of fewer than twelve people, you should be able to finish this Orientation Session in about one and a half hours.)

1. Introductions (20 minutes)

- Introduce yourself and explain that you will be leading the Orientation Session and serving as the group leader for this adventure known as *Witness: Exploring and Sharing Your Christian Faith.*

- Tell about one person who has been an important Christian witness in your life. Be sure to tell what it was about that person that made a lasting impact on you.

- Ask each of the group members to introduce him or herself by name and to follow your lead in (a) naming an important Christian witness in his or her life and (b) explaining briefly why this person's witness was important. You may go around the circle or recognize people as they are ready to speak.

- Suggest that the goal of the *Witness* journey is to enable all of us to become more like those we have just described and to help every local congregation to become more intentional and more effective as communities of Christian witness and evangelism.

2. The Video (5 minutes)

- Tell the group members to sit back and watch a video that will tell them more about what they will be doing during the course of this study. Then show the portion of the video for the Orientation, "Accepting a Challenge."

3. The Workbook (60 minutes)
Plan for 45 minutes plus a 15-minute break.

- Give each person a copy of the *Witness* workbook and a *My Witness Journal.* Give the group a moment to look at and become familiar with the books. Briefly tell the group about any other materials you have brought for display.

- Ask if there are any hikers in your group who would like to give a brief (2 to 3 minutes) testimony of the lessons learned and inspiration gained along the trail.

- Offer a personal word about your own response to this image, and explain how *Witness* uses the thru-hiker theme and journal entries from Ken to color the journey with Jesus and one another.

- Call the group members' attention to the invitation to "be stretched and challenged to discover more of who you really are" (first paragraph, page 6). Point out the **Q1** box in the side column. Explain that Q boxes throughout the workbook will form part of the group discussion. If you have time, use this first Q box now (about 15 to 20 minutes: 3 minutes for private reflection, 7 minutes for discussing in pairs, and 5 to 10 minutes for letting volunteers tell their stories to the whole group). If you do not have time, move ahead.

- Read the Acts 4:13 passage from the side column on page 6 and Luke 24:13-35 from a Bible. Perhaps a group member will be willing to read this Bible story of the two disciples walking with Jesus on the road to Emmaus. Point out that although it was late and they were tired, after they realized they had been with the risen Lord along the trail, the two disciples "got up and returned to Jerusalem" (seven miles!) and full of energy began to witness to their friends (verse 29). Explain that this is the excitement you want the group to experience along the trail with Jesus.

- Point out that the lines and space in the Camp Notes column provide a place for them to jot down their own or others' thoughts and answers.

- Move ahead to "Preparing for the Journey" (page 7). Explain the idea of the five trails, each involving four or six weeks of hiking.

- Then read the question asking for their expectations (**Q2**). Begin by telling about your own expectations (or hopes and fears) and your motivation for leading the team. Remind the other members of the group that you are a thru-hiker with them. You will not be teaching them, but all of you will be learning together. This is an important time of sharing. Help each one participate (10 to 15 minutes).

- Move next to the information about equipment needed for the journey. Explain that most of the Scripture passages quoted in the workbook will be from the New Revised Standard Version (NRSV), but that any version of the Bible they wish to use is OK.

- Read the information about disciplines, and answer any questions that are asked.

- Establish the schedule and meeting place, making sure everyone is able to attend without conflict. If you will not be meeting on particular days or weeks, or if you will be meeting in a different location, include these exceptions.

- Read through the "Getting Started" section. Explain the basic model of weekly assignments. There will be reading assignments, including daily Bible readings, journaling, and preparing for next week's session. There will also be a weekly action assignment.

- Let the group take a moment to look at the *My Witness Journal*. Explain that this book is where they will write their thoughts and ideas during their weekly Bible study. It is also where they will keep notes about their action assignments.

- If you have time (about 15 minutes), ask the group members to answer the question about God's purpose (**Q3**). They can then talk about their answers as a lead-in to Trail One. If there is not enough time to answer **Q3** together, ask the group to include this question in their assignments for next week.

- Remind the participants that if they have questions about *Witness* or their commitment to it, you are available after the meeting or during the week. Let everyone know the best times and locations (phone numbers or e-mail) to reach you with any questions they may have. Announce how they are to pay for their workbooks (unless the church is providing them without charge).

4. Closing Prayer (5 minutes)

Close this time together in prayer, using any method you desire. A brief closing prayer offered by you is probably best— thankful for the time together, for the invitation by Jesus to walk with him and witness for him, and for the privilege of growing together in the weeks ahead.

General Guidance for Sessions 2–25

As a trail guide, you will be responsible for preparing each week for the in-camp group time. Generally, each meeting will follow a common pattern:

- **an opening prayer, song, or statement of faith;**
- **discussion about the week's reading and action assignments;**
- **review and discussion of the ideas in the chapter read for the week;**
- **discussion of any assignments in Q boxes or other exercises;**
- **review of any announcements and assignments for the week to come;**
- **a closing time of prayer and/or song.**

Here are some general guidelines to help you organize the session time each week.

VIDEOS

Seven video segments introduce the goals during the Orientation Session, introduce the new theme at the beginning of each of the five trails, and wrap up the last session with a challenge to become more-effective witnesses for Jesus Christ.

OPENING

The early weeks will have a printed prayer or other guidance for how to begin the group session. As time goes by, less structure will be provided, and there will be more flexibility for prayer focused on specific needs and opportunities. You may wish to invite members to volunteer each week to bring a devotional thought or song to begin your time together.

SCRIPTURE READINGS

Six days of assigned Bible readings are included for each week in the *My Witness Journal*. These weekly assignments require that each person set aside time each day to read and reflect on the Bible passages assigned and to pray for him or herself, the church, and the people with him or her on the trail. This spiritual discipline will probably take 20 to 30 minutes a day. Participants will also need to read the information in the session to be discussed at the next camp time and to take notes on the additional Bible references that appear in the workbook material. This reading is probably best done a little at a time along with the other Bible readings, but some may prefer to do it all at one time. Our goal is not keeping rules but building disciplines for growth and staying on the trail as thru-

hikers. As the trail guide, you will be responsible for leading the Trail Talk time (10 to 15 minutes). You will guide the discussion, asking for any special insights that emerged from the assigned daily readings related to the theme of the week.

ACTION ASSIGNMENTS

The action assignments begin with listening exercises, recognizing that being a witness starts with knowing God and the hearts of people. Along the trail more action and verbal witnessing becomes the norm, as well as intentional prayer for the people the Spirit leads us to as witnesses. Eventually, the action assignments involve telling one's own faith story and the gospel to others. Some attention is also given to action assignments aimed at discovering the congregation's investment in evangelism. Your response will be to ask for any insights that emerged from the action assignments. The time given to these two aspects of the Trail Talk (reading and action assignments) will vary from week to week, but normally no more than 30 minutes (one-third of the time together) should be given to it. If you need to, remind your fellow hikers that not everything needs to be clear from the beginning. There is still more to come around the bend and over the next hill.

THE WEEKLY THEME

Each week a new theme is explored. After the discussion of reading and action assignments, offer a brief summary of the chapter material. Then ask for any special discoveries or aha's that emerged along the trail as people read the chapter. You may wish to highlight these as you review each section. Next, move on to any exercises or Q boxes related to the chapter. Additional discussion may emerge naturally from the related paragraphs as you deal with these exercises and Q boxes. You may decide to spend extra time on an item of particular interest to you or to the group. That is an appropriate and often helpful choice, but remember to keep track of the clock and leave adequate time to finish up the meeting with announcements and a closing prayer.

MOVING ON

Usually, this is a simple matter of making announcements and reviewing the coming week's assignments. Guidance is provided each week. Special prayer requests are also always appropriate.

Session 2: Biblical Images of God's Purpose, Vista One

(This week's Trail Guide is more detailed than those for later sessions. Helping the group feel comfortable and free to tell what they have been learning is at the heart of your leadership. Many of the instructions and suggestions for this session will be useful for later gatherings as well. Keep notes. Try some of your own ideas. Take it a step at a time.)

Prayer—Read the opening prayer together out loud as you begin. Notice especially the final phrase "You show me the path of life." Remind your group how appropriate this image is for *Witness* as we walk the path of life together with Jesus. You may expand this opening prayer time by asking your group if there were any special answers to prayer this week, or how they did at keeping faithful in praying for one another and for the congregation.

Trail Talk—Start the Trail Talk section by reading Ken's journal entry in the side column. Then tell the handle (trail name) that you have selected for yourself, explaining the meaning of the name (**Q1**). Ask each person to tell about his or her special identity. Make sure the participants write down the trail names of others in the group. If some have not yet managed to select a handle, acknowledge that it is not an easy task. Tell them that choosing a name will continue to be an assignment each week until everyone has one.

Next, move to the questions in the Trail Talk section: "What adventures have you had?" and/or "What dangers and delights have you encountered on the trail?" There is no need to go around the circle, but make sure everyone who wishes has a chance to offer a brief witness here.

Move on to reporting on reading assignment notes from the *My Witness Journal.* Ask everyone to offer one or two insights discovered as they read the daily Bible passages about God's design and purpose for creation and for humanity. It will be helpful while the group is still getting acquainted for you to lead with your answers and then go around the circle. Make sure each speaker remembers to clarify the day, the chapter, and the verse to which he or she is referring. If you did not complete **Q3** from the Orientation Session (page 8), let the participants read and compare their answers from last week with this week's answers in **Q2**.

Read the three questions in the text regarding the action assignment and report your own results. For variety, go the other way around the circle, or ask participants to talk in the order of their birthdays (month/day). This kind of ice breaker can get people talking and help everyone get better acquainted.

Before moving on, ask if anyone would like to tell a short campfire story of how he or she came to discover more of the path of life and God's purpose.

Video—Show the video segment for Trail One. Explain that there will be a short video at the beginning of each trail to introduce the theme of the trail. Note that the first trail is "Exploring God's Purpose."

Trail Markers—Emphasize again the theme of God's purpose and read the key words listed: *shalom, salvation,* and *eternal life.* Recall any other key words they have recorded in **Q2**.

Shalom—Tell any special insights you gained from the examination of peace as God's ultimate purpose. What did others find especially interesting or challenging in this overarching Bible theme of God's purpose (**Q3**)? Did any in the group do additional research on the concept of *shalom?* Who were the people named as examples of witnesses to this gospel of peace (**Q3**)? How would our lives be different if we were more active witnesses to this gospel of peace (*shalom*)?

Salvation—Ask how many already knew the meaning of the sign of the fish. It was one of the earliest forms of Christian art. In times of persecution, Christians would identify one another simply by drawing the outline of this symbol in the dust and thus know they were "one in the Spirit" and claimed Jesus both as God's Son and Savior. Several extra Bible passages were referred to in this section. Ask for any new insights discovered or any favorite passages about salvation. Let one or two volunteers read a favorite passage, and/or ask someone to read aloud Ephesians 2:1-10.

Moving On—Review the highlights of your first camp gathering. Clarify the assignments for next week. Remind everyone to continue to pray for one another out on the trail. Close in prayer, perhaps reciting together again Psalm 16 (page 10). You may want to close the session by saying, "See you on the path!"

Session 3: Biblical Images of God's Purpose, Vista Two

Prayer—A prayer from Psalm 25 is provided, but feel free to add other ingredients, such as (1) telling about answers to prayer from the week or (2) selecting prayer partners (trail companions). Trail companions might meet as pairs for 5 minutes at the start of each week's camp time to talk together and pray for each other.

Trail Talk—Use the questions in the text to prompt group discussion about the reading and action assignments. Note: For this reporting, you may wish to keep the group together. Or you may wish to divide the group into twos, threes, or in half. If you divide into groups, ask everyone to come back together after 15 minutes for group discussion about the assignments. Throughout the remainder of *Witness*, use variety and your own creativity to open this initial period of reporting. About a third of your group time together will be focused on this Trail Talk reflection.

Eternal Life—You may wish to read or recite the Apostles' Creed as a way to get started. Then ask **Q1**. Make sure to emphasize that eternal life is not primarily a time or place but a relationship with the eternal God (John 17:3). Discuss **Q2**.

New Covenant—Ask group members to tell about what they underlined or highlighted in this section. Emphasize the promise in the Isaiah 46:9-10 passage. Notice that covenant is about relationships, not just rules or laws from the beginning of the Bible. Discuss answers to **Q3** and focus on Ezekiel 36:26-27. Make it clear that the new *testament* is the new *covenant*. What's new? How did Jesus accomplish this new covenant?

Glory—Ask if they had considered before that the purpose of God was related to God's glory. Help them see the vista of the earth "full of the glory of God." What would that look like? Jesus is the light and we are the light. How does a dark world become light? Ask **Q4**. How does the 2 Corinthians 3 passage (Day 4) help connect the new covenant with glory?

The Kingdom—Notice that speaking about the Kingdom is high on Jesus' teaching agenda, both before his death (Matthew 6:19-33; 13:44-52) and after his death and resurrection (Acts 1:3). Paul also teaches about the Kingdom right up until the end of his life (Acts 28:30-31). Ask **Q5** and

Q6. What are the witness implications of God's purpose as "Christlikeness universalized"?

Moving On—Pray the Lord's Prayer with different people praying one phrase at a time. Join together with "for thine is the kingdom, and the power, and the glory, forever. Amen."

Session 4: The Human Problem: Sin

Prayer—Begin as you wish, giving a few minutes to trail companions (see "Prayer" in Session 3 on this page) or some kind of group sharing. Finish by praying together aloud the selection from Psalm 51.

Trail Talk—It may be best to keep the whole group together for talking about notes and lessons from the week's assignments. Then divide the group into dyads (twos) or triads (threes) to answer the three questions in the Exercise (page 22). Bring the group together again, and ask if any special insights emerged that would be helpful for all to hear.

Sin Is Serious—Start with **Q1**. (If any are struggling with the concept of what sin is, allow some discussion; but then affirm that an understanding of sin's destructiveness is central to the biblical message.) Ask if the images of a defiled heart or "wellspring of one's desires" help to clarify sin's seriousness. Is there any special underlining or highlighting in this section from the week's reading?

Sin Distorts and Destroys—Ask and discuss **Q2** and **Q3**. Are there several interesting definitions of sin, or do most agree on a common definition? Are there any special highlights from the week's reading?

Sin's Solution—Ask and discuss the answers to **Q4**.

Waters of Life—Does the Bible have hope-filled solutions to the sin problem? Is the image of living water or a healing river familiar to any? Discuss the answers to **Q5**.

Moving On—Ask what the group members have liked best and what they are looking forward to. Review next week's assignments. Then close with a prayer circle. Give thanks for God's healing in our own lives, and offer silent or vocal prayers for nations, situations, and people who need a fresh start and the taste of living water.

Session 5: God as the Evangelist

Prayer—Follow your developing pattern for opening the meeting with prayer. Lead without a break into the singing of Charles Wesley's "O For a Thousand Tongues to Sing." If singing is not possible in your group, read the words of the song aloud.

Trail Talk—Ask each person to read his or her answer to **Q1**. Notice any common features or significant differences.

The Evangel Words—Ask the group to tell one another about their action assignment. What attitudes were noticed? How did these attitudes compare with the attitudes reported in the first paragraph of "The Evangel Words" section? How do participants feel about Wadi's journal entry about Hard Rock (page 28)? Ask **Q2**. Read aloud various translations of the verses in the Exercise. Did anyone realize in a new way that our English translations may have biased the meaning of the word *evangelism* toward preaching?

God the Evangelist—Discuss the Bible passages from the *My Witness Journal* and **Q3**. Can anyone tell about an experience (wedding, funeral, sermon, conversation) when hearing a single phrase, idea, or sentence profoundly impacted him or her? Ask **Q4**. Did anyone discover the meaning of his or her name for the first time? Ask **Q5**. Let them recite the verse. Or read it aloud, if necessary. Remind everyone that the group is moving their feet along the *Witness* trail, hoping to become more-beautiful messengers of God's grace.

We Are All Witnesses—Review the names of those identified by the participants as evangelists and witnesses (side column). Were there any surprises? Was anyone from the group named? If so, how did that person respond to being named?

Something for the Trail—Discuss the image of witnesses as a "fragrance" (2 Corinthians 2:14). Highlight the three ingredients of the 1 Peter 3:15-16 passage: our relationship with Christ, our readiness to talk about our hope, and the ability to answer with gentleness and respect. Remind the group that they are working on all three as part of the *Witness* journey.

Moving On—Choose one or more of the questions suggested in the text. Remind the group that Trail One has focused on getting a feeling for the journey. Now they will head up the mountain with Jesus. End with prayer and/or singing another verse of "O For a Thousand Tongues to Sing."

Session 6: Jesus as Prophet-Teacher

Prayer—Use the printed prayer in the opening prayer time.

Video—Show the video segment for Trail Two to introduce the theme of "Up the Mountain With Jesus."

Trail Talk—Lead the discussion of insights and experiences emerging from the *My Witness Journal* assignments. Remember to use dyads, triads, half groups, or the full group as you think each model will be helpful. Write notes to yourself in your workbook so that you will know when to shift from one cluster model to another.

Jesus as Prophet—Ask and discuss **Q1** and **Q2**. Then explore the participants' answers to **Q3**.

Jesus as Teacher—Ask and discuss **Q4 and Q5**. Then encourage the participants to talk about what they found in the Bible passages in the Exercise.

Moving On—Read Wadi's journal entry (page 38). Then read Psalm 18:1-3 as a part of your closing prayer time.

Session 7: Jesus as Son of Man and Son of God

Prayer: A Statement of Faith—Conclude your opening time of prayer by reading together the portion of the Nicene Creed in the text.

Trail Talk—Tell insights from this week's Bible readings and from the conversations about who Jesus is.

Son of Man—Use the opening questions on page 40 to begin the discussion. Let the participants read their list of characteristics for a picture of Jesus **(Q1)**. Then read the passages from Hebrews (pages 40 and 41) before discussing **Q2**. What does the group think was the reason Jesus preferred to use the title Son of Man?

Son of God—Discuss **Q3**. End by inviting anyone who wishes to tell about his or her own journey from one way of understanding Jesus to another **(Q4)**.

Moving On—Make any announcements and clarify the expectations for next week's action assignment. Close by asking two or three participants to offer prayers of thanks to God for the gift of Jesus, Son of Man and Son of God.

Session 8: Jesus as Messiah, King, and God

Prayer—The opening prayer is different this week. Read aloud the entire "Prayer" section (pages 45–46). Next, read aloud Matthew 18:20 from the top of page 46. Say: "Praise God for what you have been learning," and give them a couple quiet minutes to do so. Next, read the sentence "Offer yourself again…" and pause for two minutes. Then read "Pray again…" After two more minutes of quiet prayer, have someone slowly read the Lord's Prayer (side column, page 45).

Trail Talk—Hear reports on last week's action assignment. Ask the questions in the text to get started. When finished, move to hearing reports on the reading assignments.

Jesus Messiah—Did anyone already know that *Messiah* (or Christ) means anointed? Ask **Q1** and discuss the answers. Reflect on the meaning of Jesus' death as Messiah/suffering Servant. Point out the difficulty other religions have with this idea of a dying Messiah. Discuss **Q2**. Someone in the group may wish to research this challenge of communicating to people of other faiths.

King Jesus—Ask for any highlighted or underlined thoughts from this section. Then ask and discuss **Q3**. If Jesus is our King, what might we really be asking for when we pray, "Thy kingdom come, thy will be done"?

Jesus, God Incarnate—Ask which, if any, of the biblical texts in this section proved particularly helpful or interesting to your group. Ask and discuss **Q4** and **Q5**. Read the portion of the Nicene Creed found at the beginning of Session 7 (page 39), and ask if the creed makes more sense now.

Moving On—Review the reading and action assignments for next week. Then lead a closing time of prayer.

Session 9: Jesus as Savior, Lord, and Friend

Prayer—Open with prayer, using the printed prayer (page 51).

Trail Talk—Read aloud the member vows (**Q1**). Then discuss the usefulness of these vows. Discuss the week's reading assignments, using the questions on page 52 as a guide. Let the participants tell what God has done during the week (**Q2**). Although "What a Friend We Have in Jesus" is located at the end of this session (page 56), you may choose to sing the first verse before moving on.

Jesus as Savior—Ask and discuss **Q3**. Have someone read aloud Luke 15:11-32. Ask and discuss **Q4**. Have hymnals available to read or sing favorite hymns. Consider "O Love Divine, What Hast Thou Done," "O Sacred Head, Now Wounded," "Alas! And Did My Savior Bleed," "What Wondrous Love Is This," and "Just As I Am." Let any who wish tell their story of coming to Jesus as Savior.

Jesus as Lord—Refer to Wadi's journal entry (page 55), and ask for thoughts on making it difficult for some to come to Christ as Savior because we fail to make Christ Lord. Consider the thought that all Christians have a witness, either for or against the gospel. What will ours be?

Jesus as Friend—Discuss **Q5**. Discuss witnessing as being friend-makers for God. Read aloud 2 Corinthians 5:17-20. (Read it from *The Message* translation if you have it.)

Moving On—Clarify the action assignment as a continuation of last week, but with more emphasis on making friends for God. Make any needed announcements. Sing together "What a Friend We Have in Jesus." Close in prayer.

Session 10: Spirit of the Holy Trinity

Prayer: A Statement of Faith—Open in prayer. Read together the Nicene Creed (page 58). Read and discuss answers to **Q1**, noting similarities and differences. Sing together the prayer to the Holy Spirit in the side column before moving on to the video.

Video—Show the video segment for Trail Three to introduce the theme of "Into Life in the Holy Spirit."

Trail Talk—Begin with conversation about **Q2**. Then move to the insights and discoveries found in the Bible readings.

Who Is the Spirit?—Review the biblical words for *spirit* and their various meanings. Note the various words used for *spirit* in Ezekiel (**Q3**). Note how Jesus draws on this wind-spirit relationship in John 3:8. What, do you think, is Jesus trying to say to Nicodemus?

The Spirit as Person—Discuss **Q4**. Read Wadi's surprising recollection of the Spirit speaking to him years before the moment of realization (page 62). What stories of becoming aware of the Holy Spirit are present in your group?

The Spirit of the Holy Trinity—Create a group list from **Q5**. Talk about the adjectives they listed in **Q6**. Remind them that the Spirit's task and nature is to reveal the Father and the Son. Romans 8 reminds us that the Spirit is the Spirit of God and of Christ, and that the Spirit awakens us to recognize Christ the Son and the Father as our *Abba* (meaning Daddy or Papa). Ask if Saint Augustine's explanation of the Trinity as love (page 61) helped. (You may want to read more about this in *The Contagious Witness*, by Ron Crandall; pages 29–37.) The unity and diversity found in the Trinity is what the Spirit does in the church to reveal the love of God to the world (John 17).

Moving On—Clarify next week's assignments. Two passages (Romans 8 and 2 Corinthians 3) have been read previously. This time we are looking for new insights about the work of the Spirit. The action assignment continues to focus on others, but also on the Spirit's work to melt, mold, fill, and use us. Begin each day this week with the prayer song "Spirit of the Living God" (page 58). Close by singing it to the Holy Spirit.

Session 11: Spirit of Creation and New Creation

Prayer—Use the hymn as a prayer of invocation to the Holy Spirit. The words may be read, or they may be sung to the tune of "Angels From the Realms of Glory."

Trail Talk—Begin with conversation about this week's action assignment, ways that the Spirit can melt, mold, fill, and use us. Sing "Spirit of the Living God" (page 68). Then talk about insights and discoveries found in the Bible readings.

The Spirit of Creation—Follow up on "This camp is a songfest," the closing words of the Trail Talk. Read through some hymns of praise, especially those quoted in the last paragraph of the "The Spirit of Creation" section ("Joyful, Joyful, We Adore Thee" and "This Is My Father's World"). Notice how many stanzas capture the spirit of wonder and praise. Ask and discuss **Q1** and **Q2**. How many first sensed the reality of God through nature? What are the ramifications of this for Christian camps and retreats?

The Spirit of Creativity—Ask and discuss **Q3** and **Q4.** Then go back and ask their thoughts on the statement that says churches reaching seekers today use the arts (page 64). Discuss the dance image, the hymn "Lord of the Dance," and **Q5.**

The Spirit of the New Creation—This section summarizes this week's Bible readings. The gospel is an answer to our sin problem. Did the participants recognize this? Did the

summary seem accurate? How did they answer **Q6**? Sing Charles Wesley's hymn "Sinners, Turn: Why Will You Die" to the tune of "Take My Life, and Let It Be."

One Last Image—Discuss the image of the Trinity from John 15:5, 8 and Tertullian. Sing "Spirit of the Living God" (page 68) as part of your closing.

Moving On—Emphasize that next week's assignments focus on the Spirit's role in making God's saving grace real to us. Continue in prayer and bearing witness to those special ones to whom the Spirit leads you. Close in prayer.

Session 12: Spirit of Amazing Grace

Prayer—Open with prayer for your group and for the people participants prayed for during the week. The prayer hymn can be read or sung to the tune of "Faith of Our Fathers."

Trail Talk—Discuss **Q1**. Is grace a problem? Do people really want what they earn? Do any in the group have other stories of people who have overcome through faith, discovering grace even in suffering. Read aloud Romans 5:1-5 and discuss **Q2**. Let the participants tell about their insights from the week's Bible readings.

The Spirit of Grace Before Salvation—Begin with **Q3** and the first action assignment question about the working of the Spirit in their own lives. Discuss the reading assignments from Days 1 and 2. Did the author's story (side column, page 70) help the group understand prevenient grace? Ask **Q4** and **Q5**.

The Spirit of Grace in Salvation—Ask the second question from the action assignment and **Q6**. Discuss the reading assignments from Days 3 and 4.

The Spirit of Grace for Full Salvation—Discuss the third action assignment question and the reading assignments from Days 5 and 6. How familiar is the group with the concept of sanctification, holiness, or Christian perfection? A word used extensively in the New Testament for Christians is *saints*, which means those set apart as holy. (See the salutations in Paul's letters.) Discuss **Q7**. Ask if the group understands the symbolism of the cross and the flame (a United Methodist symbol of the Holy Spirit from Pentecost). The gospel is a full salvation: justifying grace and sanctifying grace.

Moving On—Clarify assignments. Read or sing Charles Wesley's hymn "Love Divine, All Loves Excelling." Then close in prayer.

Session 13: Spirit of Ministry and Witness

Prayer—The prayer hymn emphasis is witness and giving to Christ "whatever I can be." The Spirit enables this can-be giving. The prayer can be sung to the tune of "Rock of Ages."

Trail Talk—Discuss the evaluation questions for the halfway point from the *My Witness Journal*. Note in Wadi's journal entry (page 75) that a lot of people have no idea that what we Christians take for granted is even a possibility.

A Word on Spiritual Gifts—Discuss the reading assignments from Days 1 and 2 and talk about **Q1**. If any have been through a spiritual gifts inventory, let them tell about their experience. Ask: "Based on this week's prayer and reflection, what spiritual gifts do you think the Spirit has given you?"

What SHAPE Are You In?—The SHAPE program is described in Rick Warren's book *The Purpose Driven Church: Growth Without Compromising Your Message and Mission* (available from http://www.pastors.com/pcom). Discuss the participants' notes in **Q2** and **Q3**.

The Spirit and Your Ministry—Discuss **Q4**, **Q5**, and **Q6**. Seek responses to the illustration about seeking a new personal ministry (page 78).

The Spirit and Your Witness—Discuss the reading assignments from Days 4 through 6. Then talk about the ways the group's understanding of Christian witness has grown over the past weeks (**Q7**).

Moving On—Clarify the expectations and the assignment. You may wish to join Wadi in a halfway ice cream celebration. If you are taking a break before Trail Four begins, be sure everyone knows when to return for the next session.

Session 14: Biblical Images of the Church

Prayer—Welcome the group back and make sure this opening time of sharing and prayer includes everyone.

Trail Talk—Have the participants summarize, in small groups (3 to 4), their *My Witness Journal* notes for the first half of the *Witness* journey. Then have someone from each group report common answers, special insights, and so forth.

Video—Show the video segment for Trail Four to introduce the theme of "The Church and Its Witness."

The Church Is Born—Discuss **Q1**. Review the group's work on the action assignment in the *My Witness Journal*. Use **Q2** to begin a discussion about the group's understanding of the purpose of the church.

The Three Images—Review the three images of the church: the body of Christ, the bride of Christ, and the temple of living stones. Ask which image the participants like best, and why.

Moving On—Clarify the assignment for next week. Then close in prayer or song.

Session 15: The Church as Evangelist

Prayer—If the group hasn't already been telling about experiences and prayer requests from their witnessing efforts, encourage them to do so from now on. Read or sing the prayer hymn.

Trail Talk—Ask **Q1**. Read the last paragraph of this section (page 88). Then ask for any thoughts about the questions. Follow this discussion with a discussion about the insights gained from this week's reading and action assignments.

The Evangelism of Pentecost—Begin with **Q2**. Explain that from now on there will be times when they will be asked to use their Bibles to find some of the Bible references. **Q3** should prove to be an interesting discussion. Can the group agree on five to seven key ideas?

The Church as Evangelist—Discuss **Q4**, **Q5**, and **Q6**. The group may reveal helpful ways to approach unchurched people (**Q6**). Fill in the blanks in the text and check to see how many remembered that the prayer for our oneness is in John 17 (**Q4**).

The Evangelistic Work of the Church—Read Wesley's concern for his day (side column, page 89). Are there similar concerns today? Consider the questions in this section of the text, and encourage the participants to keep notes on the lines provided in **Q7**. What other issues emerge?

The Evangelistic Word of the Church—Consider the questions in the text and the discussion of which issues are most important for your church today (**Q8**).

Moving On—Pray for special requests and for your team's part in being salt and light in the church and in the world.

Session 16: The Great Commission

Prayer—Talk about your witnessing experiences during the week and then pray for special witnessing requests. Read or sing the prayer.

Trail Talk—What are the participants' thoughts on Wadi's witness (side column, pages 93–94)? Read and discuss the questions in the last paragraph on page 93 about what a disciple is. Let the participants tell about their experiences with this week's action assignment.

The Great Commission—Discuss the Great Commission using **Q1** and this week's reading assignments. Did Paul's commission to go to the Gentiles add anything to the meaning of the Great Commission?

Matthew 28:16-20—Read these verses together and discuss **Q2** and **Q3**.

The Great Commission Plan—Discuss **Q4** and the question about your congregation's efforts at *going*. Continue the discussion for the questions about baptizing (**Q5**) and teaching to obey (**Q6**). Review together by filling in the blanks for Matthew 20:18-20 (side column, page 97). Follow up with the questions about how your congregation is doing at reaching out to people of all nations (page 97). Conclude with the recognition of Jesus words: "I am with you always." Discuss **Q7**.

Moving On—Does your church have a mission or purpose statement? If so, make sure everyone has a copy. Is it a *great* commission? Clarify assignments and close in prayer.

Session 17: A Disciple-Making Fellowship

Prayer—Tell about experiences from the week's witnessing, and pray for special requests. Read the prayer together.

Trail Talk—Wadi grew up in a Christian family, but he had to find how to claim the Christian faith for himself. Llama had little exposure to Christ and the love of God except through her contact with Wadi. Patient, natural, bold, caring witness led her to faith and freedom in Christ. Immediately, Wadi began to help her dig deeper into all that her new faith would mean. What does is mean to be a disciple? Discuss this week's action assignment, **Q1**, and helpful insights from the Bible reading assignments.

Four Marks of Discipleship (Love, Word, Cross, and Fruit)—Reflect briefly on the biblical passage in each section about the marks of discipleship as you discuss **Q2**, **Q3**, **Q4**, **Q5**, **Q6**, and **Q7**. Include the questions in the text as you discuss. (Here are several references to help with **Q4**: Romans 12:10, 12:16; 13:8; 14:13; 15:5, 15:7, 15:14; 16:16.)

Moving On—A great variety of discipleship models exists. How did the group respond to this model of the four marks of discipleship? Discuss what is happening in these areas in your congregation. Close in prayer.

Session 18: Our Witness in Our Community

Prayer—Talk about the week's experiences, and pray for special requests. Read or sing the opening prayer.

Trail Talk—This week's focus is on witnessing in our community, with special concern for those who are hurting. Talk about Wadi's confession (side column, pages 105–6). Can others in your group identify with Wadi's experience? How does Paul's counsel (1 Corinthians 10:12-13) help? Unless we know what it feels like to be lost and hurting, we may find it difficult to reach out to others in these conditions. But this is what we are called to by our Lord. Discuss the week's action assignment, and talk about how your church is doing at offering hope to those in trouble.

Jerusalem and Judea—Clarify the concept of expanding concentric circles of ministry represented by these geographic areas: your immediate community and your larger community. Discuss briefly **Q1**, **Q2**, and the questions in the text of this section. Recognize that these questions could be part of a much larger congregational effort to plan and evaluate your ministry and witness efforts.

Seeing the People—Take a moment as you begin this section to ask for any new insights that may have emerged from the reading assignments for this week. Then move through each of the groups identified (children and youth, the troubled, seekers) by discussing **Q3** and the appropriate checklists and related questions in the text.

Moving On—Let concerns for special groups of people, which emerged during the session, help focus the closing time of prayer. Also pray for your church's ministries to these people. Clarify assignments and read aloud Acts 1:8 (witnesses in Jerusalem and to the ends of the earth).

Session 19: Our Witness in Today's World

Prayer—Tell about experiences from the week and pray for requests. Read or sing the opening prayer.

Trail Talk—As members of Christ's body, we are part of God's mission to the whole world, even today's constantly changing world. Discuss **Q1**. Talk about the action assignments. What experiences have your members had in cross-cultural settings?

Hebrews and Hellenists—Discuss Acts 6:1-7 (Day 2) and its lessons for crossing cultural boundaries in faithfulness to Christ's Great Commission. Wadi was reminded that he could not run away from culture (page 112). When have members of your group learned this lesson? Discuss **Q2**.

Samaritans—Discuss Acts 8 (Day 3). Who are the dual-culture Philips in your congregation, who help you reach out to people who are not like you? Has the Spirit sometimes had to force you to open up to new ideas and people of different cultures? Discuss **Q3**.

The Ends of the Earth—Discuss Acts 10 (Day 4). Have any in your group experienced such a conversion? Talk about the "Checklist for Worldwide Witness" (side column, page 115). Following the Spirit's leading to reach new people with the gospel changes us, not just them. Faithfulness to this vision almost always creates discomfort and even conflict in the church. Review 1 Corinthians 9:19-23. (Note the translation from *The Message*, side column, page 114.) Discuss **Q4**.

Witnessing in Today's World—Discuss some of the questions in this section.

Moving On—Let each person tell one insight concerning the church as Christ's witness. Clarify that they are to do both action assignments for next week. Plan to introduce any guests who come to church with others in your *Witness* group. Close in prayer.

Session 20: My Witness and Christ's Presence

Prayer—Tell about experiences related to the first action assignment for this week. Read and discuss the opening prayers written by your members, and then pray for one another. Tell about the week's experiences related to the second action assignment. Pray for the people who were contacted during the week.

Trail Talk—Give each person a piece of paper, and ask them to write out, as best they can, the verses they were to memorize (1 Peter 3:15-16a; John 15:5; and Galatians 2:20). Don't collect the papers when they are finished, but ask them how successful they were at remembering. In good humor read Romans 12:15. Celebrate and encourage. Read Wadi's journal entry (side column, page 118). (Many excellent books are being written on Celtic Christianity.) Discuss **Q1** and then each of the memorized verses.

Video—Show the video segment for Trail Five to introduce the theme of "My Life as Christ's Witness."

Staying Contagious—The circle diagram and **Q2** can help people visualize Christ's lordship in their lives. As Christians, we should not be afraid or consider it bragging to acknowledge that Christ is the center or king of our lives. However, Christ is not only our ruler but also our companion. Let the participants talk about how they felt about this exercise. Handle **Q2** and **Q3** with wisdom and sensitivity, perhaps in smaller groups or one-on-one. Do not force answers or embarrass anyone, but give an opportunity for them to acknowledge any obstacle to Christ's full lordship in their lives. Pray for one another. Have someone read aloud 2 Corinthians 5:14-15. Then ask: "What do these verses say about the meaning of Christ's lordship in our lives?"

Knowing Christ—Review the week's reading assignments. Discuss **Q4**. Ask if they would add anything to the seven gifts for knowing Christ (top of page 121). Discuss **Q5**. The Holy Spirit transforms our lives, but we are responsible to "renew our minds."

Two Priorities—Remind them that Scripture and prayer are two priorities that they should consider as they plan to strengthen their use of the gifts of knowing Christ.

Moving On—Clarify the reading and action assignments for next week. Close in prayer.

Session 21: My Witness and Prayer

Prayer—Have the group members write the memory verses, or let each participant draw a memory verse reference from a hat and then try to repeat the verse from memory. Talk about the witnessing experiences related to the action assignments for the past week. Read and discuss the opening prayers written by your members. Then pray for one another. Pray for the people who were contacted by group members during the past week.

Trail Talk—Wadi confesses that it was not easy to pick up his pack every day. Have some of your members felt the same way? Yet Wadi acknowledges that the five months on the trail changed his life. This change is our goal as well. Discuss some of the questions listed in the text.

In School With Jesus—How aware were participants of the importance of prayer in Scripture and in Jesus' life? The words *pray, prayer,* and *praying* occur more than 250 times in the Bible, and references to prayer occur 150 times in the New Testament alone. Check for the answers to filling in the scriptural references. Discuss **Q1, Q2,** and **Q3.**

Praying Without Ceasing—Did this section expand anyone's understanding of prayer? If prayer is conversing with God, then we can pray anywhere and everywhere. Discuss **Q4.**

Interceding for Others—When we hold people in our hearts, we are better prepared to act on the Spirit's leading as agents of grace and hope. Discuss **Q5, Q6,** and **Q7.**

Moving On—Discuss **Q8.** Then clarify the assignments for next week. Close in prayer as the Spirit leads.

Session 22: My Witness as My Story

Prayer—Begin again with a review of the memory verses. If drawing from a hat, include all the memorized verses up to this point. Let each group member read his or her personal prayer of thanksgiving. Tell about any experiences related to the second action assignment. Then pray for any special concerns or opportunities.

Trail Talk—Discuss **Q1** and the idea that stories often connect to the heart, which is just below the surface. Let each participant read the outline for his or her autobiography. Allow for questions. Have fun! Discuss **Q2.**

The Bible as Story—Recognize the unique *real* and *story* nature of the Bible. Was the "honest to God" nature of Psalm 77 familiar to everyone, or was it a surprise to some? Discuss **Q3** and **Q4.**

Your Story as Christian Witness—Discuss the various kinds of stories found in the Bible passages for the week. Divide the group into threes, and give each person 5 minutes to rehearse his or her story and receive feedback (Exercise,

page 131). Introduce the ABC model. Then ask each group of three to discuss **Q5, Q6,** and **Q7.** Bring the group back together to talk about **Q8.**

Moving On—Memorizing Scripture is useful for our own lives, but it is even more helpful as we move to the next level of Christian witnessing. Knowing what the Bible says about God's story and where to find it is fundamental in offering others a chance to connect their lives to Christ. Next, we will get comfortable with two ingredients in God's story: God's Purpose and Our Problem. Encourage the group to pick up their packs and keep climbing. We're almost there. Close in prayer.

Session 23: My Witness as God's Story, Vista One

Prayer—Begin again with a review of memory verses. Remind everyone that the goal of memorizing is to become familiar with key verses and to know where to find them. Talk in smaller groups about the additional verses compiled for the first action assignment. Then have everyone come together to read the personal prayers of thanksgiving.

Trail Talk—Sing or read "I Love to Tell the Story." Ask if anyone knew the background of this song. Ask if it becomes more meaningful when they know the background. Most people we witness to know some of the words to God's song, but they may not know much about background or the Author. That's why we witness. Would anyone like to tell how his or her loving to tell the story is coming?

The Story—Fill in the blanks and discuss **Q1, Q2,** and **Q3.**

The Ingredients—Discuss **Q4,** which relates to the second action assignment. Then examine, one at a time, the participants' preferred statements and source texts for each of the four ingredients.

Some Models—Review each model and discuss **Q5, Q6,** and **Q7.** Discuss the questions in the last paragraph of the "Some Models" section.

Moving On—Review the assignments for next week. Remind the group that next week everyone will have a chance to roleplay (5 to 10 minutes) how he or she would explain the gospel to someone who is interested. Talk about any needs or prayer requests. Close in prayer or song.

Session 24: My Witness as God's Story, Vista Two

Prayer—Begin with the memory verses. Some of these verses are longer and may be a challenge. Discuss how each passage could be helpful in our witnessing. Let them read their written prayers.

Trail Talk and Roleplay—Set up the roleplaying exercise. Pair people (perhaps by birthdays, by counting off, by drawing numbers, or so forth). If the group number is uneven, you will become someone's partner. The person whose birthday is first in each pair will begin. The other person will start by saying, "But aren't we all Christians?" or "How did you get to be so religious?" or "I guess I don't really understand what you mean by being Christian." Give each person 10 minutes (five if time is limited) to present the gospel in the form of one of the models examined last week. If the witness finishes with time still left, let the listener ask questions. After 10 minutes, switch who is witness and who is the listener. After a second 10 minutes, give each pair 5 minutes to offer helpful insights to each other. Bring the group together for 5 to 10 minutes to talk about the challenges, lessons, and benefits of the exercise. The journey itself offers its own reward. Today we look at another way to invite others to come exploring with us: telling a gospel story that connects with their story.

The Power of Story—Discuss the idea that all of us love stories. Discuss **Q1** and **Q2**.

Telling Gospel Stories—The purpose of spending week after week in the Bible is so that we can use many different starting points to talk naturally about the gospel. Discuss **Q3**. Complete the exercise (side column, page 144). Discuss **Q4** and **Q5**. Suggest Rebecca Pippert's book *Out of the Salt Shaker and Into the World: Evangelism as a Way of Life* as additional reading.

Moving On—Tell the group that this week's assignment is to look back over the whole trail. Encourage them to review their notes and highlights as they complete the assignments. Close in prayer.

Session 25: Partners With God

Prayer—If appropriate, have refreshments ready when people arrive. Begin by praying together the prayer of Saint Francis (page 147). Have participants choose a favorite line in the prayer and explain why they like that line.

Trail Talk—Focus briefly on the idea of encountering God in the wilderness. Ask for volunteers to tell about a burning bush (special encounter with God) they experienced during these weeks on the trail.

Remembering—Discuss briefly the importance of memory and remembering. Encourage the group to talk together about their answers to Exercises 1 and 2.

Refocusing—Discuss the importance of refocusing (adjusting our vision) when we move from one context to another as we continue to witness on the trails of our everyday life. Discuss Exercise 3. Then explore Exercise 4, and determine if the group would like to meet again. If so, assign someone to set up the meeting. You may wish to indicate that you will meet at the same time and location the following week, or in two weeks. Before discussing Exercise 5, remind the group that the changes you want to discuss are not personal preferences, but changes related to enhancing your congregation's witness. Have each person simply read his or her ideas. Go quickly around the circle, and then look for common trends.

Refuturing—Review the concept of shaping a new future as Christ's witness. Will we simply get off the trail and try to go back to the way things were, or will we shape a different future? Discuss some of the lessons the group has learned, which were listed in the fourth paragraph of this section as one through five. Let volunteers tell about at least one commitment she or he is ready to make (Exercise 6).

Video—Show the last section of the video, "The Trail Ahead."

Moving On—Read Ken's (Wadi's) final thoughts (page 151) and affirm God's faithfulness for your group through this journey. This is a time of consecration and prayer. We all are moving on. Move into the Covenant Renewal prayer, asking each person simply to rename his or her new commitments (from Exercise 6). Or you may find it more meaningful to have everyone (one at a time) sit in a chair in the center of the room and have the group surround him or her and in prayer to consecrate new commitments and his or her life as Christ's witness. Close with the Covenant Renewal prayer and maybe a song or hymn. Sing praise to God!